Faith Horror

*Cinematic Visions of Satanism,
Paganism and Witchcraft,
1966–1978*

LMK Sheppard

Foreword by Peter Laws

McFarland & Company, Inc., Publishers

Jefferson, North Carolina

This book has undergone peer review

All illustrations are by Simon Pritchard

ISBN (print) 978-1-4766-8161-0
ISBN (ebook) 978-1-4766-4416-5

LIBRARY OF CONGRESS AND BRITISH LIBRARY
CATALOGUING DATA ARE AVAILABLE

Library of Congress Control Number 2022005130

Front cover: (clockwise from top left)
Rosemary Woodhouse (Mia Farrow) from *Rosemary's Baby,*
Widow Fortune (Bette Davis) from *The Dark Secret of Harvest Home,*
and Damien Thorn (Harvey Stephens) from *The Omen*
(illustration by Simon Pritchard)

Printed in the United States of America

*McFarland & Company, Inc., Publishers
Box 611, Jefferson, North Carolina 28640
www.mcfarlandpub.com*

This book is dedicated to my unholy trinity:
RICHARD SHEPPARD, MARK JANCOVICH
and DEREK BARRATT.

Table of Contents

Foreword by Peter Laws　1

Introduction　5

Section I.
Witchcraft, Satanism and the Apocalypse

ONE. Consumerism, Secularism and Faith
　in *Rosemary's Baby*　27

TWO. Predestination, Secrecy and Conspiracy
　in *The Omen*　56

THREE. The Cult of Youth in the "B" Horror Film　78

Section II.
Paganism as an Alternative Culture

FOUR. Ritual and the Rural in Anglo-American
　Co-Productions　111

FIVE. A Clash of Convictions in *The Wicker Man*　141

SIX. Paganism, Witchcraft and the Feminine
　in American Horror　165

Conclusions, After-Thoughts and Legacies:
　The Conjuring, The Witch, Midsommar
　and the Post-Millennial Faith Horror　195

Chapter Notes　229

Bibliography　243

Index　253

Foreword

Peter Laws

I was sitting in the congregation of a huge Christian event once. It was an evening and the event had followed an unusual week for me. For the last five days I'd joined thousands of churchgoers who had spread across the city of Manchester. Not to preach at people or tell them they were filthy sinners. It was just to do odd jobs, really. We tidied pensioner's gardens, we painted neglected school fences, we hosted free barbecues on an estate to help neighbors get to know each other.

And on the last night I heard one of the organizers stand on a stage and sum up the point of the week. He said, "It's about time Christians stopped being defined by what they are against, and became known for what they are *for.*"

The comment struck me because he was right. Religion really does have a P.R. problem. In fact, up until I was twenty, I was actively anti–Christian. And why wouldn't I be?

All I could see of the faith seemed hateful or cruel and anti-everything. I found the church very easy to dismiss because when you only define a community by what it opposes, it naturally becomes one-dimensional. A flat caricature. Ideal for a joke punchline or a black and white story arc, but not deep enough for a life choice.

LMK Sheppard's book makes the persuasive case that this doesn't just happen with Christianity. *All* groups and organizations can become a victim to this sort of binary thinking. Including Satanism, Witchcraft and Paganism. Particularly when explored in terms of horror movies.

One of the reasons I love horror is that the genre sparks so much analysis and discussion (whether that's in an academic text or over a post-cinema pint). Yet, Sheppard makes the point that when it comes to occult or folkloric communities in scary movies, we often seem make sense of them in terms of their relationship with what we *think* they oppose. When Satanic groups feature in a horror film, we sum them up as simply a

1

symbol of rebellious liberation from the outdated shackles of Christianity, etc. Or when a flowers-in-their-hair pagan community parades through a folk horror, they are seen as little more than a rural rebellion designed to critique the capitalism that defines our cities and towns, and so on.

But what if these groups have an identity of their own. One that doesn't require a counterpoint to make sense. I mean, do Satanists really spend every meeting just thinking up ways to blaspheme Christianity? I know a few, and they don't. Do Pagan communities wake up each morning fixated on their one true goal, defying the concrete landscapes they have rejected. Again, my pagan friends seem to have more interesting to do lists than that. Might these people be just getting on with what they value and what believe will bring positivity to the world?

Granted, in horror films that positivity might seem frightening to audiences, but that's often just through a lack of familiarity with a new worldview. Indeed, my own faith, Christianity, was once the mainstream, but it's slipped further and further into the files marked "quirky," "irrelevant" or "dangerous." No wonder that the church has become a rich source of horror films.

Some people can enter a church building these days and feel a sense of awe and peace. Many of us, however, see a raft of strange esoteric symbols, goblets of blood and wooden crucifixes, and we get a shiver of fear. The alien nature of Christianity creates a space that leaves some feeling more scared than sacred.

I certainly felt that, growing up. I was very antagonistic toward Christians, figuring that all church wanted to do was to get me to reject science, lose my individuality, wear socks with sandals and (heaven forfend)…stop watching horror films! These lazy presumptions were often based on my limited, movie-inspired views of what Christianity was, rather than what is actually *is*.

When I started to meet Christians in my early twenties, I was flummoxed when some of them were intellectual, reasonable and kinda normal. I was intrigued by that, enough to explore it for myself, but I'll never forget the throb of fear I felt when I tried out a church. The robed vicar stood up in a spooky sanctuary (that looked weirdly similar to the one from the last scene of *The Omen*). Then he spoke some holy sounding words…*and the congregation spoke back in unison.*

This was freaky. Up to that point I'd *never* experienced a crowd of people talking in unison. Sure, I'd heard groups cheer and applaud. I'd heard thousands sing together at a concert. But a mass of people talking in one monotone voice? Nope. The only place I'd seen that was in a hundred late night horror movies where spooky devil cults gathered in the forest and chanted their allegiance to the Goat of Mendez.

Yes, horror informs our view of religion, Christian or otherwise. Yet I soon learned that it is sensible to have a little humility sometimes. To realize that we might not have the full picture, after all.

So, as you dive into Sheppard's book, try not to paint yourself as the main character of a horror movie who stumbles into the path of a weird and kooky pagan cult. And try not to assume that this cult exists purely to destroy *your* way of life and all that *you* believe. Instead, imagine that you're just a background cast member. A traveler, who strolls into one of these communities. Only you're lucky enough to not rock up at the scary, whacky part of the village. You know, the one where the folks like to crucify Christians upside down in wicker baskets with a black chicken stuffed in their anus.

Instead, you've happened to walk into the moderate, every-day part of town. So take a moment to sit down with those folks and talk about how the fundies in that village are certainly getting the name out about your group, but not always in a positive way.

You're about to explore the occult and folk horror trends of a particularly fertile period in horror cinema. Yet along the way you'll learn that these stories are doing more than just "rejecting the common norms." They're offering *new* paths of their own, which in some ways are actually echoes of the old ways, in new wineskins.

These are films that do indeed present fabulously spooky and rich horror stories, but they also shed light on the complex way our society has grappled with a freaky paradox which is as relevant today as it was in the '60s and '70s. We are a society who, on the surface, appear to want to step away from religion. Yet the spiritual itch remains.

Maybe we dismiss all manner of spiritualities simply because we've been defining them for so long as what they are against. Yet something deep and stubborn inside us, remains enticed by a simple, glowing question.

What might these spiritualities actually be for?

Peter Laws is a novelist, journalist, podcaster, ordained church minister and horror fan. He wrote The Frighteners: Why We Love Monsters, Ghosts, Death and Gore *and writes a monthly horror film column for* The Fortean Times *magazine and is the creator of Creepy Cove Community Church, which offers horror-themed church services.*

We believe in the dignity and indeed the sacredness of the individual.
Anything that would violate our right to think for ourselves, make
our own decisions, live our lives as we see fit,
is not only morally wrong, it's sacrilegious.[1]

The richness of horror fiction testifies
to the complexity of the cultural changes
which have taken place in the last two hundred years.
But the continuity of its rhetoric, its narrative methods,
and its symbolism also reveals that the ground-conditions
for fantasy projection of this kind have not passed away in the least.[2]

That is the big theme I see all over society.
People focused on their own thing.
—GEORGE ROMERO[3]

Introduction

The first time that Sergeant Neil Howie and Lord Summerisle meet in the 1973 film *The Wicker Man*, sparks fly, both literally and figuratively. Howie, portrayed by then television actor Edward Woodward, arrives on Summerisle with a mission to solve the disappearance of a missing girl. However, from the moment he sets foot on this fictional outermost Hebridean isle, he is thwarted by local residents who first claim that the girl does not exist, and then that she exists but not in human form after being transmuted into a hare upon her death. Howie navigates any and all obstacles put in his way as a result of his dedication to his role as a police officer and his devotion to his Christian faith, the latter motivating the former. His duty to both man and God is to restore order, to reward and protect the just and to punish the sinner. The primary and most immovable impediment standing between the sergeant and his calling is Lord Summerisle himself. Played by iconic Hammer Horror star Christopher Lee,[1] the Pagan community leader is likewise driven to keep Howie at bay owing to his own spiritual views, motivations only revealed at the end of the film. As Howie approaches Summerisle Manor, he passes a group of young girls who, naked and chanting, jump over an open fire enacting an ancient Pagan fertility rite. Puritanical Howie is incensed. He barges into the manor house, confronts the Lord and demands to know the reason for what he just witnessed, no doubt considering it to be a perverse sacrilege. He asks how the unholy leader of this foul isolated community could condone such acts of patent ungodliness. Lord Summerisle, towering over Howie, retorts, "Your God had his chance. He blew it."[2]

This film and indeed all the works discussed in this book were produced during a period beginning in the mid–1960s and continuing throughout the 1970s. At this moment in history, as suggested by the scene described above, there arises a considerable outcropping of alternative religious practice horror films. Significantly, these works exploded onto the scene at a time when, concomitantly, there were vast ecumenical changes occurring from within and from without, revisions not only to religious dogma itself but also to socio-political alliances with these spiritualties. An era popularly discerned as being at the crux of modernity and post-modernity, this body of work also coincides with debates relating to the necessity for and legitimacy of universal grounding systems overall. These include familial alliance, generational legacy and traditional faith mechanisms, precepts which potentially sparked such transformations to religion overall. Indeed, faith and family historically act in tandem, the family being the means by which religion is taught and disseminated from generation to generation, and religion acting as the tie that binds the family together as a cohesive unit of shared belief.

This book will focus on what will come to be known as Faith Horror. These narratives not only present non–Christian religions including Satanism, Paganism and Witchcraft as being viable alternatives to more historically traditional faiths, but equally foreground such unorthodox and indeed radical spiritualties as being agents of potential social cohesion and individual grounding. It could thus be argued that these films and their adaptive literary sources both discuss and disseminate contemporaneous debates involving the battle between spiritual traditionalism, religious radicalism and secular skepticism overall. Admittedly, engagement between the horror cinema and religious debate is not necessarily altogether new, for in many ways, horror has been the means whereby issues of religion and faith have been addressed since its inception as a genre. This trajectory begins with the Gothic and filters through classic horror cinema, which adapted many archetypal Gothic aesthetics including its villains, Dracula and Frankenstein's monster, and its locations, the remote castle. This generic cycle then continues through the 1970s to the present day, both eliciting and engaging in discussions related to shifting contemporaneous religious paradigms, as will be explored in depth throughout this manuscript. However, whereas film and cultural theorists alike argue for the importance of religion for these earlier horror works,[3] the late 1960s and 1970s horror cinema, while engaging in such debates with equal vigor, have not been considered as disseminators of such discourses. Indeed, even given the ways in which these films were received by the secular and religious press alike as being imbued with themes related to faith, these concerns have not been taken seriously either contemporaneously or retrospectively in academic analyses.

To pose questions with regard to spiritual alliance and increasing secularism during a time in which these issues were coming to the fore made the horror film quite controversial during this moment in history, marking the extent to which these debates were being foregrounded and furthered. While classical horror, a generic cycle argued to espouse traditional values, is not seen by secular or religious film critics as posing a serious ideological or moral challenge, conversely, since Alfred Hitchcock's *Psycho* in 1960, viewed by many film theorists and cultural critics including Stephen Prince and Tony Williams as the first "modern horror film," eight such works have been condemned by the United States Conference of Catholic Bishops (USCCB), formerly the National Legion of Decency: *Rosemary's Baby, The Devils, The Exorcist, The Wicker Man, The Omen, Carrie, Dawn of the Dead,* and *Friday the 13th.* Of these films, all are discussed as being denigrating to orthodox religious practice. For example, a review of *The Omen* published by the USCCB notes the potential for defamation of traditional religion when it states:

> The American ambassador to Great Britain (Gregory Peck) finds himself the foster father of the Antichrist in director Richard Donner's slick, expensively mounted but essentially trashy horror show. Though it refers to scripture and religious beliefs, its only interest in religion is in terms of its exploitation potential.[4]

The review for *Rosemary's Baby* seems to share similar concerns, as the reviewing body argues:

> Directed by Roman Polanski, the production values are top-notch and performances completely chilling, but the movie's inverted Christian elements denigrate religious beliefs.[5]

Furthermore, *Psycho* and *Rosemary's Baby*, in being directed by two serious cinematic auteurs, Alfred Hitchcock and Roman Polanski respectively, also gain a certain cultural cache as representatives of serious high art cinema. Additionally, *The Exorcist* and *The Omen*, in starring respected actors such as Max von Sydow and Gregory Peck, while being directed by traditionally non-horror directors, William Friedkin and Richard Donner respectively, may be defined as being mainstream cultural products, rather than horror genre works that merely rest on the fringes. It is due to this newfound legitimacy that Faith Horror was able to garner larger audiences than previous horror genre films had achieved. For example, *The Omen* ranked number one on box office charts for its opening weekend, grossing $4,273,886 within the United States alone, while *The Exorcist*, with a total lifetime gross of over $225,000,000, is one of the most popular horror films of all time. Even given this overwhelming popularity, the influence of this group of films remains underrated when it comes to its articulation of contemporaneous debates concerning faith.

When researching this period, discourse surrounding the 1960s and 1970s horror film focuses on works considered to be progenitors and components of the Slasher Film, arguably one of the sub-genres most referenced by academics and critics alike as being visually ground-breaking, theoretically innovative and historically influential for the future of this generic film production. These works include, but are obviously not limited to, *Psycho* (1960) and *The Texas Chainsaw Massacre* (1974) as proto–Slashers, and *Halloween* (1978) and *Friday the 13th* (1980) as being amongst the first properly Slasher films. Out of the analysis of these later films, the final girl theory developed wherein spectatorial identifications with violence and terror was addressed. Admittedly, these films did not present religion as being of import, nor were they recognized as doing so. However, when works that did come to represent alternative religion are mentioned, film theorists and historians tend to group these texts into two sub-genres, neither of which focus on religion as a primary concern.

The first of these subgenres is what has been referred to as the Evil Children narrative. This group focuses on films that demonize children as a way of addressing the limitations of reductive, restrictive and repressive social norms including familial structures and gender roles—for example, the female/mother figure as being the primary caregiver and the male/father as being the primary bread winner in a constellation that is absolutely heteronormative. Titles considered to be Evil Children narratives include *The Exorcist, Rosemary's Baby, Alice Sweet Alice*, and *The Omen*, to name a few. The second subgenre, as will be discussed in relation to *The Wicker Man* later in this book, is the Folk Horror Chain, a group of seventies British Horror films and teleplays that engage with debates surrounding the rural and the urban, the rational and the irrational, and the ways in which the former debates support the latter. For the Folk Horror, the urban universe is one of skeptical rationalism, which is pitted against the rural, a world steeped in the irrational, folkloric, and legendary. Films in this group primarily include what has been referred to as the unholy trilogy, such as *The Wicker Man, The Blood on Satan's Claw, Witchfinder General* and the films that have been influenced by them.

Both of these designations, Evil Children and Folk Horror alike, position mid–1960s and 1970s films and their thematic concerns as not really being about faith at all. Instead, scholars such as Robin Wood, Adam Scovell and Mark Jancovich regard their discussion of spiritual affiliation as being symbolic of larger concerns regarding a breakdown in systems of authority, an establishment of socially accepted mechanisms of repression, or both. Indeed, rather than religion being about religion, spirituality is instead located as just one of many signifiers of debates surrounding the viability of, the repressive tendencies in, and a necessity for traditional institutions of power. Alternatively, what this book will showcase is the way in which Faith Horror functions as a powerfully relevant cultural disseminator, making a historical socio-political analysis of the religious discourse offered up in these works as important and indeed as necessary as it was for other horror cycles throughout history. In other words, faith and the faith community is just as important for this group of mid–1960s and 1970s horrors as it was for the Gothic and for the classical horror cinema alike, and to deny this, to fail to realize this discursive trajectory, would, in this author's humble view, be a grave oversight.

A History of Horror as Religious Discourse

To begin, Gothic fiction (mid–1760s to the present), an arguable progenitor for both literary and cinematic horror alike, arose in a cultural climate that was founded upon the dual legacies of the Enlightenment and the Reformation. In articulating this historic shift away from what was considered to be irrational, these texts debated the efficacy of beliefs associated with the supernatural over the more rational pursuits into scientific inquiry.[6]

The Gothic novel, in fact, warns of the danger in an overarching attempt to rationalize all aspects of the universe. As essentially conflicted as its contemporaneous culture, these novels also warned of the dangers of adhering to traditionalism. This literary movement was at once decidedly anti–Catholic, deriding an alliance to a traditional sacramental religion which valued faith, revelation and supernatural intervention over reason, while equally remaining spiritually grounded. More simply put, the Gothic universe is neither purely rational nor purely irrational, and its existence has a supernal dimension which alone can give it meaning. This thematic concern is evidenced through a critique of characters who held to a belief in complete human autonomy. The Gothic would argue that there is a price for an existential hubristic rebellion wherein man attempts to adopt a God-like nature. Like Satan in Milton's *Paradise Lost,* humanity is punished for conceding to a domineering feeling of mastery over the world gifted to them. In the Gothic, scientific rationality is overwhelmed by a lurking uncanny fear for that which cannot be assimilated, understood and conquered.[7] In giving voice to this existential dread, the Gothic privileged all that was defiant, frenzied, elaborate, and excessive. Further, in an attempt to eschew an increasingly pervasive secularism, the Gothic enacted a return to the primitive past, wherein the supernatural exists and only absolute rationality is illusory. Regarding this idea, David Punter, author of *The Literature of Terror*, argues, "The Gothic was the archaic, the pagan, that which was prior to or was opposed to, or resisted the establishment of civilized values and a well-regarded society."[8] In other words, even as Gothic fiction was wary of traditionalism, which was simply ordered, it was nonetheless literally and figuratively haunted by it, as if through making the past manifest, it reinvented while at the same time recaptured history for its own purposes. Punter refers to this as traditional threat, discussing it in the following way:

> When thinking of the Gothic novel, a set of characteristics spring readily to mind: an emphasis of portraying the terrifying, a common insistence on archaic settings, a prominent use of the supernatural, the presence of highly stereotyped characters, and the attempt to deploy and perfect techniques of literary suspense. Gothic fiction is the fiction of the haunted castle, of heroines preyed on by unspeakable terrors, of the blackly lowering villain, of ghosts, vampires, monsters and werewolves.[9]

In the Gothic novel, the supernatural becomes an active force for both good and evil. Although good is granted with supreme power, likewise, evil is presented as being both real and robust. Malevolence is both subtle and deadly, its efficacy lying in the deception of beauty, and the danger of playing God, a conflict brought to life in the Gothic fiction as a body of work.

This concern with the battle of good versus evil is revisited in classical horror cinema, although in a much more ordered and predictable form. The classical horror film sets up clear narrative conflicts wherein those who have Christian faith were on the side of "good," while those who practiced other faiths, or who held no faith whatsoever, were regarded as decidedly "evil." It was, in fact, a prerequisite for the altruistic narrative protagonist to wield their faith, and by extension powerful symbols of righteousness such as the cross, the Bible or vials of holy water in the service of defeating evil antagonists, whether they be monsters, vampires or demons.

Indeed, from the 1930 film adaptation of the classical Gothic novel *Dracula*,[10] all the way through to the 1960 Hammer classic *City of the Dead*, those characters who come to rely upon tradition, historical knowledge, and the tenets of orthodox religion successfully defeat evil. Van Helsing, arguably the protagonist of *Dracula*, although a scientist, is also willing to accept the possibility of the supernatural, and thus uses supernatural means, in the form of religious implements, to defeat his evil foe. In brandishing the cross, the symbol of the power of God, to defeat the devil, the efficacy of traditional Christianity is reiterated.

Even in a more modern context, the 1960 film *City of the Dead*,[11] protagonist Richard Barlow defeats the Satanic cabal led by Christopher Lee using these same traditional means.

While those who are deemed to be on the side of good are those who accept the power of traditional religion, those who practice alternative faiths, such as Satanism and Witchcraft, are decidedly regarded as being evil. Dracula, a classical horror villain, is defeated because he does not abide by the laws of God, just like Alan Driscoll, who actively worships Satan in *City of the Dead*. Paul Leggett, film historian and fellow McFarland author, argues that classical horror, like its Gothic predecessor, should be understood as a spiritual allegory, the classical horror ultimately presenting a Christian worldview.

Another connection between these two horror cycles has to do with the setting. In the Gothic novel, just as the conditions of reality became fantastic thematically, through calling upon the supernatural in the service of overwhelming rampant rationality, the locations of these tales may be said to equally articulate a distancing from societal norms.[12] The castle, the most common of all Gothic edifices, not only exists on a remote mountain in an even more distant country but is itself an enactor of isolation. The heroine of the Gothic novel, trapped within this labyrinth, increasingly separated from the external culture and the present time, first becomes lost and is then driven mad.

Interestingly, this landscape is equally offered up in the classical Hollywood horror cinema. Within this film genre, like its ostensible literary antecedent, the isolated, remote and foggy landscapes, what horror theorist James B. Twitchell calls "Horror Art," are likened to dreams in producing "marvelous" inexplicable imagery that is not only literally distant in being set in a remote locale, but equally distant in being set apart within a dreamlike realm wholly separate from reality. Indeed, the settings, like the characters, reflect this elusive quality in being predominantly located in the perennial "over there," foggy, dark and obscured spaces beyond the realm of human experience. Classical horror in this way may be defined as an "Art of Occlusion," a text which offers up diegetic monsters that are fundamentally unknowable because they exist on the peripheral line between the conscious and the subconscious. However, whereas the Gothic enacted aesthetic isolation in the service of criticizing contemporaneous cultural norms and mores, the classical horror film remained distant while nonetheless espousing traditional values inherent to the era. Ironically, while distancing was used, it need not have been a concern, for, as suggested above, thematic controversy was not an issue.

If it could be argued that the Gothic articulated an attack against a privileging of the rational over the supernatural both aesthetically and thematically, and if the classical horror cinema might be considered to have carried on these debates by presenting a conflict between benevolent religiosity and rational skepticism, reconfigured as a battle of good versus evil, then a new wave of horror text began to emerge in the late 1960s and throughout the 1970s. Simply put, the Gothic and the Faith Horror might be conceived as generic bookends within a trajectory that includes the classical horror text sandwiched in the middle. Indeed, the Gothic was formed in response to an ushering in of modernity, and the focus of this book, Faith Horror, not only shares a similar thematic concern with debates of skeptical rationality and supernatural faith, but was established in response to another cultural paradigmatic shift at the advent of postmodernity. Like the Gothic, Faith Horror has to do with a privileging of the supernatural, for as horror historian Andrew Tudor argues in *Monsters and Mad Scientists*, the 1970s represents a boom with regard to supernatural horror films, and indeed thus continues the deliberation regarding the importance of religion, a concern shared by Punter, who writes:

> And finally, we have the 1970s and the coming of a new range of films ... which if we are to follow through any argument about the social significance of the forms of terror, must be considered in a more detailed way.[13]

He goes on later in the same chapter:

> Alongside the development of the "traditional" horror film there [has] arisen a genre more designed to cope with specifically contemporary perceptions of terror: what is harder to understand is that in the 1970s both of these forms appear to have been temporarily supplanted, at least in terms of commercial success by a third form, which returns to the age-old themes of Satanism and possession.... The first important exponent of the form was Roman Polanski himself in *Rosemary's Baby*.[14]

However, such a concern may not represent a third form, but instead, to a certain extent, a shared thematic and formal sensibility reminiscent of the Gothic tradition, and equally suggestive of the integral relationship of religion to the horror films of the 1960s and 1970s.

By the 1970s, the dominant image in the horror film is chaos, as once again culture is divided from spirituality. The first break from classical horror to Faith Horror might be located in the breakdown of standard narrative development. It is this closed and arguably happy ending that is also problematized in the modern horror text. Horror historian Andrew Tudor seems to support this when he argues:

> The horror movie worldview suggested by these developments is one in which typical threats have increased in intensity and become more focused.

We, in our familiar domestic and everyday settings, are the unwitting prey of graphically presented horrors created by our failings or by invasion from a seemingly malevolent natural world. Victory is no longer assured.[15]

The fact that these threats are left unresolved poses an additional threat, for, to return to Tudor, "If the fears here represented are undefeated, then the cultures within which such narratives make sense must surely be less secure than they once were."[16] The crowning example of modern horror, for many theorists, is *Psycho*, directed by Alfred Hitchcock in 1960. As Stephen Prince argues:

> Classical horror happened in a remote location. "Things have changed in the modern period, with *Psycho* (1960), being one of the threshold films that mark a separation between eras.... Hitchcock put horror in the here and now."[17]

However, setting the horror in an isolated motel far off the new main highway definitely positions this text as not being in "the here." Equally, the setting of the Bates mansion behind the all-but-deserted motel is also described as being antiquated inside and out. This is suggested in the novel upon which the film was based: "Here everything was orderly and ordained; it was only there, outside, that the changes took place."[18] If, as Vivian Sobchack suggests, "since the 1960s, the events of family life and social life have been commonly and increasingly experienced as convergent.... The displaced 'There' has been replaced with 'Here,' and 'Then' and 'When' have been condensed as 'Now,'"[19] then *Rosemary's Baby*, which will be discussed in detail in the first chapter of this book, presents a more accurate marker for a universe that is radically, realistically articulated. Thus, this work could in fact be considered one of the first works of horror in espousing an ethos reminiscent of modernity in its rejection of the traditional, and its foregrounding of concerns with the here and now. Indeed, in being set in the urban mecca of New York City, and in being imbued with contemporary references to the New York City blackout and the Pope's visit to the "Big Apple," this film and its adaptive novel seem to be rooted in the present in a far more radical sense than even *Psycho*. Additionally, in referring to 1966 as year one, and in incorporating the *Time* magazine issue, on the cover of which was emblazoned "*Is God Dead?*," the film equally refers directly to the debates surrounding religion that were coming to the fore during this time period.

The Faith Horror and Theological Debate

During the mid–1960s through the 1970s, the horror film's thematic concern with monotheistic religion became less grounded. Just as a paradigmatic shift in terms of spirituality, arguably, issued forth the Gothic, so too did the culmination of modernity and inception of post-modernity issue in new concerns and debates with regard to religious connectivity.

During this era, culture was becoming open to a vast array of choices when it came to spiritual affiliation. From reforms in the Catholic Church to new ways of disseminating the Christian message, from the opening up of alternative faiths including Satanism, Paganism and Witchcraft to a renunciation of faith altogether in the form of secularism and atheism, the allure of spirituality as a force for personal grounding and social connectivity became a key trope, especially when it came to horror. In an article published in the *New York Times* entitled "In Horror Movies Some Things Are Sacred," critic Leonard Wolf argues that this is a special appeal of the modern horror film, a lure beyond its ability to scare audiences. He suggests:

> [T]he lurking religious [content] gives many [horror films] their special power to attract. It seems bizarrely true that the cinema of horror provides its highly secularized audiences with their last—perhaps their only—opportunity to experience mystery and miracle as if they were dreadful; as if they were aweful.[20]

These modern horrors were also, as noted by Punter, "more designed to cope with specifically contemporary perceptions of terror ... [by returning] to age-old themes of Satanism and possession."[21] However, what is interesting about these texts is not only the very fact of their depiction of radical faith mechanisms, including Satanism, Paganism and Witchcraft, but, more specifically, how they position these belief systems as viable alternatives, often cloaked in the garb of traditional religion. Using biblical vernacular or Latin and traditional religious robes, while incorporating traditional religious rites, these films offer up an alternative religion that is at times, ironically, even more orthodox than the orthodoxy of the period.

Indeed, following the Second Vatican Council, wherein under the banner *aggiornamento* the Church sought to make Catholicism more relevant and in accord with other Christian faiths, certain tenets of the faith were undergoing transition, including but not limited to: the preaching of liturgy in the local vernacular versus using the traditional Latin; reforming the hierarchy of the Church to account for the rights of individual conscience that moved away from the long established belief that the Church was the only true teacher and disseminator of Truth; and the establishment of dialogues with other faiths and the secular community, all of which, for religious historian Hugh McLeod, "presented a mainly positive view of contemporary culture."[22] However, even as the Catholic Church was becoming less orthodox, the religions presented in these films were, at times, articulated as being highly traditional, relying on the historical traditions that are associated with what is referred to in these works as being "old religions." This element was also noted in the ways in which these works were received. To return to Wolf:

> The great frenzies of chaos, creation, disobedience, disaster, solitude and evil which have been rendered vague or bland in the ivell-bred church and synagogue services of the 70's are restored to their terrifying proportions in the half-light of the movie theaters. Priests of the horror cinema still recite incantations that count; Satan, in his foul and gorgeous panoply, appears; sacrifices are still offered or refused; and men (or creatures) still die to save the world.[23]

What is interesting in regard to these films is not only how they, in many cases, depict traditionalism as efficacious, but more importantly how these texts ushered in a new era of legitimacy for horror altogether, increasingly making it a mainstream cultural product. *New York Times* film critic Vincent Canby sums this up in an article for this popular secular publication:

> [The devil is] the biggest thing at the box office this summer no matter what you call him: Satanism has always been an interesting, though not a very respectable form of movie myth. The subject was usually left to the "B" picture makers ... but it was never considered worthy of the attention of the makers of "A" films. Roman Polanski's *Rosemary's Baby* ... started to change that.... It is to overemphasize the point, I suspect, to say that this renewed interest in Satanism represents what psychologists and sociologists describe as a need to externalize evil.... The fictional process itself is a way of externalizing ideas and feelings, the better to understand them. The existence of Satan is part of our mythology.[24]

Indeed, these works offer up a religion that was, like these films, an inherent part of the socio-political milieu.

On the one side, conservative faiths were undergoing transformation. This renovation, following the Second Vatican Council (1962–1965), includes a reworking of Catholic liturgy into parochial vernaculars and alternations to the hierarchical organization of the Church itself with the aim of becoming more inclusive. This was coupled with an increase in membership to Evangelical congregations such as Billy Graham's ministry, who, through his personal, broadcast and televisual crusades, reached global audiences with his message of salvation through being born again in Christ. On the other side of the conservative/liberal divide, countercultural alignments with Eastern faiths,

including Hinduism and Buddhism, co-existed with more radical affiliations such as Paganism, Witchcraft and Satanism to form potential,
if not altogether widely acceptable, alternatives to Christianity. In the
middle ground of this spectrum of belief, Agnosticism and Atheism
were becoming increasingly tolerable in public forums for those who
possessed either a lack of faith or an uncertainty when it came to the
existence of a deity. This plethora of viable faiths from which to choose
as well as the option of exhibiting no faith whatsoever represented an
opening rarely before witnessed in Western civilization.

Speaking to this era's popularization of radical alternative spiritual
alignment, historian Theodore Roszak asserts:

> [This] youthful political activism of the sixties ... reveals itself in the unprec-
> edented penchant for the occult, and for exotic ritual which has become an
> integral part of the counterculture.[25]

Investigating figures within popular culture, the occult did indeed take
on a special fascination. Mick Jagger of the Rolling Stones, for example,
not only dedicated a song entitled "Sympathy for the Devil" to Satan in
the title track of the 1968 *Beggar's Banquet* album but was also slotted to
appear in Kenneth Anger's *Lucifer Rising*, a film based on the teachings
of esoteric guru Aleister Crowley. Jagger was not alone in his alignment
with the occult, however, and celebrities including Jimmy Page, Marianne
Faithfull and Dennis Hopper all contributed in some way to Anger's production, while other seminal rock music icons, The Beatles, went so far as
to include an image of Crowley in their 1967 album *Sgt. Pepper's Lonely
Hearts Club Band*. As a result of this collective cultural referencing and
revering of radical religions, it should thus seem as no coincidence that
during this time not only did a resurgence of interest in Crowley's Church
of Thelema emerge, but equally an increase in membership to Anton
LaVey's Church of Satan. In fact, the Satanic Church gained an unprecedented number of members at this time, resulting in the mainstream publication of *The Satanic Bible*[26] by Avon Books in 1969.

In terms of occult philosophy and practice, Aleister Crowley and
Anton LaVey represent a continuum of alternative belief moving from
a spirituality that focused upon scientific and rational foundations, as
is the case with Crowley's *Magik*, to a faith that was more grounded in
superstition, religious ritual and rite, as is the case with LaVey's Church
of Satanism. In other words, whereas Crowley, on the one hand, adopts
an inherently logical and methodological framework for the understanding of spiritual ritual, LaVey, alternatively, sought to found a
church that filled what he considered to be a gap left by a privileging of
the rational over the supernatural universe.

For Crowley, *Magik* was a "science of life" handed down from the ancients. It encompassed a study of what he regarded as the laws of nature from a rational vantage point. Crowley argues:

> [T]he mind should be trained by the study of any well-developed science, such as chemistry or mathematics. The idea of organisation is the first step, that of interpretation the second.[27]

The magician therefore relates to the world by privileging the objective over the emotional. In order to do this, the self and any self-interest must necessarily be reined in. An understanding of the occult and its practice can only be achieved when the "ego-idea" is overcome. He states: "[A]ttainment means first and foremost the destruction of the individuality. Each of our ideas must be made to give up the Self to the Beloved.[28]" However, even while rejecting the concerns of the individual, *Magik* at the same time refused to adopt a political stance. Crowley argues: "You will cease to be interested in controversies, politics, ethics, religion will seem so many toys and your Magical Will will be free from these inhibitions.[29]" Twenty years after his death, interest in Crowley was being resurrected, possibly due to these modern theories that he foregrounded regarding science over sentimentality.

Interestingly, while Crowley championed a devaluation of the self in favor of attaining a certain connectivity to a higher power, Anton LaVey and his Church of Satan was founded upon a tendency toward hedonism and an almost diametrically opposed focus upon freeing the self and the will of the individual above all else. In a section entitled "The Infernal Diatribe" from the larger work, *The Satanic Bible*, LaVey asserts, "Life is the great indulgence—death the great abstinence. Therefore, make the most of life—HERE and NOW."[30] Again, later in the same section, the author suggests, "Then all my bones shall say pridefully, 'Who is like unto me? Have I not been too strong for mine adversaries? Have I not delivered MYSELF by mine own brain and body?'"[31] This hedonistic glorification of the self may then be contrasted with the spiritual philosophy of Crowley, who suggests that it is not an embrace but an abhorrence of the individual that enacts a unification with the higher power and thus attains fulfillment. It is, ultimately, this selfsame debate posed by occult practitioners that is revisited within the larger culture of a period defined as the "Me" generation. Specifically, should the individual be reverenced, or, conversely, should the ego remain in check? These existential queries feed into the larger debates of this era, debates related to the necessity and efficacy of traditionalism and liberalism, concerns regarding cultural shifts and the crux of modernity and postmodernity, and the potential grounding and freeing of individuals inherent to discussions surrounding religion versus secular skepticism, debates that form the basis for this study of Faith Horror.

Faith Horror and Issues of Pedagogy

The films that were chosen for this book, like the debates that they further, should not be regarded as comprehensive, but instead as being representative of the larger trends specifically within this Faith Horror discourse. The first of these are works that were included because they present two faiths, namely Satanism and Witchcraft, as being synonymous. The second group of films was engaged for their articulation of Witchcraft as being more aligned with Pagan polytheism. It is thus that the two sections of this book are organized. As will be suggested in section one, adherents of Satanic Witchcraft all seem to desire to take over the world as apocalyptic narratives enact a battle between believers and those of little faith. The second section involves Pagan Witchcraft and those who desire not to overthrow, but instead to exist in isolation, keeping their rituals in secret from the selfsame skeptical milieu. Then within these larger thematic trends, discrete concerns allied with this contemporaneous culture are offered up, foci that align to debates over traditionalism and the counterculture: consumerism, determinism, naturalism, and feminism. Indeed, these films are not viewed in isolation, but are considered as cultural outputs as well as textual constellations. In incorporating not only the films and teleplays themselves but also their adaptive literary sources and novelizations, a more privileged reading can be achieved not only in terms of narrative and thematic development, but also, and even more significantly, in terms of socio-political connectivity,[32] because rather than seeking to evaluate the primacy, validity or fidelity of the "original" versus the adaptive work, focusing upon textual differentiation, this methodological underpinning foregrounds intertextuality and cultural embeddedness. As Thomas Letich suggests in "Twelve Fallacies in Contemporary Adaptation Theory":

> Though novels and films may seem at any given moment in the history of narrative theory to have essentially distinctive properties, those properties are functions of their historical moments and not of the media itself.[33]

If it could in fact be argued, as Leitch does, that any text is by definition intertextual in nature, then to study how they expand upon one another rather than how they may be seen as merely possessing unique systems of signification, a primary focus of adaptation studies, may open up insights into how these works in fact reveal a constellation of meaning within larger contemporaneous cultural debates. With this in mind, not only novels and their adaptive filmic counterparts will be engaged, but equally, the primary televisual texts that were critically related to these cinematic works, as well as their adaptive literary sources. As a result of this thematic expansion in some cases, these works were made and marketed outside of the American context, as is the case with the BBC production *Robin Redbreast.* Thus, while the thrust of this book is in relation to American Faith Horror, certain British productions have been added, more specifically those that were funded by American dollars, or those that had an influence upon key Faith Horror texts. Also, it should be noted that to include televisual plays into a study of film suggests the primacy and potency of religious debate at this moment in history across media platforms.

A second difficult consideration for any film historian, in addition to textual inclusion, has to do with periodization. Indeed, when considering precedents, scholars have forwarded a veritable plethora of formulations with regard to how the time periods of the 1960s and 1970s might be delineated.[34] For the purposes of this study, after a careful review of the primary sources and secondary sources listed in the bibliographic section at the end of this book, I have commenced with an historical analysis of the mid–1960s, and more specifically with the year 1963, and concluded in the mid–1970s with the year 1978. One precedent for this timeframe follows the work of Andrew Tudor, who suggests, in his seminal discussion of the horror film entitled *Monsters and Mad Scientists,* that it was in 1963 that a change occurred within this discourse, a shift that he refers to as a period of "American Decline." During this period, the effects of *Psycho,* arguably, the first modern horror film, were truly felt, as he contends:

> The internal incoherence of the supernatural sub-genre reflects a general tendency in sixties horror movies. The period of American Decline illustrates exactly that: the American horror-movie forms are either changed or rendered insignificant.[35]

In fact, the argument offered up in this book relates exactly to this transformation from classic to modern horror—a shift that, as discussed above, is directly related to debates regarding the efficacy of traditionalism, which were key components of this era and its media output.

Equally, in the larger socio-political context, this year was also quite significant in terms of a shifting traditionalism that resulted in landmark events with regard to religion and civil rights. One example of this can be the death of Pope John XXIII and the election of Pope Paul IV as the head of the Catholic Church. Reform had, admittedly, already begun within this religious institution, resulting in the opening of the Second Vatican Council in October 1962; however, it was in 1963 that the reins of the Council, and indeed the Catholic Church overall, were effectively handed over to Pope Paul IV. The choice of this new spiritual leader was symptomatic of the larger concerns of the era itself. Indeed, Paul IV was popularly discerned as a man who was instrumental in implementing the certain reforms suggested by the Council and who equally was thought to have fostered improved ecumenical relations between Christian factions including Catholicism, Protestantism and Eastern Orthodox churches. This was also the Pope that appeared and preached in Yankee Stadium, offering a new and more liberal face to Catholicism. Outside of a strictly religious forum, and more specifically in terms of the counterculture and civil rights movements, 1963 was also the year in which Betty Friedan's *The Feminine Mystique* was first published, a text that was popularly discerned, although not unproblematically, as being the watershed moment with regard to Second Wave Feminism. Further, this was also the year that Martin Luther King, Jr. engaged his March on Washington, culminating in one of the most famous proclamations of his career, the "I Have a Dream" speech.

If 1963, for the reasons specified above, then serves as an opening, with *Eye of the Devil* produced in 1966 and its literary antecedent, written under the name of *Day of the Arrow*,[36] published in 1964, being the first text chronologically to be considered, then the ending date would fall in the mid–1970s, and more specifically 1978. It was during this year that the final text to be herein considered, *The Dark Secret of Harvest Home*, was produced. Additionally, within the larger cultural context, this was the time when the religious right was on the upswing, and when conservative candidate Ronald Reagan was beginning his campaign for President, being on the verge of coming into office in 1980, effectively ending what may be regarded as a period of "getting loose." This was also the year that Andrew Tudor identifies as the end of the 1970s boom in supernatural themed horror and the beginning of the genre's sustained growth.[37] Indeed, if the early to mid–1970s was a time of uncertainty and lack of cohesion, then the late 1970s appeared to get its ducks in a proverbial row, signaling a solidifying of the debates and tensions that were inherent to the mid–1960s to mid–1970s era, both socio-politically for the United States and thematically for the horror cinema.

Lastly, it should be kept in mind that the majority of the research engaged in preparation for the writing of *Faith Horror* was conducted in the years spanning 2013 and 2017. Additional research with regard to the concluding section was engaged in 2019 so as to make manifest the relevance of this study for contemporary film theory. With this in mind, there might be several referential omissions of work produced between 2017 and 2019, works that might be addressed and included in future iterations of this book. It should be understood that any such oversights are not intentional, nor are they reflective of their importance or their theoretical influence for this author specifically or for film studies overall.

Section I Overview: Witchcraft, Satanism and the Apocalypse

This section delineates the first type of alternative religion text—those works that share a thematic concern with Satanism and Witchcraft, the two being closely aligned and pitted against more traditional religions such as Catholicism and Protestantism. Although it is suggested by media historians and critics alike that this conflict is one involving good versus evil, in which the former, Satanic Witchcraft, is regarded as evil, and the latter, traditional Christianity, as being good, this section will suggest that this is not as simple as it initially appears. This is true because in most instances, Satanism is configured as being traditional in adopting links to both historical imperatives and generational legacies. This "alternative" orthodoxy is then pitted not against Christianity, but on the condition of disbelief and disconnectedness inherent to modernity as an ethos. In this way, this group of films discusses and disseminates contemporaneous cultural debates with regard to the apparent efficacy of both modernity and traditionalism within this period.

Chapter One: "Consumerism, Secularism and Faith in *Rosemary's Baby*" discusses *Rosemary's Baby* and the role of consumerism in providing a grounding for the individual and, by extension, the society. In this film and novel, it is suggested that the central conflict is not one of good versus evil, or even traditional versus alternative faith mechanisms, but instead belief versus disbelief.

Chapter Two: "Predestation, Secrecy and Conspiracy in *The Omen*" focuses on the first film in *The Omen* trilogy and the subsequent novelization written by the screenplay writer of *The Omen*. As with the film and novel versions of *Rosemary's Baby*, *The Omen* in both forms problematizes the conflict of good versus evil and traditionalism versus modernity by presenting Catholicism and Satanism as being equally traditional, specifically with regard to the concept of predestination.

Chapter Three: "The Cult of Youth in the 'B' Horror Film" deals with several other horror texts that share a similar thematic concern with the works discussed above. Included in this analysis are the film and literary versions of *The Witches*, as well as the films *Race with the Devil* and *The Brotherhood of Satan*. Once again, these three films not only present a conflict of belief versus skepticism, as opposed to a more traditional conflict of good versus evil, but also address a concern with the cult of youth.

Section II Overview: Paganism as an Alternative Culture

Section II focuses on a second group of works that deal with Paganism and its connection with the counterculture movement. In addressing a spirituality essentially based upon the worship of nature, these texts at once align and differentiate the Pagan from the back to earth movement, as both simultaneously divorce themselves from the modern urban mecca, while at the same time concomitantly diverge in terms of the popular "hippie" ethos of getting loose.

Chapter Four: "Ritual and the Rural in Anglo-American Co-Productions" involves an analysis of two texts that share a thematic concern with the Pagan rites and rituals as discussed by Sir James Frazer in his seminal anthropological text *The Golden Bough*. *Eye of the Devil*, its literary antecedent *Day of the Arrow*, and the BBC *Play for Today* installment *Robin Redbreast* all connect Pagan spirituality counterculture while at the same time presenting this belief as being inherently stratified, historically rooted and, as a faith based upon personal sacrifice, a challenge to the self-interest that seemed to characterize the era.

Chapter Five: "A Clash of Convictions in *The Wicker Man*" brings together the discussion of the three works discussed in the previous chapter by suggesting their connection to an infamous work entitled *The Wicker Man*. Whereas the aforementioned texts pit modern skepticism against alternative orthodox religions, *The Wicker Man* is unique in concerning itself with a battle of faiths, between the Pagan and the Protestant. In being regarded as equally efficacious, this text and its novelization, written by the screenplay writer and director, suggest an opening up of religious alternatives, a contemporaneous concern following the Second Vatican Council.

Chapter Six: "Paganism, Witchcraft and the Feminine in American Horror" discusses two American Pagan works, *The Season of the Witch* and *The Dark Secret of Harvest Home*, in light of feminist philosophies. In this chapter, as is the case with all of the discussions throughout this book, simple dichotomies involving traditionalism, patriarchy and modern feminism are problematized.

In "Conclusions, After-Thoughts and Legacies: *The Conjuring, The Witch, Midsommer* and the Post-Millennial Alternative Religion Horror," the tenets established with the Post-Millennial Faith Horror will be analyzed in more contemporary horror cinema texts. In presenting this connection, it will be argued that the works discussed throughout this book have an enduring legacy and, given the current concerns with and debates surrounding religion, are worthy of further serious consideration as socio-political documents relevant as much today as they were at the end of the age of modernity.

SECTION I

Witchcraft, Satanism and the Apocalypse

ONE

Consumerism, Secularism and Faith in *Rosemary's Baby*

Cinema gives you the chance of making a play into something that is real, and not stagey, so that it's like life.... You have the weather around you, the night or the sun, you can step out of the door even if you don't want to "open it up" as they say.[1]
—ROMAN POLANSKI

Before Ira Levin, horror always happened somewhere else. Regular ordinary people were forced to pack their luggage and kennel their dogs and had to leave their homes and schlep seemingly forever to Transylvania ... or the Bates Motel.... Horror never occurred at home.[2]—CHUCK PALAHNIUK from the introduction to the novel version of *Rosemary's Baby*

When I suggested that Vidal Sassoon himself should come to Hollywood to cut Mia's hair, Bill Castle decided to hype the occasion into a spectacular "photo" opportunity for the Hollywood Press. Bleachers were set up on a soundstage, and there in front of photographers and TV crews, Vidal removed Mia's locks. Throughout, like the true hippie she was, Mia kept up a verbal assault on the press for covering such a minor function instead of applying their investigative energies to the plight of the deprived and underprivileged American Indians.[3]—ROMAN POLANSKI on the role of commercialism during the filming of *Rosemary's Baby*

Introduction

In an early scene from the film version of *Rosemary's Baby*, protagonist and housewife Rosemary Woodhouse is depicted as being wholly consumed with setting up the homestead. She supervises the painters as they "brighten up her home tremendously,"[4] applying white paint to the natural dark wood adorning her midtown apartment.[5] She arranges costly, recently purchased furnishings within this large urban domestic space. She hangs curtains and designs matching window seat cushions. She reads edition after edition of *House Beautiful* magazine[6] to come up with the latest interior design products and techniques to render her universe fashionable. The only time for pause in her furious homemaking comes in the form of two significant interruptions. The first occurs when she stops to watch her husband's television commercial for the *"swingin'* world of Yamaha."[7] Then, later she is distracted from her work once again by a nosy neighbor, Minnie Castevet, who comes to welcome Rosemary to the Bramford apartment house, to introduce herself, and to see the apartment, which has recently been vacated by the elderly matron's dear and now deceased best friend. The first visitor to enter Rosemary's private space, Minnie comments upon the brightness of the home and its modern design. She flatters Rosemary even as she questions the cost of these adornments. Picking up the cushion of a newly delivered chair, still in shrink-wrap, Minnie wonders how much such a chair would cost. Rosemary responds that she is unsure. While sitting at the kitchen table, which is uniquely placed as a result of an ad in *House Beautiful*, Minnie continues her role as inquisitor. She dons her glasses, replete with a chain to keep them handy, and goes on to ardently read the price stickers on the cans that Rosemary is in the process of arranging in her cupboard. She ends her visit at the door. Handing Rosemary her mail after rifling through the envelopes consisting only of ads, Minnie insists that Rosemary and her husband come for dinner that very night. Minnie asserts that she will not take "no" for an answer. That it would, in fact, be doing the older couple a favor to have their company. Rosemary promises that she and her husband will undoubtedly attend. However, this social engagement seems less likely upon her husband's return from work. Guy comes home in a state of anger and depression because he was not chosen for a desired starring role on the Broadway stage. Guy tells his wife that even if the play folds, a likely eventuality given the dubious quality of this play, this is a part that "gets noticed." He complains that this was the role that could have jump-started his career and set him on the road to riches and fame. Guy, it seems, is lost in himself and simply does not feel like becoming involved. This is especially true of making the acquaintance of an elderly couple across the hall who at first glance seem irrelevant to any of his concerns regarding stardom. Perhaps they remind him of the parents he has already rejected coming back again to control him.

When taking a close look at this early scene, *Rosemary's Baby*, both as a film and a novel, may be seen from the outset to engage with many contemporaneous cultural and ideological debates. More specifically, these deliberations involve the efficacy of and need for traditionalism, a concern which is pitted against cultural modernity. Whereas a conservative ethos, incorporating such elements as orthodox religion, generational legacy, gender positioning and familial bonds, possessed the positive attributes of a stable, known quantity, it was at the same time also perceived as being stultifying and repressive. This is especially the case when compared to the enticing freedoms offered by a non-conformist secular culture dominated by consumerism. As modernity gave rise to postmodernity, the

(Clockwise) Guy Woodhouse (John Cassavetes), Minnie Castevet (Ruth Gordon) and Rosemary Woodhouse (Mia Farrow) from *Rosemary's Baby*.

vast socio-political and cultural shifts that have come to characterize the mid– to late 1960s had many implications for the individuals living during this moment in history. In light of the changing mores, affiliations and goals, the future of those living within this period became increasingly uncertain. Questions arose as to whether the outcomes of contemporaneous debates involving traditionalism and modernity would ultimately lead to a looking back or a forward focus. Would a resurgence of conservatism be instilled, or would the liberalism of the counterculture movement come to dominate? Would both of these be eradicated by a hedonistic consumer culture?

In turn, *Rosemary's Baby*, in both the film and novel versions, seems to pose more questions than to offer solutions to the above cultural conundrums. Resting on the fence, much like the culture out of which they spring, the Woodhouses may not only be aligned with traditionalism in the form of religious affiliation and gender roles, but also liberal ideologies in their ties to secularism and more contemporary mechanisms of identification, such as rampant consumerism. As will be discussed in this chapter, textual protagonist Rosemary Woodhouse is the character who is most divided in this regard. She is presented as a lapsed Catholic with binding, albeit subconscious, ties to the Church, and an equal connectivity to the secular world as a result of her ties to her husband. She is also a housewife whose primary role, as suggested in the scene above, is to take care of her husband and their home. Although surrounded by objects of a consumer culture that dominate this space, and indeed most of the private spaces of this period, Rosemary is apparently unaffected by its lures, not even aware of the value of these accouterments. Her only desire is to orchestrate a pleasing space for her husband, even more than for herself. This is evidenced in her seeking approval in all her endeavors, even including lining the shelves with paper. In other words, as a result of her familial ties, first to her family and then to Guy, she is torn between her ties to her Catholic faith and her ties to the consumer culture. It is only as a result of an addition to her family, the birth of her child, and her maternal instinct that she might be swayed. The film ends with her rejecting her spouse, and on the brink of deciding whether to assume the role of mother if not of wife. In the book, this vacillation is increased between killing the child, going to a priest for help, or assuming the role of mother on her own:

> [S]he couldn't throw him out the window. He was her baby no matter who the father was. What she had to do was to go to someone who would understand. Like a priest.... It was a problem for the Church to handle ... not someone stupid like Rosemary Reilley from Omaha.[8]

In the final pages of the book, she appears to make a more definitive decision than the film allows. First, she names her child Andrew John Woodhouse, and then she acknowledges her link to him: that although he was half Satan, he was half hers as well, and that her influence might be equally as strong as that of a supernatural malevolent entity. She decides that if she worked against them, Andy could turn out for good as opposed to evil. Whether this ultimate desire to assume her maternal role is the result of influence from the Church, the media or her own independent action is a question that must be considered and cannot easily be answered.

Guy's identifications, on the other hand, seem less troubled. It might at first appear as if being a married man who assumes the traditional role of husband and sole breadwinner might align him with a conservative ethos. However, when stripping the paint from his exterior, it is revealed that such affiliations are only manifestations of his need for self-aggrandizement. As a part of the media industry, he is, in fact, an unwavering product of conspicuous consumption. His beautiful and doting wife, his immense urban apartment in the sought-after Bramford apartment complex on New York's Central Park West, and his acting career are all signals of his desire to be admired: to reinforce his ego by surrounding it with things of apparent cultural cache. His innate impulse to measure his worth and the value of others by things acquired is in turn supported by his control of domestic funds. In charge of both cash and credit reserves, Guy has a relatively unchecked rein to populate his universe with the trappings of success. Further, due to his secularism, neither his overblown sense of self nor his spending is curbed by religious teachings. It could be argued that Guy would sell his soul and his wife's body to anyone to achieve what he desires. It just so happens that the Satanists get there first. The true danger that Guy and Rosemary ultimately face as a result of their failure to fully and consciously connect to more traditional mechanisms of stabilization makes them particularly susceptible to the Castevets. Without strong connections to family, faith or anything outside of themselves, this couple has no support system on which to rely should this acquisitive impulse fail.

While the Woodhouses' identifications are complex, aligned at once with both conservative and liberal ideologies, their neighbors Minnie and her "hubby" Roman Castevet, alternatively, seem to be less troubled. As an apparently traditional couple, they more solidly exemplify one side of this cultural dichotomy. Indeed, Minnie and Roman are an elderly couple whose very lives extend back to an earlier era. They have been married for decades and live in a tightly knit religious community established by Roman's father. Their clothes and their décor are fiercely "un-hip" and disconnected from the vagaries of modern taste. They work together in the familial legacy of multiplying the Church and forwarding its mission on earth. Their actions, in turn, seem to speak to this faith: they dote on Rosemary and Guy, both of whom are estranged from their respective families, and likewise care for others before themselves, taking in a young, starving, drug-addicted woman found lying near-dead on the street.

When regarding the text in this way, it would appear as if the characters of Rosemary and Guy Woodhouse are determined by an interplay of acquisition and loss. In other words, their identities are constructed in the midst of the objects which they have acquired, and in their exteriority to the beliefs that they have lost. The Castevets are, in turn, defined by the people to whom they are connected through a spiritual belief that they hold dear. Further, when considering not only the film, but also the novel version of *Rosemary's Baby,* such contemporaneous paradigmatic shifts become, in many ways, the debates of this narrative itself. Indeed, it appears as if rather than the good versus evil conflict that characterized classical horror narratives of the first half of this century, the essential debate presented in both versions of *Rosemary's Baby* is one of the old versus the new, the conservative versus the liberal, and the congregational versus the consumer culture. This debate is redoubled in its setting: New York City. This major urban metropolis boasts being the home of media in the form of the popular press, being the heart of commodification in the form of the stock market trading floors, as well as being the hub of the American theater in the form of Broadway. This text offers a perennial *right here* as opposed to a distant *over there,* as was noted in the reviews at the time of the film's release. *New York Times* reviewer Renata Adler suggests that the filmic adaptation as grounded in the here and now makes perfect sense:

> One begins to think it is the kind of thing that might really have happened to her. That a rough beast really did slouch toward West 72nd Street to be born. I think this is because it is almost too extremely plausible.[9]

Indeed, in terms of identification, plausibility and location, this work once again breaks with classical horror, not only in terms of character and theme, but also in terms of setting. This is not the "horror of occlusion," in the sense described by James B. Twitchell in *Dreadful Pleasures,* but instead the horror of inclusion.

For these reasons, it may be argued that *Rosemary's Baby* represents one of the first truly modern horror narratives. What makes this textual constellation both compelling from an analytic perspective and horrific from an emotional perspective is the extent to which all who engage with this work can indeed locate themselves within this text and thus connect with its characters—the antagonists possibly even over the protagonists—and how, when looking at the bright white paint on the surface of this text, it is easy to align with the apparently benevolent parental figures of Roman and Minnie Castevet. This obfuscation continues until the true mission of Roman's church is revealed.

It is confirmed later in both the film and novel versions of *Rosemary's Baby* that Minnie and Roman are actually Satanists, attempting to conjure the living devil so as to take over the world. Once made manifest, the fact that the Castevets, complicit with Guy, offer Rosemary up as an unwilling sexual object who will be used in a ritualized rape to conceive the Antichrist is an overwhelmingly disturbing revelation. The true horror of both the novel and the film thus rests in the fact that nothing is as it appears, that the things that seem the safest are in fact the most dangerous. We are lured by the white paint and fail to see the unadorned wood beneath. The threat of the apparently innocuous is not only revealed in this text, but equally in most of the films discussed in this book, most notably in *The Omen*, the topic of the subsequent chapter in this section.

Thus, rather than framing *Rosemary's Baby* as primarily addressing issues of patriarchy, as does Tony Williams in *Hearths of Darkness* and Reynold Humphreys in *The American Horror Film*, institutions including religion, consumerism, and sexual repression will not be collapsed into one troubled mechanism of a phallocentric universe. Instead, as is suggested by the film and novel versions of *Rosemary's Baby*, these institutions are significantly at odds with one another for dominance, a struggle that figures as one of the main conflicts of this text. While there are also examples of conspiracy throughout *Rosemary's Baby*, a trope common to many films of this period that were informed by the melting pot of Kennedy assassination theories culminating with the subsequent 1974 Warren Commission, these conspiracies are perpetrated by a religious coven, a group that is collapsed into figures of authority in the work of authors such as Mark Jancovich when he argues, "Despite the continual discussions about the death of God, it is authority that is the problem, not the loss of religious faith."[10] It is indeed the absence rather than the fear of stabilizing institutions such as spiritual communities and strong familial ties that allow the individuals that populate *Rosemary's Baby* to become prey to potentially destructive mechanisms including narcissistic self-interest and the lures of consumer culture, not to mention an international Satanic cabal. Kim Newman goes on to argue in *Nightmare Movies*:

> To his credit, Ira Levin admits that the demonology in *Rosemary's Baby* is secondary to the Big Scary Idea that the heroine is pregnant with the monster. Lapsed Catholicism and chic witchcraft are vital to the atmosphere, but the mechanics of the horror would work without these elements.[11]

However, as will be presented in this analysis, rather than mere window-dressing, a common reading offered by both Newman and Jancovich, religious faith and spiritual community are central not only to this text, but to the period overall, making it a legitimate concern, even if not consciously addressed by Levin as part of his creative process.

Another popular reading of this text, as suggested in the introduction to this book, is to consider *Rosemary's Baby*, and indeed *The Omen*, as evil child narratives that address the ambiguity, ambivalence and contradiction manifest in a culture that has not come to terms with debates between traditionalism and modernity, what Vivian Sobchack regards as "wholly culture's own."[12] Barbara Creed, in her book *The Monstrous Feminine*, goes on to locate the horrific child as the primary signifier of female abjection. However, by interpolating psychoanalytic theory, these authors not only fail to address the significant ways in which consumerism and religion figure into this equation, but equally run the risk of offering an a-historical argument, a palimpsest of the socio-political connectivity that this book seeks to reveal. Finally, those who focus on the demise of the family as the predominant concern of *Rosemary's Baby* come at issues of repression and patriarchy from yet another angle. Tony Williams concludes that those who take the spiritual debate within this text seriously reassure themselves that the disintegration of the family is the result of supernatural intervention rather than social breakdown, while Reynold Humphreys also warns against critiques that regard *Rosemary's Baby* as dredging up, in the words of "that hoary old chestnut, the fight between *good* and *evil*."[13] Indeed, as Humphreys suggests, and as will be revealed in this chapter, while addressing the debate between the supernatural and the secular world in which this text is located, the conflict of *Rosemary's Baby* is not one that can, in fact, be reduced to such classical horror tropes. As is the case with the culture out of which it arises, the conflicts are much more problematic and thus require significant, complex consideration.

This analysis will, in fact, take up the call offered by Reynold Humphreys by interpolating the concerns of the contemporaneous culture back into this text while at the same time offering an intervention into current discourse by suggesting that, as mentioned in the introduction to this book, the debates surrounding spirituality, faith and religious communities should be taken seriously, not as signifiers or symbols but as concerns in and of themselves at this moment in history. All this fear, uncertainty and debate begs to be considered within the context of the contemporaneous culture. Lest we not forget, the story is set within the familiar streets of midtown Manhattan and, moreover, in buildings and locations that actually exist and could be visited. This, when combined with the references to current events including the visit of the Pope to New York City, the blackout, and industrial action strikes, adds a new dimension of terror to this fiction-cum-*reality*. Ira Levin comments on his process writing the novel version of *Rosemary's Baby*:

> I anchored my unbelievable story in the reality of Manhattan in that season—as much to make myself believe it as to win the belief of readers. I saved the daily newspapers, checking back through them on the transit strike, the incoming shows, the mayoral election, writing always a few months ahead of Rosemary and Guy's calendar.[14]

David Punter concurs with the effect of such referential treatments when he suggests, "Fear is at its fiercest when it is seen to invade the everyday contemporary world."[15]

The Isolation of Modernity

One of the characteristics that render Guy and Rosemary Woodhouse most vulnerable to the horrors perpetrated upon them by Roman and Minnie Castevet and their coven is apparent isolation. This is first suggested by a lack of significant ties to family, a common concern of modernity, which sought to eschew all bonds considered to be repressive. Indeed, Rosemary and Guy's respective families become a significant structuring absence. As revealed in the scene between Minnie and Rosemary that opened this chapter, the families do not appear to write to the couple, nor are they portrayed even once throughout the film version. The only allusion to familial history comes in a scene between Minnie and Rosemary during their first social engagement. At this dinner party, Rosemary and Minnie go into the Castevet kitchen to do the washing up while Guy and Roman retire into the living room to quaff brandy and smoke cigars. While separated from their spouses, engaged in so much "women's work," Minnie and Rosemary's thoughts naturally turn to things domestic. While Minnie washes the dishes and Rosemary wipes them dry, they begin to discuss Rosemary's plans for the future. Rosemary tells Minnie that her family, at present, consists of Guy alone, but that she plans on having a total of three children. Minnie inquires as to Rosemary's extended family, and Rosemary offers that she has three brothers and two sisters, as well as sixteen nieces and nephews. Minnie replies that as she obviously comes from fertile stock, she should have no problem getting pregnant and having as many children as she wishes. While Rosemary's family is mentioned just this once, almost in passing, Guy's family is never mentioned at all in the film. This is slightly different in the novel version, wherein both Rosemary and Guy's respective backgrounds form a minuscule part of the narrative, if only to underpin their isolation from them. In his novel, Levin writes that as Rosemary and her husband begin to set up house, she finds that she has no one with whom to share her joy in her new married life. The novel suggests:

> They were all hostile now ... not forgiving her for (a) marrying a Protestant, (b) marrying in only a civil ceremony, and (c) having a mother-in-law who had two divorces and was married now to a Jew up in Canada.[16]

This schism is increased by her decision to move away from her home-town of Omaha and to the Big Apple. The novel suggests of her family and her place therein:

> She was the youngest of six children, the other five of whom had married early and made homes close to their parents; behind her in Omaha she had left an angry, suspicious father, a silent mother, four resenting brothers and sisters.... In New York she felt guilty and selfish.[17]

Like Rosemary, Guy's family lacks a significant role both in the narrative and in his life. Levin mentions Guy's mother in a scene wherein she visits him during the tour of his hit Broadway show.[18] Nonetheless, Guy is presented as not being close to his family, and, like Rosemary, actively shuns any meaningful familial connections as he himself feels shunned. This isolation, as the book suggests, creates a longing in both Rosemary and Guy resulting in their creating alternative parental role models.

For Rosemary, this figure is Hutch, an older gentleman who has assisted her since she first moved to New York City. If Minnie Castevet is the first uninvited visitor of the Woodhouses, then Edward Hutchens is their first invited guest. He comes with historical knowledge of the apartment house and its former residents, including a pair of sisters who purportedly ate small children, an unnamed perpetrator of infanticide not to mention a warlock and his coven. Ironically calling the Bramford "happy house," he tries to warn Guy and Rosemary of potential danger. Indeed, if Roman, the son of the aforementioned coven leader and his wife, wants to make the Woodhouse family feel welcome, Edward Hutchens wants them to clear out as soon as possible. This warning is presented not only consciously, in her meetings and conversations with Hutch, but also unconsciously. In a dream that will be discussed below in detail, Rosemary is embarking on a journey on a yacht with members of the Catholic community. Her friend, left ashore, suggests that they are in for rough weather: a typhoon lurks ahead. In addition to Hutch, the Pope and John Fitzgerald Kennedy also figure in this dream, all attempt-ing to navigate this stormy passage. In *Hearths of Darkness*, Tony Wil-liams suggests that Hutch, the Pope and Kennedy all take on the role of father figures, and like Dr. Abraham Saperstein, her obstetrician, all of these figures of authority fail to protect her.[19]

For Guy, the need for surrogate parents is satisfied by the narrative antagonists, Roman and Minnie Castevet. As Rosemary observes:

> She saw that Minnie and Roman had become deeply important to him. It wasn't surprising; his mother was a busy self-involved chatterer and none of his fathers had been truly fatherly. The Castevets were filling a need in him, a need of which he himself was probably unaware.[20]

Just as Guy unconsciously acts based upon a structuring absence of family, so too does Rosemary. However, for the heroine apparent, this unconscious drive manifests itself more in her loss of faith than in her loss of family.

Indeed, Rosemary is portrayed as being in a state of angst with regard to her separation from the Church, an existential crisis that is exhibited in involuntary actions like her crossing herself in times of stress, and in her dreams, as suggested above. This psychological dissonance is noted not only in the text itself, but also in the reception of Ira Levin's novel. According to a book review of *Rosemary's Baby* published in *Time* magazine, the lack of religious connection experienced by this protagonist results in the primacy of the Catholic guilt that Rosemary experiences. Equally, this thematic concern also acts an important narrative device when it is suggested that Levin "proceeds to create suspense by operating on the theory that a little Catholic guilt can go a long way."[21]

Roman and Minnie use this guilt first to lure Rosemary into their circle by appealing to her sense of propriety. Once they have succeeded, they hold her by assuming the role of nurturers. Minnie acts as a surrogate mother, making Rosemary nutritious shakes using home-grown herbs and spices, offering to do her shopping, and even saving her from a panic attack while Rosemary wanders alone in the city, one of the only times she is shown within the exterior urban landscape. The Castevets even appeal to her unconsciously rooted Catholic morality. By choosing her to be the mother of the spawn of Satan, they know that she will not only bear the child but also care for it, regardless if the father is Guy or Satan himself. In fact, as a result of her upbringing in faith, she will consider it a sin not to do so.

While Roman and Minnie overwhelmingly succeed in their desire to keep Guy and Rosemary right where they are so as to fulfill their religious calling, Hutch, even given his superior knowledge of history, ultimately fails in his mission to protect his surrogate daughter and son-in-law. Acting alone, he has no one to protect him and thus falls victim to the malevolent forces within this text. Leaving a glove behind at Rosemary and Guy's apartment, he is cursed by the coven, goes into a coma and eventually dies, a fate that might have been altered were he not alone in his beliefs regarding the efficacy of the Castevet coven. Socio-political theorist Robert Bellah supports this argument as he asserts repeatedly in his seminal study of this period entitled *Habits of the Heart* that within the United States, religion was, up until this time, one of the most pervasive mechanisms for individual and social stabilization. Likewise, C. S. Lewis in *Mere Christianity* further avers that faith is not effective unless it is shared. He states, "the only real instrument for learning about God is the whole Christian community.... Christian brotherhood is, so to speak, the technical instrument for this."[22] To be powerful and effective within the world of *Rosemary's Baby* is to be spiritually unified. Throughout this text, the radical secular individual is, alternatively, to be doomed to failure.

The Role of Religion and the Lure of Traditionalism in *Rosemary's Baby*

In the novel version of *Rosemary's Baby*, Ira Levin describes Pope Paul's visit as establishing social cohesion. He suggests:

> It was Monday, October 4, the day of Pope Paul's visit to the city, and the sharing of the event made people more open and communicative than they ordinarily were. *How nice it is*, Rosemary thought, *that the whole city is so happy.*[23]

This depiction of the event illustrates the way in which religion has the power to draw people together and form communities, even though, it could be argued, the majority of New York City citizens are not faithful Catholics. This unifying principle is also suggested in the etymology of this religious ecumenicism. The name given to the Catholic faith derives from the Greco Latin *catholicus*, meaning "universal." To be *catholic* meant to be affiliated with the Universal Christian Church, a faith that, from the time of the Middle Ages, linked an ever-increasing majority of the world.

This unifying effect is not reducible to the names and practices of traditional orthodox faiths, however. It is equally an ardently held belief in a supreme power that binds Roman Castevet to his wife, to his home and to his flock of followers. Roman was indeed born in the apartment in which he currently resides, an architecture of powerful supernatural force as a result of its long history in housing a Satanic community, as suggested by Hutch in the previous section. Roman uses this physical battery in the service of carrying on his father's spiritual work by attempting to conjure the living devil. Minnie is a devoted wife who is both physically and spiritually entwined to her husband. Because they are joined by God, although admittedly not the Christian deity, they perceive themselves to be of one body, one mind and one spirit, and they act accordingly. She further aids him physically by assuming the role of the dutiful housewife and supports his spirituality through offering advice regarding important decisions made within the coven.[24] Likewise, he takes her counsel into account in the running of not only their home, but also their congregation. Surrounding the Castevets in the Bramford apartment house are Roman's religious followers, members of his spiritual circle who unquestionably support the couple and their mission, thus forming a connected and committed religious community. The novel goes on to suggest of this faith community in relationship to the outside world around them, "the stubborn fact remains that whether or not *we* believe, *they* most assuredly do."[25] As film scholar Tony Williams has suggested, the Castevets are portrayed as being both spiritually and historically connected to a traditional mechanism of faith:

> Satanists [practice] another older religious order, having its own religious rites alongside the Catholic ones. The Castevets represent the historical, knowing older thespians, practicing an ancient religion.... Satanism and Catholicism presented as equally conservative.[26]

Beverle Houston and Marsha Kinder, like Williams, further discuss the religious overtones of *Rosemary's Baby* in the following way:

> The story takes the traditional Christ myth and dresses it in its equally traditional Satanic disguise. The ... myth parallels the New Testament, with the divine figure as father of the child, Rosemary as the chosen vessel, the starting of the new era with the birth of the messiah, and the adoration of the child.[27]

This establishment of Satanism as an orthodoxy by linking it to Catholicism can, in fact, be found to be a key trope throughout both the novel and the film. Symbols of these two faiths are time and time again doubled so as to make this connection manifest. However, what is even more controversial than this alignment is that it appears as if Satanism, at least within the world of *Rosemary's Baby*, is the more ardently held belief, one that, in fact, comes even to dominate over its Catholic other.

Rosemary's dreams provide an entry point into this concern. In the first dream sequence, which occurs as Rosemary is drugged and raped by an incarnate Satan to conceive the Antichrist, the novel describes her hallucination of the event:

> Guy came in and began making love to her. He stroked her with both hands—a long, relishing stroke that began at her bound wrists, slid down over her arms, breasts, and loins, and became a voluptuous tickling between her legs. He repeated the exciting stroke again and again ... and when she was ready, more than ready, he slipped a hand in under her buttocks, raised them, and lodged his hardness against her, and pushed it powerfully in.... Brutally, rhythmically, he drove his new hugeness. The pope came in.... "Jackie tells me you have been bitten by a mouse," he said. "Yes" Rosemary

said, "That's why I didn't come to see you." She spoke sadly so he wouldn't suspect she had just had an orgasm. "Am I forgiven father?" she asked. "Absolutely," he answered.[28]

In the film version, Roman Polanski portrays this scene in a way that closely approximates the original text, except without the mention of the size of the devil's member, or the fact that Rosemary has an orgasm as the result of it. What is included in the film that is not alluded to in the book, however, is a scene wherein the Pope forgives Rosemary of her sins and proffers his ring, which she kisses in an act of contrition. This holy Catholic symbol, the ring of the Pope, is the exact double of the amulet given to Rosemary by the Castevets, a good luck charm filled with an ancient herb, tannis root, or the devil's pepper, and thus an object connected to the practice of Satanism. Not only does the ring double the necklace, but the necklace also acts as a double for a rosary, a Catholic chain of prayer beads. The novel suggests of this conflation of symbols: "If only prayer were still possible! How nice it would be to hold a crucifix again and have God's ear: ask him for safe passage through the eight more months ahead.... Suddenly she remembered the good luck charm, the ball of tannis root; and foolish or not, wanted it—no needed it around her neck."[29] Whereas the Catholic symbol is no longer open for her, this symbol of luck filled with tannis root, the *devil's pepper*, offers a likely substitute for supernatural protection.

In this sequence, it is not only the link between the Pope's holy ring and the coven's charm, but further the fact of the devil, a supernatural being, procreating with a mortal woman to produce an heir on earth, that highlights the connectivity established between these two faiths. Even though the demonic impregnation is obviously much more overtly sexualized, and completely non-consensual—a rape, in fact—there still remains a strong and indeed troubling connection to its divine counterpart. The annunciation is described in the following passage taken from the first chapter of Luke, verses 26 through 38:

> And in the sixth month the angel Gabriel was sent from God unto a city of Galilee, named Nazareth, to a virgin espoused to a man whose name was Joseph of the house of David; and the virgin's name was Mary. And the angel came in unto her and said, Hail *thou that art* highly favored, the Lord *is* with thee: blessed *art* thou amongst women. And when she saw *him* she was troubled at his saying and cast in her mind what manner of salutation this should be. And the angel said unto her, Fear not Mary: for thou hast found favor with God. And behold thou shalt conceive in thy womb, and bring forth a son, and shalt call his name JESUS.... Then Mary said unto the angel, How shall this be, seeing that I know not a man? And the angel answered and said unto her, The Holy Ghost shall come upon thee, and the power of the

Highest shall overshadow thee: therefore, also that holy thing which shall be born of thee shall be called the Son of God.[30]

This establishment of Satanism as a traditional faith by association, finally, can be drawn from the film and novel's depiction of the birth of the Antichrist taking place in a lowly location, replete with gift-bearing travelers who have conducted a pilgrimage to witness the newborn savior, a scene akin to the depiction of the gifts of the Magi from the Bible. Further cementing this relationship is the doubling of the location of the birth of Jesus and the location where Adrian Castevet, Sr. met his death. The narrative states, "Do you know where Adrian Marcato died? In a stable on Corfu because they wouldn't let him into the hotel. '*No room at the inn....* So, he died in the stable.'"[31]

The socio-political resonance of this connection between Satanism and Catholicism is also noted in the analysis of the film by Kinder and Houston:

> In the extraordinarily powerful scene where Rosemary conceives the son of Satan, there is a merging of images from at least three mythologies: Satan and the witches from the demonic, the Pope and Michelangelo's creation of Adam from traditional Christianity, and the Kennedyesque yachting captain from the modern myth of power.[32]

However, while these authors view these "mythologies" as being inherently separate and mutually exclusive, they may actually be interconnected. All of the aforementioned representations may indeed be seen as archetypes of conservative traditionally grounded values, just like orthodox religion. The reference to Jack Kennedy in the hallucinatory dream, for example, acts as a similar reference to that of the virgin birth and the gifts of the Magi: a tool foregrounding the importance of faith to culture. Indeed, not only was Kennedy the first Catholic president of the United States, but once elected, he continued to point to the prominence of religious affiliation at the time. In his inaugural address delivered on January 20, 1961, for example, Kennedy makes apparent his belief in tradition and traditional values:

> We observe today not a victory of a party, but a celebration of freedom—symbolizing an end, as well as a beginning—signifying renewal, as well as change.... The world is very different now. For man holds in his mortal hands the power to abolish all forms of human poverty in all forms of human life. With a good conscience our only sure reward, with history the final judge of our deeds, let us go forth to lead the land we love, asking His blessing and His help, but knowing that here on earth God's work must truly be our own.[33]

The president insisted that Americans begin to realize their potential that was inherited from the Revolutionary War, suggesting that to look to the traditions of the past would secure the future of the country. Finally, by invoking God, Kennedy seemed to have not only a social and political imperative, but a moral one as well—a belief that was rooted in religion as much as historical nationalism. Indeed, the values that the symbol, if not the man, seemed to embody are lost in the protagonists in both the novel and the film versions of *Rosemary's Baby*.[34]

This focus does not, however, lie solely in the mythology as related to the fundamental texts of Christianity, but also extends to the depiction of religious symbolism offered through artistic representation and dream condensation. As she goes in and out of consciousness during the same dream sequence mentioned above, she begins to imagine scenes from the Sistine Chapel wherein God breathes life into Adam. Significantly, the fall of this first divine progeny results in the necessity of the second coming, an event that is doubled at the conclusion of the film with the birth of Adrian/Andrew, the Antichrist.

This connection between faiths is also depicted in both versions of the text in yet another dream sequence. Rosemary, once again teetering on the verge of reality, overhears Minnie Castevet speaking through the wall. Minnie's voice is incorporated into Rosemary's dream of her former Catholic school. The words her neighbor speaks become that of the nun in the dream. This time the conflation is one of key religious figures—Minnie, the wife of the head of the Satanic cabal, and the Catholic nun, a wife of Christ.

However, as suggested throughout this chapter, it is the ways in which the novel and the film differ that provide the most interesting fodder for analysis, and the depictions of the Pope's visit is yet another example of this. As discussed in the description that opened this section, Levin makes a point to present the cohesive effect of this religious figurehead. The film presents an almost opposing concern: isolating as opposed to coalescing. The same visit of the Pope to this New York secular landmark is described through the eyes of Guy as he watches the head of the Catholic Church enter Yankee Stadium. Sitting in their television room, which will soon become their nursery, he shouts to Rosemary, "It's the Pope at Yankee Stadium. Christ what a mob." He also alludes to the fact that this event would be an excellent spot for his Yamaha commercial. While Guy watches, Rosemary lies alone in bed in another room, struggling with an unbearable abdominal pain brought on by her pregnancy. If the Pope acts to bring New York together in the book, this unity is received within the Woodhouse apartment in isolation. Not only are Rosemary and Guy physically apart during this event, but also their understanding of it is wholly dissimilar. Rosemary, as a lapsed Catholic, would receive the presence of the Pope in humility and reverence, as suggested by her dream. Guy, however, only sees the significance of the visit as a means to self-aggrandizement. As a victim of such feelings, he is prey to the Castevets, based not on a concern of religious faith, as is the case with his wife, but instead as a result of his acquisitive impulse.

Rosemary's Baby and the Role of the Acquisitive Impulse

Within the film version of *Rosemary's Baby*, as Guy and Rosemary Woodhouse view what will become their new, hip, urbanite, New York City apartment for the first time, a conversation ensues between the couple and the building manager, Mr. Nicklas:

> NICKLAS (TO GUY): Are you a doctor?
> ROSEMARY: No, he's an actor.
> NICKLAS: Have I seen you in anything?
> GUY: I did *Hamlet* a while back, didn't I Liz, and ... the *Sandpiper*.
> ROSEMARY: He's joking. He did *Luther*,[35] *Nobody Loves an Albatross*, and a lot of television plays and commercials.[36]

As is revealed in this scene, from the moment Guy Woodhouse is introduced, he is seen to be a chameleon, acquiring a new identity at will. In this way, the ironic comment made by Guy speaks not only to his sense of humor, but also his sense of self as being fluid. Not only does he not deny the misconception that he is a doctor, but later in the same exchange he pretends to be Burt Lancaster. In other words, within this narrative, both his on and off-screen personas are both literally and figuratively consumed with the assumption of roles for gain. In this case, the choices are designed so that Guy will appear more important and successful. Many might already regard the profession of acting, especially on the New York stage, as being a symbol of status, both financially and as an artistic pursuit, but this is qualified later in the scene as Nicklas comments:

> NICKLAS: That's where the money is isn't it? In commercials?
> GUY: Yes, and the artistic thrill, too.[37]

Although the comment was also, admittedly, made tongue-in-cheek, it is later revealed that the primary way in which Guy has, in fact, made his money is through commercials, rather than more "high art" endeavors. In the novel version, Levin writes:

> In 1964, Guy had done a series of Anacin commercials that, shown time and time again, had earned him eighteen thousand dollars and was still producing a sizable income.[38]

This selfsame method of success is equally revealed in the film, as described in the introduction to this chapter with Guy's Yamaha advert. When comparing the novel to its adaptation, yet again, it is the way in which the original is modified that is particularly noteworthy for the purposes of this discussion. In the film, Guy's financial boon comes from a motorcycle, advertised as being "swingin'," while in the novel, it is an advertisement for Anacin, an over-the-counter analgesic. The Yamaha ad seems to thus be selling a lifestyle as opposed to a utilitarian mode of transport. The Yamaha bike is also a distinctly masculine, non-family orientated thing. A motorbike, like Guy himself, is designed to go in one direction very fast, without heeding danger or responsibility. It is decidedly not a safe and economical family sedan. The reliability of this mode of transportation is of no consequence, and thus is not mentioned in the commercial. It would appear that the value of owning one is that it will make you hip. Anacin, on the other hand, although a name-brand aspirin product, is nonetheless a pharmaceutical known for reducing fever and potentially saving lives, making the former superfluous when compared to the latter when it comes to advertising technique as well as actual product usefulness. In this way, the film seems to align Guy even more strongly as a product of the impulses of conspicuous consumption.

Not only is the projected identity, media persona, and the livelihood of this young urbanite man derived from commercialism, but, additionally, consumer magazines, as suggested above, influence Rosemary and Guy both in the way that they live and also in the choices that they make. This is indicated not only by Rosemary taking clippings from *House Beautiful* for ideas in decorating, but equally by her getting the "very in" haircut from top stylist Vidal Sassoon, whose work was made internationally famous by media pop icon Twiggy.[39] Likewise, Guy is not just a producer of media image creation, he is also a product of the same. Just as Rosemary falls prey to certain allures of the consumerist media culture, Guy makes fashion choices as a result of media advertising, as evidenced by his buying the latest shirt that was advertised by the *New Yorker*. However, while Rosemary is surrounded by the culture of commodity as a result of being Guy's wife and thus influenced by him, Guy's whole identity seems to be completely subsumed. In this way, Guy is presented to be a product of postmodernity, both literally and figuratively. As Jean Baudrillard claims, one of the signals of postmodernity is the characterization of commodities not merely in relation to their use-value and exchange value, but more significantly in terms of their sign-value. For, as Baudrillard suggests in *The System of Objects*,[40] *For a Critique of the Political Economy of the Sign*,[41] and *The Consumer Society*,[42] as the expression and mark of style, luxury, prestige, and power become increasingly dominated by commodity and consumption, so too does the extent to which the individual is defined not by who he or she is, but indeed what he or she owns, uses, and trades. To return to the metaphor of the painted wall, if Rosemary allows herself to be painted over, Guy is the paint itself as well as the paint store salesman.

It is this connection between commodification and identification that is specifically noted in a critical analysis of the film and literary text offered by cultural historian Mark Jancovich in an essay entitled "Post-Fordism, Postmodernism, and Paranoia: The Dominance of the Horror Genre in Contemporary Literature." Jancovich suggests:

> Unlike the film, the novel is saturated with references to the media and media events. It presents a social world in which the population is constantly being ... told what to think and how to behave.[43]

However, whereas the novel does indeed present these issues of media influence, the film does so to an even greater extent as evidenced by the film's foregrounding of the draw of commercials, the role of television, and the prevalence of the press as mechanisms for the building of a self agency. Once again, it is not the similarities, but in the ways in which certain elements of the film adaptation have diverged from the novel that are of particular interest when it comes to these debates. Another deviation between the two texts significant to this discussion occurs in the scheduled meeting place for Rosemary and her close friend, mentor and general father figure, Edward Hutchens. Once Hutch discovers the fact that Rosemary might be prey for a Satanic cult, he schedules to meet Rosemary at the *Time* & *Life* (two commodities Hutch will shortly run out of) Building, whereas in the novel, the rendezvous point is the Seagram Building. Although Seagram's Gin is, admittedly, not a necessity of life, *Time* and *Life* magazines are particularly significant with regard to issues of acquisition and status, because they represent key vehicles for the transformation and dissemination of middle-class values. Indeed, it is the middle class that is most affected by the self-defining attributes of consumerism because this group is neither automatically positioned in powerful roles, like the aristocracy, nor is this group chiefly concerned with subsistence, like the lower class. Daniel Bell suggests that *Time* magazine became not unlike a bible for the disenfranchised middle class. He argues:

> The genius of Henry Luce ... was to take traditional American values, the belief in God, in work, in achievement, and to translate these, through the idiom of the coming urban civilization into the creed of American destiny.[44]

Luce, who, in one of his own publications, namely *Time* magazine, was lauded as being one of the most influential private citizens in America, not only published *Time,* but also *Life, Sports Illustrated* and *Fortune.* In total, these publications not only report on every facet of American life from business to leisure, but also interpret and comment on them so as to influence every aspect of middle-class existence. Through manipulating traditional rhetoric and applying it to a consumerist culture, Luce effectively sold a style of life to which the middle class adapted, and the working class aspired. Equally, the reference to *Time* foreshadows not only Rosemary's transformative haircut, as discussed above, but even more importantly, the religious debates that *Rosemary's Baby* will also address.

Both the novel and the film present one of the most controversial issues of *Time,* a black covered, red-lettered edition upon which "Is God Dead?" is prominently emblazoned. While this is only shown in the film, a magazine that Rosemary picks up while, appropriately, waiting for her obstetrician appointment,[45] it is directly discussed in the Levin novel.

At a party hosted by Guy and Rosemary for their young and hip friends, a man remarks of the feature article, "His name is Altizer, and he's down in Atlanta, I think; and what he says is that the death of God is a specific historic event that happened right now, in our time. That God literally died."[46]

Another example of the influence of commodification and the media occurs at another party given by the Castevets for the Woodhouses. During dinner, a conversation ensues regarding religion and the Pope's visit to New York City, an exchange that is present in both the film and the novel:

> **Roman:** No Pope ever visits a city where the newspapers are on strike.
> **Minnie:** I hear he's going to postpone and wait until it's all over.
> **Guy:** Well, that's showbiz.
> **Roman:** That's exactly what it is.
> **Minnie:** I think we're offending Rosemary.
> **Rosemary:** No ... no....
> **Minnie:** You're not religious, are you?
> **Rosemary:** Well, I was brought up a Catholic. Now, I don't know. Well, he is the Pope.
> **Roman:** You don't need to have respect for him just because he pretends that he's holy.
> **Minnie:** When I think of what they spend on robes and jewels.[47]

The Pope is also referenced later in the narrative in Guy's reaction to the papal visit, as suggested earlier. Like the consumerism that figuratively consumes Guy, it would appear as if Catholicism, at least within the world of this narrative, has lost its identity under the influence of secular consumerism. It is indeed reduced to, at least for these characters, just another product of and victim to commodified media hype.

Another apropos bone of contention that in some ways further problematizes these concerns has to do with links between Catholicism and commodification. More specifically, this has to do with what might be regarded as a spiritual get-out-of-jail-free credit card: the indulgence. An indulgence, in the form of a payment made to the Church on behalf of oneself or a loved one, could limit the time one spends in purgatory. It would appear as if the live-for-now-and-worry-about-the-consequences-another-day ethos of the consumer culture oddly conformed to the oldest and most conservative of Christian ecumenicisms. It was this practice that was, in fact, first protested by Martin Luther, the father of modern religious reform, as one of his Ninety-Nine Theses. The added consideration that Vatican City at that time as today is popularly renowned as the richest sovereign state per capita in the world does little to assuage these doubts. This critique of Catholicism was something that was noted in the reception of the film, as will be shown later in this chapter, and is also noted by Ira Levin himself. Levin suggests of the adaptation of his novel:

> The movie of *Rosemary's Baby* attracted some of the hostility I had worried about while writing the book. A woman screamed "Blasphemy!" in the lobby after the first New York preview, and I subsequently received scores of reprimanding letters from Catholic schoolgirls, all worded almost identically.[48]

The critiques offered by both the novel and the film versions of this text were somewhat holistic when it comes to the contemporaneous consumer culture. Historically speaking, though money could be used to free one from the burden of sin through the purchase of an indulgence, as it could be used to surround oneself with the icons of status in the form of creature comforts, up until this time it could not extricate the individual from familial ties and general legacy. It was only at the advent of modernity that money seemed to fulfill all of the aforementioned goals: it was not only a road toward atonement and self-gratification, it was also a road toward reinvention. This was liberating in many ways, as those without traditional position or upper-class affiliations could thus rise in station with the material wealth garnered through hard work rather than by birthright alone. This is the crux of the American Dream, which equally promised all the right to life, liberty and the pursuit of happiness. New York City became a symbol for this promise of freedom, housing not only Ellis Island, but also the Statue of Liberty, whereupon these words are engraved:

> Give me your tired, your poor, your huddled masses yearning to breathe free, the wretched refuse of your teeming shore. Send these, the homeless, tempest-tossed to me, I lift my lamp beside the golden door![49]

Even though this promise extended to the poorest members of society, it equally provided for potential increased insecurity: unchecked avarice.

In the past, tendencies toward overaccumulation were curbed by ascetic Protestant religions, such as Puritanism instilling the belief that the moral man was one who toiled and delayed satisfaction in order to please God and increase his kingdom. However, as Daniel Bell argues in *The Cultural Contradictions of Capitalism,* an economic ethos based upon the delayed gratification inherent to the traditional Protestant ethic, what he defines as "bourgeois capitalism," effectively surrendered to a neo-capitalist impulse during this period. This brought with it opportunity for monetary growth and an increase of status even as it destroyed the "keystone of character unleashed by the revolution of the consumer-durable culture,"[50] namely humble thrift. It is for this reason that religion is often considered socio-politically vital, not only because it functions to hold society together, but also because it fosters a belief in something outside the realm of the self and self-interest. In this way, religion held the radical individualist in check and hampered any hedonistic tendencies. However, as appetites were awakened in the mid–1960s and 1970s, a culture poised at the pinnacle of modernity effectively effaced many of these limitations that a healthy culture must necessarily establish. In a society that links accumulation with self-worth and success, individual agency in and of itself was in danger of becoming just another commodity to be bought and sold, as was the traditional spiritual community that held it together.

Rosemary's Baby as a Modern Gothic Text

Like this textual constellation, the Gothic literary movement provided a critique of the mechanisms of traditionalism, such as orthodox Catholicism, while equally setting itself up in opposition to modernity and a growing consumer culture. As David Punter suggests in *The Literature of Terror,* this fictional genre "strove to eschew the contemporary world, the world of commerce."[51] In other words, just like in the 1960s and 1970s, the eighteenth century was equally embroiled in debates regarding the role of traditionalism. In this way, *Rosemary's Baby* may be seen not only as a modern horror narrative, but moreover a modern Gothic tale, for not only does it address themes common to this earlier literary movement, but also uses its aesthetic conventions.

Indeed, just as the contemporaneous culture was embroiled in uncertainty at the culmination of the modern era, so too can its artistic output be regarded as being equally unsettled. If it could be argued that

Roman Polanski's work reveals, as cultural historian and Gothic scholar David Punter suggests, "The terrors of everyday life, which prise apart the bland surfaces of common interaction to disclose the anxieties and aggressions which lie beneath,"[52] and Ira Levin addresses a reawakened interest in the supernatural in the form of the occult by writing, "a popular, yet well-informed, book on the most bizarre of its facets ... with its unnerving revelation that the 'black arts' of the Middle Ages are alive and well, if secreted in such 'caves' of modern cities as the Victorian apartments of the Bramford,"[53] then it could indeed be argued that both the film and the novel thematically and visually reinforce a connection to the Literary Gothic.

From the very opening title sequence of the film, the iconic Gothic edifice of the Bramford apartment building begs to be considered an important, central character, so unlike the Chrysler and Empire State buildings that have come to stand for a modernist aesthetic and agenda, which are indeed never pictured throughout the film. Rather than these new and shiny steel structures, the Bramford is old, antiquated, and falling apart. It is not angular and linear, but instead overly decorous, rococo, and replete with cavernous depths, long winding corridors: mazes that confuse, isolate and entrap. This is the first indicator of the way in which the film seems to suggest a tendency to stand apart in a perpetual past, all the more noticeable when compared to the surrounding city. This setting can thus be located as being opposed to the modern, as an inherently Gothic internal universe. When this aesthetic concern is combined with a theme involving religion and a prevalence of the supernatural, *Rosemary's Baby*, in many ways, rejects the modern even while it equally supports key elements of the Gothic literary tradition. On the most obvious level, the film and novel versions of *Rosemary's Baby* focus on the need for a belief in the possibility of the supernatural. Indeed, while Guy exists in the outside public world of entertainment and commerce, Rosemary, while admittedly affected by the external world of commodification, is nonetheless increasingly relegated to the interior spaces. She is in fact only seen within the modern external world of Manhattan three times in this film. In all of these excursions, she is either accompanied by or avoiding the males who have come to dominate her. She is freer, ironically, in her internal domestic space, where she can roam unreservedly. She even comments to Hutch that it hurts less when she moves around. It is only when these men who attempt to control Rosemary actively invade her world, a world which she attempts to bar them from, that she is driven mad. Much like her Gothic heroine predecessors, once driven to the brink of madness, it is only when she denies the rational and comes to accept the possibility of a supernatural world that she begins to relinquish her fears of sub-jugation—to accept and understand the world in which she has been trapped. On the surface, these fears with regard to the actual versus the perceptual are portrayed as having a scientific basis, as the product of a woman under the influence of what is, according to Guy, "Prepartum I-don't-know, some kind of hysteria."[54] However, as revealed in the final scene of the film, once she removes the carefully lined shelves that she had previously been drawn to paper, she acts to expand her universe, rupturing its confines. Taking action to pass a barrier that she was previously forced through, the potential for freedom from her fetters is literally opened up. Much like the Gothic heroine in "The Yellow Wallpaper," also in the throes of the supposed "postpartum crazies," she locks her husband out and strips back the wallpaper of the world to which she had been confined. Once Rosemary's yellow papered shelves have been removed, she acts based on her own agency for the first time. She denies seeing Roman Castevet, "I don't hear you. You are in Dubrovnik."[55] She spits in Guy's face when he tells her that she was not mortally affected by his actions: that the ends justify the means to his selling her body to the devil for fame and fortune. She is worshipped by the coven as being an alternative Mary, the mother of the Antichrist: the book in fact ends with the coven chanting "Hail Andrew…. Hail Rosemary, mother of Andrew…. Hail Satan."[56] For the first time in the narrative, she takes control of what was hers to control all along as the protagonist of this text. The narrative does, in fact, follow Rosemary in her actions and thoughts, unlike any of the other characters, in what amounts to a first-person point of view without the use of the personal pronoun, and information is only revealed as she is made aware of it. Thus, it can be called into question until the very end as to whether she is under threat from a Satanic coven or only prey to what Guy and others attempt to dismiss as deluded fantasies so as to deny the reality behind their actions. As suggested earlier and as will be explored in detail below, it is in this deception that the horror of *Rosemary's Baby* rests. It is also in circumventing Rosemary as an active female agent that this work addresses important concerns surrounding the contemporaneous feminist movement, as will also be addressed in a later chapter, a topic that could equally be applied to this text as well.

The thematic concerns of the Gothic can indeed be seen to directly comment on female agency, as the irrational supernatural still seems to be associated with the female as a way of belittling her. At various points in the film, Rosemary is told to not read books—it is an order from Dr. Sapirstein and her husband, the latter of whom resorts to placing *All of them Witches* on a high shelf where she cannot reach it. The former,

Dr. Sapirstein, also tells her not to take mass-produced vitamins. This very Gothic separation of a female protagonist from the world of science, books and rationality, and pushing her towards irrationality is archetypal.

The Religious Reception of *Rosemary's Baby*

When analyzing the reception of the film, it is specifically this religious thematic concern with Satanism as being not only an alternative orthodoxy, but equally a grounding mechanism that makes it particularly controversial, as is suggested by Levin in the introduction to this chapter and equally in a review of the film published in the *New York Times* on June 21, 1968, just following the release of Polanski's version of *Rosemary's Baby*. This article reported that the film had been condemned by the National Catholic Office for Motion Pictures (formerly the National League of Decency) for the way in which traditional Christianity was depicted. According to the reviewer, "Much more serious [than the scenes of nudity] is the perverted use that the film makes of fundamental Christian beliefs surrounding the birth of Christ and its mockery of religious persons and practices."[57] The aesthetic value of the film seemed to pose an additional threat, as the National Catholic Office goes on to suggest: "The very technical excellence of the film serves to intensify its defamatory nature. They [the National Catholic Office] feel that if the film becomes a big money maker it will mean a further decline in the influence of the group."[58] Additionally, in a similar film review published by the United States Conference of Catholic Bishops (USCCB), the film was given an "O," meaning morally offensive:

> Directed by Roman Polanski, the production values [of *Rosemary's Baby*] are topnotch and performances completely chilling, but the movie's inverted Christian elements denigrate religious beliefs.[59]

Thus, the film was regarded by the religious press as presenting a challenge to traditional morality, a challenge all the more damaging given the film's standard as being a more "high art" discourse.

Extratextual Considerations of *Rosemary's Baby*

As with *The Omen*, which will be discussed in detail in the subsequent chapter, the film *Rosemary's Baby* takes on added significance when a consideration of the associations provided by cast and crew are taken into account. Like with *The Omen*, *Rosemary's Baby* in many ways transcends the marginalized horror genre categorization by attempting to appeal to a much wider swath of the population. In targeting the art house, teen/B-cinema, television and classical Hollywood viewer, the film can indeed be considered to be engaged with consumerism in a more direct sense, just as it addresses this theme within the text itself.

First, Paramount Pictures attempted to garner the old Hollywood audiences by including actors associated with classical Golden Age Productions. For the role of antagonist, Roman Castevet, Sidney Blackmer was cast. Blackmer, considered to be a character actor, as opposed to a leading man, was featured in over 120 films spanning from the post–World War I period, beginning with the serial *The Perils of Pauline*, to the early 1970s. He also lent the production a bit of legitimacy by virtue of his Tony Award–winning performance in *Come Back Little Sheba* in 1951 on Broadway. Ralph Bellamy, although obliquely connected to classical horror cinema for roles in Universal's *The Wolf Man* and *The Ghost of Frankenstein*, also had a more mainstream career dating from the silents to the talkies. Hollywood paired him with the likes of famous staple actors including James Cagney, Cary Grant, Jean Harlow and Clark Gable, and awarded him an Academy Award for Best Supporting Actor for his performance in the *Awful Truth*. Elisha Cook, Jr., the apartment superintendent, was also a well recognized bit player who had been cast in films including *The Big Sleep* and Stanley Kubrick's *The Killing*.

Not only did the film target audiences from old Hollywood, but also television, arguably the main competitor for viewers during this period, as noted in *Rosemary's Baby* itself. British actor Maurice Evans (Hutch) had also appeared on Broadway, but was more renowned for his television roles in the 1960s, including the role of The Puzzler for the campy superhero series *Batman* and the narrator of Disney's animated feature *Winnie the Pooh*. However, ironically, his most famous role is probably that of Samantha Stephens's father, the warlock Maurice, on the television sitcom *Bewitched*. In this series, a witch marries a mortal man and both must work to accommodate each other's lifestyles—hers as a magical being and his as an advertising executive—all within middle-class American suburbia. Although diametrically opposite from *Rosemary's Baby* in terms of tone, this sitcom did nonetheless bring the witch and concept of practicing witchcraft into the American home.

As suggested above, as an international art house director, Roman Polanski lent the film a certain level of respectability, not only historically and culturally speaking, but also in terms of the larger viewership of this work. In addition to this, the inclusion of John Cassavetes, as leading male Guy Woodhouse, redoubles this consideration. Cassavetes is considered by critics and theorists alike as being the father of the American independent cinema movement, alongside other, possibly more widely recognized directors such as Woody Allen and Martin Scorsese. After graduating from the American Academy of Dramatic Arts in New York City, the future director went on to study method acting at Lee Strasberg's Actors Studio, where actors were trained in alternative approaches to developing characters through immersion in the role. One of the techniques taught by Strasberg, improvisation, inspired Cassavetes to make his first film, the largely unscripted and thus revolutionary *Shadows* (1960), a work which established him as an independent director. Further, his decision to remain in New York City, as opposed to Hollywood, set him and the indie movement in opposition to the mainstream: living on the other side of the country, self-funding highly personal works of cinema rather than works to gain profit, and breaking with standard formula.

Finally, on the other end of the artistic spectrum, the film was produced and features a walk-on part[60] by William Castle, who was well known as a B-cinema director and producer. Famous for films promoted with gimmicks such as electrified seats set to go off during screenings of *The Tingler*, the *House on Haunted Hill*'s "emergo," wherein a skeleton attached to a line above the audience's heads would fly over at key moments in the narrative, and an insurance sale whereby audiences could take out a one-thousand-dollar policy should they die of fright whilst watching *Macabre*, to name a few. Studios realized that competition from B-cinema producers such as American Independent Pictures took away a large chunk of the teen viewership, and thus including Castle would possibly appeal to this segment of the population.

In terms of political discourses and opening up of traditionalism, several members of the cast can be discussed in terms of contemporaneous debates regarding the role of cultural conservatism. First, Mia Farrow, Rosemary Woodhouse, was herself the daughter of Irish actress Maureen O'Sullivan and, like the heroine that she portrays, brought up Catholic. At the time of filming, she was famously married to singer and fellow actor Frank Sinatra. Himself an Italian Catholic, Sinatra took issue with her starring in the film. As discussed in his biography, Sinatra actually became so disgruntled that he finally ended up serving Farrow with divorce papers on the set of the film. Whether this was as a result of the theme of the film and the Catholic Church's reaction to it, Farrow's apparent nude scene (even though she was reported to have a body double), or her failure to assume the role of house wife, opting for a career instead of supporting his, the fact of the dissolution of their marriage seems to ironically align with the themes presented in the film with regard to the breakdown of conventional mechanisms of stability including marriage. Another extratextual indicator of the failure of the conservative institution of marriage comes with the casting of Victoria Vetri, who portrayed the first victim of the Castevet coven, Theresa Gionoffrio. When Terry meets Rosemary in the laundry room, Rosemary stares. When noticed, Rosemary suggests that the reason for her attention has to do, ironically, with the girl's uncanny resemblance to Victoria Vetri, the actress. An Italian American like Sinatra, Vetri became famous for being the woman whom Natalie Wood replaced in *West Side Story*. Regardless of her acting career, failed or otherwise, she was made more famous (or potentially infamous) off-screen. She was *Playboy's* Playmate of the Month in September 1967, a sexual icon that would have, arguably, made Sinatra squirm in more ways than one. Married four times and divorced three, Vetri was charged with attempted murder of her last husband after allegedly shooting him from close range inside the Hollywood apartment they were sharing. Continuing on with the issue of sexuality, Patsy Kelly, who stars in the film as coven member Laura-Louise, was infamous beginning in the 1930s for being an openly gay actress. She claimed affairs with Wilma Cox and Tallulah Bankhead. Indeed, if this film, and the era out of which it arose, were about an opening up of conservative boundaries, then this actress seemed to be paving the way.

Toward an Understanding of Where the Horror of *Rosemary's Baby* Lies

In an early scene of the film, a tracking shot follows the Woodhouses as they view the Bramford for the first time. Although this shot establishes these characters as the protagonists by literally tracking their every move, the camera is diverted away from these central figures when it stops to focus on a man installing a peephole in a door to one of the apartments. Significantly, this shot resonates, as it remains stationary for several seconds. This image could be read in a number of ways: indeed, it could be seen to foreground the notion that the spectator needs to look deeper and beyond the surface—that all is not what it seems.

Within both the novel and the film, there is a constant questioning of appearances. Guy, whose name suggests an everyman, is an attractive husband with ugly intentions. Roman Castevet, née Steven Marcato, a grandfatherly neighbor who potentially rearranged the letters in his alias to form an anagram that could easily be read as Roman Catholic, is a man so innocuous as to have a book-on-a-hook entitled *Jokes for the John*. Yet, this man is also the head of a Satanic cabal. Abraham

Saperstein, whose name is a reference to both "honest Abe" Lincoln and the biblical Abraham, a common patriarch of Judaism, Christianity and Islam, is not only a kindly and internationally regarded obstetrician,[61] but also an ethnically Jewish man and practicing Satanist. There is also the Pope, who, in the eyes of Minnie and Roman, only pretends to be holy. The first victim of the Castevets, Terry Gionoffrio, a woman who is ironically touted as looking exactly like the actress Victoria Vetri, was in fact Vetri, although oddly using the pseudonym Angela Dorian. And finally, Rosemary Reilly Woodhouse is, as per her own description, a country girl at heart. Her name, Rosemary, suggests an herb, much like one of the herbs growing in Minnie Castevet's herbarium, thereby implying that she too is uprooted and transported to an indoor urban apartment and used in the service of a Satanic coven. Nothing is, in fact, as it seems. Everything is wrapped up in a friendly and appealing guise, packaged and sold to Rosemary much like the chairs, the design ideas, and the cans that populate her world and literally consume her husband. Thus, the visual cue of the peephole and the painter both demand a looking through, a deeper look beyond the obvious exteriority of the rational world and into a world wherein superstition and the supernatural housed in a Gothic castle all abound. Herein, the supernatural is real, and those who believe gain strength even while those who doubt are thus weakened by their denial of this possibility. This same trope of mistaken appearances, the conflict of the secular world of modernity and the ancient world of supernatural spiritual affiliations, and the role of faith are not, however, limited to the film and novel versions of *Rosemary's Baby*. All of these themes are equally explored to much the same effect in a film and novelizations produced almost a decade later, *The Omen*.

Two

Predestination, Secrecy and Conspiracy in *The Omen*

With the collapse of religion, biblical references, which formerly penetrated deep into everyday awareness, have become incomprehensible.... In the space of two or three generations, enormous stretches of the "Judeo-Christian tradition," so often invoked by educators but so seldom taught in any form, have passed into oblivion. The effective loss of cultural traditions on such a scale makes talk of a new Dark Age far from frivolous.[1]
—CHRISTOPHER LASCH, *The Culture of Narcissism*

Given the enormous American emphasis on independence and self-reliance ... the survival of the family with its strong emphasis on interdependence and acceptance is striking. The family in many ways represents a historically older form of life.[2]—ROBERT BELLAH, *Habits of the Heart*

In *Rosemary's Baby* Satan decides to reverse two thousand years of Christian hegemony by sending his messiah to destroy American society from within. Polanski's film anticipates an assault that continues in *The Omen*.[3]—TONY WILLIAMS, *Hearths of Darkness*

Introduction

In the penultimate scene from *The Omen*, following the instructions of archaeologist, demonologist, and exorcist Carl Bugenhagen, protagonist Robert Thorn takes his young adopted son to sacred ground, in this case an Anglican church, wherein he has chosen to murder his heir in accordance with an ancient ritual. In order to complete this rite, Thorn has been given a series of daggers with which he will be expected to stab his child in the form of a cross radiating outward from the heart to the limbs. The whole film has been leading up to this moment, the narrative arc indeed culminating with this choice. Should the suspected son of Satan be allowed to live, or should the child be destroyed? Will Thorn be successful in this ghastly undertaking, or will he fail? Finally, what will be the outcome of these actions for staving off the impending apocalypse that the rise of the Antichrist is destined to bring about?

Once arriving at the church, followed by a trail of police officers who are attempting to stop this potential political incident,[4] Thorn prostrates the child upon the floor of the transept before the altar. As he raises the first dagger, he shouts to God asking for aid in carrying out his task. It is at this point that he is shot by

(Clockwise) Robert Thorn (Gregory Peck), Willa Baylock (Billie Whitelaw), Father Brennan (Patrick Troughton), and Damien Thorn (Harvey Stephens) from *The Omen.*

police officers, the scene ending with a close-up of the bullet as it speeds toward its target. This is a traumatic scene, not only because it offers a potential for the violent death of a child, but also because it results in the ultimate death of the protagonist, whom we have been following throughout his many trials and tribulations in this film. Further, should an ancient prophecy be believed, Thorn's failure to vanquish evil will bring about the end of days. This is confirmed in a biblical poem that figures prominently in the narrative:

> When the Jews return to Zion, and a comet rips the sky, and the Holy Roman Empire rises, then you and I must die. From the Eternal Sea, He rises, creating armies on either shore, turning man against his brother, till man exists no more.[5]

At this point in the text, historically speaking, the Jews have returned to Zion through the establishment of the State of Israel. Equally, according to the interpretation of this poem, the Holy Roman Empire has risen with the birth of the common market. Now known as the European Economic Community, this body was established with the Treaty of Rome in 1957. More specifically in terms of the Antichrist, his birth under a comet has also occurred within this narrative, as has his rise from the world of politics, the Eternal Sea, given Damien's adoptive father's role as ambassador first to Italy, then to the United Kingdom. Further, as a result of his wealth, family name, social circles and prestige, Thorn was destined (up until the point of his death, that is) to be a future President of the United States, a likelihood directly expressed by his wife and by Thorn himself upon becoming Ambassador to the United Kingdom.[6] However, now that Thorn is dead, it would appear as if his ultimate act has in fact thrown a spanner in the works, although not in the way in which he initially intended. Although alive, Damien will no longer be affiliated with the political sphere. This connection has apparently been severed by Thorn's death, and thus the prophecy rendered illegitimate. However, once again fate turns the tide. Indeed, regardless of whether Thorn heeds or ignores the signs, regardless of whether he lives or dies, it is all of no real importance. The birth, the rise and the effect of the Antichrist will be carried out no matter what diversions mortal man may enact, and the final scene of the film confirms this. Even given the untimely death of Thorn and his wife, Damien will rise from the Eternal Sea, if not as a result of his connection to Thorn, then as a result of a surrogate. At the double funeral of both his parents, Damien smiles in a tight close-up. The camera then zooms out to show the child holding the hands of a woman and a man, the latter of whom is addressed by an aide as "Mr. President." It is thus revealed that Damien has now become the adopted son of Robert Thorn's best friend, the current President of the United States of America, and will be in a prime position to claim his birthright, fulfill the ancient prophecy, and ultimately bring about the apocalypse. Indeed, what was initially regarded as being a difficult choice is in fact revealed to be no choice at all, but instead an inevitable outcome that will bring about the omen for which this film is entitled. The trailer signals this further when it begs similar questions to those posed in the introduction to this chapter. The narrator of this promotional material states in voice-over, "For generations the Thorns have been a family of tremendous wealth, position and power.... Was it an accident? Was it murder? Was it a coincidence? Or was it an Omen?"[7]

With these themes in mind, this chapter will discuss *The Omen*, another example of a film that, like *Rosemary's Baby*, presents an alignment of Catholicism and Satanism suggesting that the titular omen is no accident, but instead has religious relevance in being rooted in biblical doctrine. Likewise, these presumably orthodox faiths are then pitted against the irreligious world of modernity: the conflict offered being between spirituality and secularism. Rather than framing this struggle as involving a secular consumer culture, as was the case in the previous chapter, *The Omen* will be shown to offer debates surrounding issues of free will. More specifically, this film and its textual adaptation articulates a concern with the traditional religious dogma of predestination and familial legacy, both of which are then, once again, contrasted with the world of modernity. The protagonist of *The Omen* is Robert Thorn, a man, as suggested in the aforementioned trailer, who comes from the privilege and benefits bestowed to an upper-class industrialist family. The narrative follows him through a journey from secular skepticism to belief as he comes to discern the prevalence and efficacy of the Satanist Church, which has been masked as Catholicism within this text. Thorn must then overcome his disbelief in the predictions, symbols and warnings offered to him by religious texts and men of faith. Once he accepts the apparent veracity of the predestined role that he is to play in this apocalyptic narrative, he is forced into action: the outcomes of which, as a result of his conflicted alignment, he ultimately misapprehends.

On the crux between traditionalism and modernity, Robert Thorn is indeed, much like Rosemary Woodhouse, the protagonist discussed in the previous chapter, a character in conflict. On the one hand, he is a modern secular individual who relies upon his own moxie to establish himself within the world of politics. Not a church goer, he instead gains his power from his connections to familial legacy, being an heir to an immense fortune and all the trappings and benefits therein for a secular consumer culture. However, although monied and connected, the film makes no real mention of the Thorn family, and his and his wife's extended relations are never mentioned or depicted. As a result of this disassociation, Thorn assumes the conservative role of husband in relative isolation. He is a married man and the sole breadwinner that on the one hand is inexorably tied to the public sphere, desiring to spend a proportion of his time with his powerful political friends and alliances so as to get the proverbial "leg up" in the world, as his legacy suggests that he should. Yet on the other hand, he is also equally defined by ties to his own nuclear family. He alone thus involves himself in making decisions not only for himself, but also for his family without the aid of past generations to guide him. As the narrative progresses, these bonds become increasingly problematic: first, as a result of the psychological difficulties experienced by his wife and then by the legacy offered by his adopted son, the heir apparent and the Antichrist, both of these domestic concerns in turn leading to an inability to assume the full duties of his political office. Indeed, when regarded on the surface, it is his decision to adopt Damien, without the knowledge and consent of his wife, that leads to the difficulties that he experiences both privately and publicly, a choice that once enacted, as many theorists argue, leads to the breakdown of the family. However, as will be shown in this chapter, his choice is really no choice at all: he is as equally powerless as his wife in realizing the full ramifications of his act in furthering the omen. In other words, his actions are guided not by free will but instead by an ancient biblical prophecy that has been predetermined and is thus destined to be realized.

Likewise, the traditional Church, that figures as the other side of the narrative conflict presented in *The Omen*, is equally problematic in terms of its allegiances. On the surface, the Church appears to be affiliated with Catholicism, the oldest Christian ecumenicism; however, the text goes on to reveal that those who pose as priests or Catholic followers, both arguably representatives of God on earth, are in fact in league with Satan. Much like the Castevets, these symbols of benignity and benevolence are, in fact, engaged in establishing the reign of the Antichrist and thus bringing about the end of the world. Also, as will be discussed in this chapter, the ideological alignment of *The Omen* is further rendered problematic when considering it on an extratextual level. As was the case with *Rosemary's Baby* (and, in fact, all of the works discussed in this book), an analysis of the extratextual elements such as choice of actors, directors and their added socio-political significance might make an ideological alignment even less clearly delineated. If it can be argued, as Marshall Berman does, that "to be modern is to live a life of paradox and contradiction,"[8] then *The Omen* is, if for this reason alone, indeed a modern work.

Even given its deeply divided nature, both textually and extratextually, current academic discourse tends to focus on representations of traditional mechanisms presented in *The Omen*, such as family, gender roles, and orthodox religion, and thus position this work as being reactionary, most suggesting that this text articulates debates regarding the detriment of devaluing traditionalism. Andrew Tudor speaks to this when he argues, "One group [of seventies supernatural horror films] postulates varying degrees of demonic intercession in the world's affairs and is rooted in *The Omen*'s 1976 success."[9] Indeed, given that this film was made not even two years after the resignation of President Richard Nixon and ten years after the publication of the Warren Commission report, it would appear as if a political exorcism might not go altogether amiss.

It is this ambivalence of the contemporaneous culture that drives Robin Wood's analysis of the horror cinema of this period, and of this film in particular. He argues, "*The Omen* would make no sense in a society that was not prepared to enjoy and surreptitiously condone the working out of its own destruction."[10] For Wood, the popularity of *The Omen* cannot be wholly explained by its depiction of classic horror tropes involving Satanic threat. It is instead the connection to family horror, and more specifically its reactionary ideological position, which does not question the "goodness" of the family that forms the basis of the narrative. In other words, for Wood, the success of the film stems from the way in which this conservative institution, the family, is put into conflict against Old World evil in a modified good versus evil motif.[11] Wood argues:

> [*The Omen*] is about the end of the world, but the "world" the film envisages ending is very particularly defined within it: the bourgeois, capitalist, patriarchal Establishment. Here "normality" is not merely threatened, it is totally annihilated: the state, the church, and the family.... [T]he devil-child is its [the film's] implicit hero, whose systematic destruction of the bourgeois Establishment the audience follows with a secret relish.[12]

Cultural critic Vivian Sobchack follows Wood's foregrounding of the family-in-struggle as problematic. Likewise, she argues that it is the breakdown of the family that leads to the end-of-the-world scenario presented in *The Omen*:

> From the early to mid–1970s and coincident with bourgeois society's negative response to the youth movements and drug culture of the late 1960s ... [t]he child was figured as an alien force that threatened both its immediate family and all adult authority that would keep it in its place.... The bodies and souls of such children as appear in.... The Omen (1976) are "possessed" by demonic, supernatural, and a-historic forces that play out apocalypse in the middle-class home.[13]

This demonization of the child becomes a trope in many of the era's horror films, including *The Omen* and *Rosemary's Baby*, as was discussed in the previous chapter. It is, in fact, in this way that these two texts are usually brought together[14]: as demon child narratives equally articulating the prevalent phobia of the late 1960s and early 1970s counter culture. More specifically, it is the fear of the stifling nature of familial roles, according to Wood, that leads (or at the very least contributes) to the subsequent breakdown of the traditional family overall. Other film theorists, including Tony Williams, articulate a more generalized focus regarding the breakdown of authority. Williams suggests that the film presents demonic possession as a symbol for adult paranoia. These fears are not only directed toward the private sphere and the pending destruction of the family by the unruly *evil* children. Concern equally manifests to the potential of overly zealous and destructive government institutions which might well enact global annihilation in a relentless drive to save the world for democracy.[15]

While this chapter will follow these authors in arguing for a thematic concern that focuses on the family, this will be shown to be limited to the protagonist's own nuclear family. It will be further asserted that while the individual working alone is in fact rendered ineffectual, collective systems including religion are, alternatively, primarily effective. Indeed, individual agency is brought to its knees, while predestination and an outward focus on collective historical belief remain dominant forces that cannot be challenged or negated. In this way, spiritual orthodoxy will be shown to be of primary concern and not merely yet another symbol of restrictive patriarchal traditionalism.

The Omen and the Role of Prophecy and Predestination

Throughout this work, *The Omen* presents a thematic concern with familial connectivity and predestination, a conservative focus that is then pitted against an ethos of individualism and free will that characterizes the secular culture of this era. The conservative themes that form one side of the narrative conflict presented in *The Omen* are revealed in the prophecies regarding the birth of the Antichrist, in the lineage that both establishes and reinforces these omens, and in the roles that will be assumed by the figure who answers this call of destiny. This theme is presented from the outset, thus underscoring its importance for the narrative overall.

In the opening scene, protagonist Robert Thorn, the United States Ambassador to Italy, rushes to a Roman Catholic hospital, wherein, without the support of any other family member, his wife has just given birth to a son who has died. Upon arrival, and before seeing his wife, he is taken aside by a priest who convinces Thorn, unbeknownst to his wife, to adopt another child born at the same time as his dead child. He suggests, "It would be a blessing to her [his wife] and to the child. On this night, God has given you a son."[16] Given the fact that this hospital is run by the Catholic Church, that this hospital is located in Rome, not far from the Vatican, and that this man himself wears priestly accouterments, one comes to assume the god bestowing the child is the Christian one. However, as is revealed later in this text, the aforementioned assumption is proven to be false. In fact, the priest is part of a Satanic circle committed to the nurture and rise of the Antichrist, the very child that has just been adopted.

It is with this initial "decision," the inciting incident of this narrative, that the nature of free will is first challenged. When regarded more closely, Thorn's "choice" to adopt a son based upon an apparently random string of events proves to be no accident at all. It is instead the result of careful planning so as to fulfill the aforementioned prophecy as quoted in the introduction to this chapter. First, the seeming coincidence of the Antichrist's birth and the subsequent death of the Thorn heir is shown to be no mere coincidence. The Antichrist is indeed destined to be born just at this moment: as a certain comet crosses the sky, on an auspicious (or rather inauspicious) date and time: June 6 at six a.m. (**6/6/6:00**[17]). Likewise, the Thorn baby does not die naturally, as is later revealed in the narrative. He was, in fact, killed to make room for the surrogate to the Thorn legacy, making his death not simply a horrible random event. Also, it is, in turn, Robert Thorn who must adopt this child, yet another incidence of careful planning. The alignment of the Antichrist to the Thorn lineage specifically fulfills another prophetic indicator that establishes the identity of the Antichrist: that he shall come from the world of politics. This is the very world to which Thorn himself, not to mention his powerful friends including the President of the United States, belong.

One final prophecy solidifies the Antichrist's position as the only heir to the Thorn dynasty. Thorn is told by a priest that his wife is once again pregnant and that the Antichrist and his followers will not let the child live. When Thorn next sees his wife, the fact of her pregnancy is confirmed as well as her desire for an abortion: she does not want to have any more children. Thorn does not give heed to her wishes due to the fact that it was prophesied that the fetus would not be born. However, even given his refusal, the unborn child does die, as suggested in the prediction at the hands of Damien, who causes Kathy to fall from the upper floor of their house, injuring herself and causing a miscarriage.

The role of predestination, first established as the initial narrative conflict, indeed does continue to play a strong role throughout *The Omen*: as suggested above, this theme drives the unwitting actions of these specific characters. Moreover, by foregrounding an alignment of orthodox faiths, Satanism is rendered a powerful and efficacious force that will not be denied. In other words, the fulfillment of prophecy is the very concern that not only controls the actions of the characters and drives the narrative forward, but also establishes Satanism as a Christian other, a conservative belief system mirroring Catholicism in faith and creed. The conflict of *The Omen* is, thus, not good versus evil, Catholicism versus Satanism, or even the benevolent influence of the family versus the Satanic Church. If read via religious connectivity and prophetic revelation, *The Omen* instead offers a thematic concern with faith versus skepticism: religious belief versus modernity. Arguably, had Thorn been a religious man, knowledgeable of the biblical signs, he might have been able to wield his knowledge and his faith to enact a change in the series of events that play out in this text, for to understand the Christian is to understand its Satanic other. Further, had he been closer to his powerful family, he might have been dissuaded from making the choice that he did, given the fact that a biological heir is far preferable to an unknown contingency. However, he was in fact specifically chosen for these particular attributes, the fact of his secular familial isolation and political connectivity making him an ideal candidate to carry out the prophetic rise of the Antichrist.[18] Also, on the other side of the dichotomy presented in the narrative, much as was the case with *Rosemary's Baby*, the two historically rooted faiths, Satanism and Catholicism, are presented as being interconnected; in fact, they are offered up as being equally conservative religious systems that are contingent upon one another in their ties to historicity and reliance on dogma. It is this connectivity that is foregrounded in this work: a repeated signifying mechanism too pervasive to be ignored, to be devalued as of minor importance, or to be seen as being a mere symbol of reactionary socio-political mechanisms.

Within *The Omen*, the doubling of orthodox faiths is revealed most prominently in another conservative ideological alignment: familial ancestry. When considering the connection between faith and family, this should be of no great surprise. As discussed in the introduction to this book, the family is the institution whereby faith is instilled, furthered and forwarded. Ideally, the historic role of religion has been to provide a sense of community established by shared ethical concerns and reverence to a higher power, whose laws and teachings must first be taught and then be obeyed. The deference to the Church is first mirrored by the family: succumbing to familial law practice for succumbing to the law of God. Further, the connection between biological kinship, the family, and spiritual kinship, the Church, is directly established in the Ten Commandments, wherein to honor the father and mother is likened to honoring God himself. These beliefs are not only mirrored by but equally transmitted within the family. They are then reinforced by the Christian community at large, the family of the congregational Church. This is why, historically, parental authority, like religious authority, acted as a primary mechanism for cohesion and why when one fails to be heeded, the other falls in turn. Familial legacy, therefore, becomes a

primary force in religious texts and indeed, it is paternal lineage that is significant when analyzing the aforementioned Satanic religious prophecies presented in *The Omen* and their connection to biblical texts. Moreover, these are the selfsame ways in which the former thus informs and mirrors the latter.

When looking at the opening scene alone, Thorn, it would appear, is predestined to choose to adopt Damien as a result of his lineage, just as Joseph's adoption of Jesus was equally predetermined for similar reasons. If the way in which the Antichrist may be identified is through his familial connection to politics, then Christ could be recognized by equally being descended from the family of King David. As the Second Book of Samuel from the Bible indicates, God promised King David that Christ would rise from his future heirs:

> When your days are fulfilled and you rest with your fathers, I will set up your seed after you, who will come from your body, and I will establish his kingdom. He shall build a house for My name, and I will establish the throne of his kingdom forever. I will be his Father, and he shall be My son.[19]

In this way it is revealed that lineage is determined and rendered significant through God's election rather than being merely a biological accident in a chaotic world without meaning.

As the narrative within *The Omen* progresses, this collusion of faith is yet again suggested by providing linkage in the roles and representations of Christ and the Antichrist; it is also apparent in the implication that the generational legacy of both Jesus and Damien was one not left to chance, but instead determined and defined by biblical prophecy. These roles may thus be regarded as being inescapable and binding. It is, specifically, this constraint that comes into conflict with certain elements of the contemporaneous secular culture in which *The Omen* was created, for indeed, religious and familiar authority were primarily and equally instruments of restraint. According to social theorist Christopher Lasch in *The Culture of Narcissism*, with the modern age, the desires of the self were made a primary concern over the roles and the teachings of the family. This resulted in a destabilization of the family, which opened a potential for a subsequent breakdown of religious orthodoxy. This breakdown resulted in a further weakening in the family, in what may be regarded as a socio-cultural vicious circle. Lasch argues throughout his writings that it is the abdication of parental authority itself that installs a desire for unlimited individual agency, self-expression and exploration—freedom from the perceived constraints of a traditional and potentially stultifying ethos. Turning away from the family had to do with a turning away from the past, from tradition and from mechanisms of identification based upon posterity, genealogy and generations rather than upon self-determination and individual free will. This ethos comes into direct conflict with *The Omen*, as it is a generational legacy and the roles it instills which are rendered significant, meaningful and efficacious within this text.

To return to a consideration of the film, Damien is directly referred to as Messiah, which, according to the *Oxford English Dictionary*, is defined as, "A leader who is believed to have the power to solve the world's problems."[20] In other words, this appellation refers not merely to a way of defining or categorizing an individual, but to a role to which one must adhere from birth. The Satanic Antichrist thus provides a similar if oppositional position to the Christ of traditional Christianity, and in this way the narrative antagonist becomes imbued with an historical meaning and religious significance which cannot be denied or altered. Both Christ and the Antichrist solve the problems of the world, the former by saving the souls of sinners in the afterlife, and the latter by bringing about the apocalypse, whereby those who are good and those who are evil will be judged accordingly.

Another example of the connectivity between the family of Christ and the Antichrist that might be regarded as traditional is presented visually near the end of the film and involves maternal positioning. In terms of this maternal connectivity, before Kathy Thorn is killed, she is seen to be wearing a blue hospital gown over a white robe. As she attempts to undress, this outer garment is pulled over her head and hair. These colors, blue and white, and the configuration of her attire, a loosely fitting dress with a white shawl covering the hair, is similar to that in which Mary, the mother of Jesus, is often pictured. Although Kathy did not conceive or give birth to Damien, like Mary did of Jesus (and as Rosemary did of Andy in *Rosemary's Baby*), the heroine of *The Omen* is thus nonetheless equally aligned with her Christian counterpart.[21]

Similarly, connectivity in terms of pre-destiny is revealed through geography and a sense of place. The location that Thorn is directed to visit in order to seek advice as to how to destroy the Antichrist, for example, is Megiddo, Armageddon from the Greek, an important biblical location.[22] It is here that, according to the book of Revelations [*sic*],[23] the final battle between good and evil is destined to take place, hence the significance behind the name. Other prophecies regarding the end of days are also mentioned in the film, as discussed earlier in this chapter. One of these, the comet, takes on the appearance of the star of Bethlehem, which shone at the time and on the location of Damien's birth in the same way as the star of David did upon the birthplace of Jesus. This doppelganger relationship between Damien and Jesus is not only suggested metaphorically, through signifiers involving family, role and significant locale. Their connectivity is, in fact, directly stated, making the importance of their ties to one another more manifest than mere allegory.

A key example of this occurs at Damien's fifth birthday party.[24] In this scene, two photographers are engaged in shooting footage. One, who remains unnamed, turns to the other, Keith Jennings, played by David Warner, and inquires as to why he is not taking the opportunity to shoot photos of the event. Jennings (Warner) in turn replies, "Just saving a bit [of film] for the canonization. I don't know if we've just got the heir to the Thorn millions here or Jesus Christ himself."[25] This exchange, although again as admittedly ironic as the exchange between Guy and Nicklas in *Rosemary's Baby*, is another one of many references to the primary thematic concern for *The Omen*. Familial connectivity and predestination are both revealed to be traditionally religious signifiers that come into conflict with a contemporaneous focus upon free will and freedom of choice because of their restrictive nature.

Religious Conservatism and *The Omen*

As discussed above, in terms of theme, *The Omen* presents a conservative concern with the overwhelming power of religion, predestination, and historical imperatives through the foregrounding of the titular "omen," a portent of events that will occur in the future through the inevitable ascendancy of the Antichrist. The text suggests that if the warnings are not observed, they will result in the apocalypse, the end of the world. Academic debate also suggests that such an overarching concern might indeed render this text as ideologically reactionary. This alignment cannot altogether be denied, although not for the reasons suggested by current scholarly discourse. As has been argued, it is not the fear of the child, the constraints offered by the family, or indeed familial breakdown alone that makes this text traditional. When regarded outside of such secular contexts, it is instead the coming of the Antichrist as being predestined that presents a radically conservative mechanism from a religious standpoint. This concern, much like the aforementioned themes foregrounded by Wood, Williams and Sobchack, denies the potential for free will. In other words, *The Omen* sets itself up as being ultra-conservative by appearing to support a fundamentalist traditional philosophy wherein historical imperatives are upheld through a focus on determinism over free will.

Indeed, like the individuals, Jesus and Damien, the religions that they embody are equally aligned under the sway of orthodox determin-ism, as Christianity and Satanism are shown to share the same "omens" that are alluded to in the title of the film. This is made clear in a "bibli-cal" poem that signals the circumstances surrounding the end of days as is supposedly revealed in the book of Revelations [sic], as quoted in the introduction to this chapter. Even though not included anywhere in the book of Revelation, nonetheless certain prophecies that are con-tained therein do actually describe signs signaling the end of days. This includes the opposing armies that do battle "on either shore," and the fact that these apocalyptic events are predestined to occur:

> The revelation of Jesus Christ, which God gave show unto his servants things which must shortly come to pass…. Blessed is he that readeth and they that hear the words of this prophecy and keep those things which are written therein; for the time is at hand.[26]

These prophetic statements that are present in the Bible and fic-tionally recreated in *The Omen* suggest the nature of faith in either God or Satan as involving predestination. Indeed, each person who worships Satan is marked at birth with an indicator that does come from a bibli-cal referent:

> Here is wisdom. Let him that hath understanding count the number of the beast: for it is a human number of a man: and his number is Six hundred threescore and six…. If any man worship the beast and his image, and receive his mark in his forehead or in his hand.[27]

Although not on the forehead or hand, Damien possesses the mark of the devil on his scalp, under his hair, and Father Brennan, another fol-lower of Satan, shares a similar mark on his inner thigh. Because this 666 insignia is bestowed at birth, the suggestion is that regardless of the will or actions of man, their destiny to follow the Antichrist is in fact predestined, and, as defined above, doubly so, as both salvation and damnation are decided at the time of conception.

Father Spiletto, the man who bestows Thorn with his chosen son, becomes equally marked in a way which was, according to the text, specifically predicted. Upon narrowly escaping a fire that engulfs and destroys the hospital, wherein both the legitimate Thorn son and his changeling are born, Spiletto retreats to a monastery, takes a vow of silence, and spends his last days incapacitated, staring at statues of the saints from his wheelchair. As Thorn discovers him, it is suggested by a fellow priest residing in the monastery that the nature of Spiletto's inju-ries were, like the birth of the Antichrist, also foretold, as those who betray Christ will come to have their right arm wither and to be blinded in the right eye, signs of their pact with Satan. In fact, the predestined deaths or disfigurements of all the followers of Satan are just as inescapable as the fate of Thorn and his son Damien, as is revealed by the camera of the aforementioned photographer Jennings.

At the same party that the photographer alludes to the connection between Damien and Christ, Jennings also becomes privy to the extent to which not only the Antichrist's life and birth are foretold, but equally the extent to which the deaths and disfigurements of the followers of Satan are beyond the scope of human action to alter. This is first suggested in *The Omen* as Jennings snaps a photo of Damien's nanny, who, later at the birthday party described earlier, hangs herself from the roof of the Thorn mansion. When Jennings develops these photos, he notices what he at first believes to be a fault in the film or the development process. The image of the nanny is marred by a dark line that seems to run around the woman's neck, extending up and out of the frame—a strange coincidence given her suicide by hanging. As the narrative continues, this fault is seen to be not mere chance, but instead an indicator of the predestined fate of the characters themselves. Equally, another Satanic priest, Father Brennan, who is already marked with the sign of the devil, possesses a fate that is similarly sealed. As Jennings shoots and then develops photos of the priest, he finds a fault in the form of a line that runs through the man's torso, a mark that is repeated in all the photos captured by Jennings's camera, and which signals the impending and predetermined death of Brennan, who is impaled by an iron rod outside of a church during a storm.

After Brennan's death, Thorn, who is accompanied by Jennings, enters the priest's rooms and finds them literally wallpapered with pages from the Bible covering all the surfaces, including the windows, except for one which looks out onto his church. Equally prevalent are a veritable panoply of crosses—forty-seven affixed to the door to this chamber alone. Jennings informs Thorn that Brennan was, obviously, trying to keep something out, that something being the priest's destiny. In the same room, Jennings himself accidentally takes what today would be called a "selfie" and notices a mark that severs his head from his body. It is no surprise that later in the film the photographer meets with his predestined end as he is decapitated by a plate of glass in a "freak accident."

Keith Jennings, much like Thorn himself, is another character in conflict. This conflict of destiny versus denial is manifested as he comes to discern his fate and indeed the fate of all those associated with Thorn through the prophetic photographs that he takes. Much like the protagonist of the film, Jennings himself is a secular individual, not aligned to any faith whatsoever. Whereas he, like Thorn, comes to acknowledge the power behind the prophetic statements that must be heeded in the identification of the Antichrist and the signaling of Armageddon, he is also bestowed with scientific proof of the biblical predictions that shall come to pass as a result of the omen. This proof lies in the photographs that he takes that signal specifically who will die and the method of their demise. It is this scientific proof that begins his journey to belief; the ways in which the promises of the Bible are carried out solidify his faith in the veracity of the religious predictions offered in this text. In other words, Jennings is at once associated with both modernity and spirituality, and it is the method of his death by which his alliance to religious belief is ultimately decided.

A final connection between textual and spiritual themes lies in the character of Robert Thorn himself. As was discussed at the outset of this chapter, the climax of this film rests upon the protagonist's decision to murder his son and heir, whilst the inciting incident of the narrative equally involves choices made by Thorn in regard to the Antichrist. The priest suggests that the infant child would be a blessing to their family—a blessing, moreover from God himself. Therefore, the decision to destroy the heir would be akin to murdering not only the last known legitimate son of the Thorn dynasty, but also the blessing that was bestowed upon the Thorns by supernatural intervention. This scenario is much like the biblical tale of Abraham and Isaac. Similarly, Abraham and his wife Sarah desired a son, and although an heir was promised by God, it was not bestowed upon them until far past their childbearing years. This made Isaac's birth a clear blessing and an indicator of divine intervention. Not only was the heir a blessing to Abraham and Sarah, Isaac was in fact a blessing to the world, as it was foretold that he and his heirs would found a great nation. Indeed, Abraham and his decedents were the progenitors not only of Christianity, and Judaism, but also the Nation of Islam. However, prior to the actualization of this promise, God tested Abraham's faith by sending an angel with instructions to sacrifice his only legitimate child. Abraham takes the child to a holy altar where burnt offerings are received and is in the process of sacrificing Isaac when God stays his hand, saving the child and confirming the prophecy foretold to Abraham. Likewise, Thorn has been given a prophecy that his heir will have earth-shattering influence for future generations, and likewise, he is asked to kill the child. Thus, when, as described above, he calls on the help of God, his request might not be to assist him in the sacrifice, but instead to stay his hand from this very task. However, even though his sacrifice is indeed deterred, it is only done so as a result of Thorn's death, which occurs in the midst of this selfsame sacrificial act.

While not given credence in academic circles, the importance of the religious articulations in *The Omen* is the chief concern not only textually, but equally in the film's reception by both secular and religious media alike, a fact that once again alludes to the central importance of such a thematic concern. In terms of reception, *The Omen* was panned at the time of its release, for, as Richard Eder suggests in his review of the film for the *New York Times*, "*The Omen* takes its details with no seriousness at all. It is not a put on—it's terribly solemn in fact—but it often seems like one."[28] In another *New York Times* review, Vincent Canby supports Eder's comments in the following way:

> It takes as its text a bit of hilarious doggerel that David Seltzer, the screenwriter, would have you believe comes right out of the Book of Revelations [*sic*]. If you can possibly locate The Book of Revelations [*sic*] you might possibly locate this quote. It is nowhere to be found in the Book of Revelation, though.[29]

The religious reception of the film was equally unfavorable, as evidenced by the response from the United States Conference of Catholic Bishops (USCCB):

> Slick, expensively mounted [*The Omen*] refers to scripture and religious beliefs, [however] its only interest in religion is in terms of its exploitation potential.[30]

Thus, like *Rosemary's Baby*, *The Omen* was perceived by both the secular and the religious press as articulating a thematic concern with faith and religion, regardless of the seriousness or apparent success of such an articulation. However, this concern seems to be overlooked by academic discourse. Given the social climate of the late 1960s and 1970s, wherein traditional religion was culturally devalued, such an oversight becomes all the more glaring.

Formal Choices in *The Omen*

While the narrative of *The Omen* reveals an apparent and undeniable concern with predestination and familial connectivity, themes which render this text as being ideologically conservative, as suggested above, an analysis of the formal dimensions of the film suggest an alternative reading. In other words, while this text seems to be directly concerned with traditionalism, on a less overt level, the extratextual choices made with regard to actors show a conflicting focus that suggests a more liberal agenda.

To begin, the protagonist, Robert Thorn, is portrayed in the film by Gregory Peck, who, although a stalwart classical Hollywood actor, is nonetheless equally associated with liberal mainstream filmmaking. Indeed, in his career, Peck is most notably identified with his role as Atticus Finch in *To Kill a Mockingbird*. It was while portraying Finch that Peck received his only Academy Award, and in several interviews he describes the role as being one of his favorites. This 1962 film is rendered even more significant from an ideological standpoint when considering its release date at the height of the Civil Rights movement. Following the 1954 *Brown v. Board of Education* decision that symbolically (if not actually) ended segregation, and coming two years before the 1964 Civil Rights Act, the film challenged long standing cultural prejudice.

Peck was not the first choice to play Thorn, however. Charlton Heston was, in fact, initially offered the role before Peck. This choice of star is equally significant because, before becoming a conservative icon,[31] Heston was also aligned with a liberal agenda. In terms of his film career, his choice to play Moses in *The Ten Commandments*, a character that famously lead the Jews out of Egypt and away from persecution, and in taking a starring role *Ben Hur* as Judah, a character who equally fought for human rights and an end to tyranny, Heston, like Peck, became aligned with Democratic ideals and the Civil Rights agenda. During a period that spanned from 1955 to 1972, he was also politically active outside of Hollywood films through his endorsement of Democratic candidates for president. Indeed, Heston became known for activism not only by (ironically) signing several petitions to support the up-and-coming Gun Control Act, along with Peck and others, but also through his engagement in the Civil Rights campaign. One account suggests that in 1961 when a segregated Oklahoma movie theater was showing his movie *El Cid* for the first time, Heston joined a picket line outside; however, this action was not included in the actor's autobiography, nor does he make mention of it in the press.[32] While this account was never directly confirmed by the actor himself, he was nonetheless famous for attending sit-ins at restaurants that supported segregation, an action that he did admit to in his autobiography. This liberal alignment, for Heston, was solidified by his connection to his roles in science fiction films including *Planet of the Apes* and *Soylent Green*, two post-apocalyptic works that also supported a liberal humanist agenda.

The other starring role in *The Omen* was garnered by Lee Remick. As a graduate of Barnard, the famous liberal women's college based in New York City, Remick aligned herself with an equally liberal circle, choosing to study method acting at the Actors Studio upon graduation from the university. Her first film, *A Face in The Crowd*, like the aforementioned *Ben Hur* and *To Kill a Mockingbird*, was equally anti-conservative, telling the story of the potentially insidious nature of the media's advertising industry in luring audiences into its overarching capitalist agendas.

Finally, the two British actors in *The Omen*, David Warner and Billie Whitelaw, were also both regarded as being non-conformist in their native countries before ever coming to Hollywood. David Warner, as Jennings, began his film career in an auspicious manner by taking a role in John Osborne's *Tom Jones*, a subversive play which challenged traditional theatrical presentations by adopting a Brechtian stance that often broke the fourth wall by engaging directly with audiences. Likewise, after meeting Samuel Beckett, an equally subversive playwright, in 1963, Billie Whitelaw became indelibly associated with not only the man but also his work. Indeed, Beckett considered Whitelaw to be a "perfect actress," and it was thus that she became not only his voice, but equally a muse for whom he wrote and rewrote each play. After Beckett's death, the actress became the foremost authority on the author's work and theatrical techniques. Being an aficionado of the experimental theater of the absurd linked Whitelaw, like Warner, to anything but a conservative agenda.

Thus, while the form of *The Omen* seems to be aligned with a more liberal agenda when considering the actors and the connotations with which they are associated, this work that is considered as being ideologically conservative in academic circles may be refigured as being ideologically unsettled. This nature will be further explored through an analysis of the novelization, an adaptive text that seems to present equally divided articulations.

Much like *Rosemary's Baby*, *The Omen* necessitates a deeper look, a consideration that is foregrounded in the latter film, not only by textual, but equally by formal concerns. When it comes to the cinematographic techniques, the frames themselves are deep. Much like Orson Welles's seminal use of deep focus in *Citizen Kane*, *The Omen* creates a frame whereby the foreground, mid-ground and background are equally focused, allowing for multiple lines of action. Not only this, but the mise-en-scène is set up to allow for a variety of levels of action vertically as well as horizontally. This multi-planar action is revealed most clearly in a scene wherein Thorn and Kathy are preparing to attend a wedding.[33] While Thorn runs around in the background, the camera tilts to a shot of Kathy as she descends the stairs. Once at the bottom, she calls up for Damien to be brought down, whereupon a conflict ensues between Kathy and her nanny Mrs. Blaylock. When looking closely, and indeed deeply, the conflict of the narrative becomes clear: Thorn is in the background in terms of domestic affairs, whilst the fight for dominance in the home is figured between Kathy and Blaylock. The fact of the nanny being at the top of the stairs suggests that she will dominate in this battle of wills, which in fact she does later when she murders Kathy, pushing her out the window as described above. In other words, it is thus vital that the cinematic gaze does not rest at the surface when it comes not only to thematic but also to formal constructions.

Considerations of the Novelization of *The Omen*

In the same year as the release of the film, screenwriter David Seltzer published a companion novelization to *The Omen*, which, although similar on many of the key narrative points presented in the film, significantly digresses from the original text with regard to the nature and efficacy of the Thorn family, while at the same time further privileging the religious connectivity of this work. In other words, while both the cinematic and literary versions seem to position spiritual belief and familial connectivity as two equally vital concerns (unlike the film, which links posterity and traditional religion as successfully operating in tandem), the novel seems to offer up these two themes as being in a state of disintegration.[34]

This failure is first presented through descriptions of the Thorn family. Both the original and the adaptive texts depict the Thorns as being an inseparable married couple on the surface—a fact which ironically brings about the ultimate downfall of husband and wife. It is, in fact, through this connection that Robert Thorn is first exposed to the Satanists in both the film and the novel.[35] In the film, the strength of family is foregrounded visually as much as thematically. This is achieved through several montage sequences that document Robert and Kathy's investment in Damien's early years, photographs contained within the mise-en-scène, including several of Kathy kept by Thorn in his office and by his bedside. However, unlike the film, in the novelization the family is in a state of disintegration, in trouble from the start. Their happiness is described as being a façade: "The brick wall that everyone else took for reality."[36] Likewise, in the film, Kathy Thorn is portrayed as a strong woman who becomes increasingly unstable throughout the course of the narrative—an instability that is attributed to the lie perpetrated by Thorn, and the concomitant introduction of the Antichrist changeling into their nuclear family. This is not the case in the novelization, however, as Kathy is directly referred to as being insecure and unstable from the outset. With regard to the pregnancy, in the adaptation Seltzer suggests that the birth of the child would be, for Kathy, the only mechanism to stave off madness. It also goes on to tell of the previous attempts at procreation that ended badly, a detail that is not present in the film. Seltzer writes, "It was the third time now, and Thorn knew it was the last. If this time something went wrong, it would be the end of her sanity."[37] It is this assertion that suggests why the substitution of the devil child for the lost Thorn heir is an imperative in a secular if not religious sense.

Just like the film, the novel also describes the importance of history, tradition and familial alliance. However, unlike the film, this tradition is seen to be failing. One example of this, the history of the Bugenhagen family, is described in the following way:

> It was a Bugenhagen, who in the year 1092 found the first progeny of Satan and devised the means of putting it to death. It was again a Bugenhagen in 1710 who found the second issue and damaged it to the point where it could summon no earthly power. They were religious zealots, the watch dogs of Christ; their mission, to keep the Unholy One from walking the face of the earth.[38]

In an attempt to deny his heritage and the actions his forefathers take in destroying the Antichrist, Bugenhagen literally buries himself in Meggido, a place of protection described in the book as being "the site where the Bible itself was created."[39] Later in the narrative, Bugenhagen confesses as much: "The city of Jezreel, the town of Meggido, my fortress, my prison. The place where Christianity began. Geographically, this is the heart of Christianity. So long as I remain within, nothing can harm me."[40]

The other differences between the novel and the film are also significant in regard to faith. For example, while the film opens with Thorn being rushed to the hospital already being aware of the news of his son's death, in the novel version, the opening provides a preface to the Thorn story. It begins with the comet, one of the signals of the end of days. Seltzer describes the dark glowing star as arriving at the precise moment that was predicted in the Old Testament. He further suggests that this is indicative of the moment when the history of the earth would change, similar to the events that occurred following the arrival of the star of Bethlehem that signaled the birth of Jesus:

> Now democracy was fading, mind-impairing drugs had become a new way of life, and in the few countries where freedom of worship was still allowed, it was widely proclaimed that God was dead. [B]rother had turned against brother, father against children; school busses and marketplaces exploded daily in the growing din of preparatory lust…. Clearly, it was a conspiracy of events. The Book of Revelations [*sic*] had predicted it all.[41]

Thus, the novel, like the film, seems to foreground the collusion of predestination and religion with regard to prophecy and place from the opening of text.

This foregrounding orthodoxy continues throughout the novel. For example, the changeling is presented in Seltzer's text as part of "God's plan,"[42] and the child itself as exhibiting "angelic perfection."[43] As the dark star reaches its apex, the priest, who states, "For the sake of your wife, Signore, God will forgive this deception," further convinces Thorn: "On this night, God has given you a son."[44] Finally, the religious connection is solidified as Thorn, who cries tears of joy as he gives the baby to his wife, quietly thanks God for "showing him the way."[45]

Although religion becomes an increasingly important thematic trope, the characters themselves are portrayed as being agnostic:

> The Thorns were both of Catholic parentage, but neither of them were religious. Kathy was given to occasional prayer and visits to church on Christmas and Easter, but more out of superstition and sentiment than a belief in Catholic dogma.[46]

However, the film only alludes to the fact that the Thorns are not religious. It is only through a failure to show them entering into a church until Damien is five years old (when they finally enter a sacred space for a wedding and not for worship) that their religious connection (or lack thereof) is noted.

While indeed there are many significant differences between the original and adaptive works, there are also many significant similarities between the two, specifically with regard to the representation of the alignment of Catholic and Satanic spiritual beliefs. More specifically, just as the prophecies are shared between faiths, so are the tenets and histories, as suggested throughout this chapter. In this way, belief becomes a key theme in this text not only in terms of religion, but also for personal stability. This is evidenced in a description of Thorn during one of his speeches, the success of which is attributed to the fact that "he stirred people, and they believed in him.... He was the image of a champion, and more important even than his own innate abilities, was that he could make the people believe."[47] Indeed, Thorn is portrayed as a figure that inspires belief, but who is not himself a believer. However, although Thorn is agnostic, the roots of the Catholic faith still reside in him, as evidenced in the book:

> It was as though they had entered the medieval ages, and the presence of God, of spiritual holiness could be felt as though it were a physical living thing.... Thorn was deeply upset, his knees trembling as though insisting he fall to them and pray.[48]

This seed of faith that refuses to die is represented not only in the characters, but also in the locations of religious significance, equally vital to both works as being signifiers of the persistence of faith. This is revealed in passages such as, "Rome itself was a hotbed of energy; the seat of Catholicism ... the core of Satanism throughout the world. The atmosphere fairly crackled with power."[49] Further, the monastery where Tassone (in the film, Father Spilletto) lives is venerated as being on historic hallowed ground:

> It had stood on its mountain here in the southern Italian countryside since the time of Herod and persisted in standing through all the sieges that followed. At the outset of World War II, all the monks within were shot by invading German forces who used it as a headquarters and cabal. In 1946 it was mortared by the Italians themselves, a retribution for the evil work that had gone on within.... Santa Benedictus was a holy place ... rising upwards from the very vaults of history.[50]

Finally, Cerveteri, the cemetery wherein both the mother of Damien and the murdered Thorn heir are interred, is another ancient locus described in the film, but more adequately so in the book as being an ancient Etruscan burial ground, a place that God-fearing men avoided. In the novelization, it is revealed that the location was a shrine to Techulca, the Etruscan devil-god, thus described as ancient holy sacrificial ground.[51] Indeed, it appears that just as historic Christian locations can be imbued with religious significance throughout time, so can those of a Satanic nature.

Overall, the themes presented in *The Omen*, like those of *Rosemary's Baby*, position Satanism and Catholicism as equally orthodox faith mechanisms. This then ultimately begs the question as to whether or not these works provide a critique of traditionalism, or in fact call for a return to orthodoxy. It could indeed be argued that the fact of the antagonists ushering in the end of the world by establishing an oppositional, yet nonetheless orthodox, faith relates to anxieties with regard to the retrenchment of traditional historical religion, thus falling in line with its contemporaneous culture, as the Gothic did two hundred years earlier. However, it could equally be argued that by the very fact of making this religious configuration efficacious in its goals, while, at the end of the day, vanquishing those who hold no belief whatsoever, could in fact be calling for the return of religion as a means of stability. Regardless, as has been discussed here and as will be addressed in the following chapter, within the world of horror, religion and religious debate form an integral component that cannot be denied.

THREE

The Cult of Youth in the "B" Horror Film

We find in the great historical religions a fear of the demonic, of human nature unchecked. In effect, the culture—particularly modernist culture—took over the relation with the demonic. But instead of taming it, as religion tried to do, the secular culture began to accept it, explore it, and revel in it.[1]—DANIEL BELL from *The Cultural Contradictions of Capitalism*

The rivalry between the young and the adult in Western society during the current decade is uniquely critical.... For better or worse what is presently happening that is new ... is the creation of a youth who are profoundly, even fanatically alienated from the parental generation, or of those who address themselves primarily to the young.[2]—THEODORE ROSZAK reflecting on the late 1960s

Introduction

In the final scene from the film *The Brotherhood of Satan*, the antagonists, all elderly members of an isolated desert community, engage in a ritual whose outcome promises to restore their youth. To achieve this result, the coven must first pledge their souls to the devil as part of a ceremony held in Satan's honor. In return for their allegiance, the followers will come to inhabit the bodies of the film's sacrificial victims: all local children who have been abducted and imprisoned by this religious group. While these community elders worship Satan, the younger members of this village are shown as being configured into conservative nuclear families: mothers, fathers and children who not only live together and eat meals surrounding the dining room table, but also pray in unison to their Christian God before each repast. For support, they turn not only to their own families, but also to the community at large, including their neighbors and local law enforcement. Additionally, and indeed significantly, these families also seek guidance from the local parish priest in an attempt to vanquish the threat posed by the older Satanists who are abducting their children. What is truly horrifying about the titular Satanic brotherhood is thus not only that they are on the surface benevolent elderly figures, but also the fact that they represent the extended families of their victims. In other words, the antagonists not only seem grandfatherly and grandmotherly, but they are literally the grandparents of the

Visions of *Race with the Devil*.

children whom they abduct and plan to destroy. Equally horrifying is the fact that against these apparently evil characters, the "good" families eventually succumb, as do their children.

However, what is interesting about this text, and indeed all of the works discussed in this book, is, once again, not a thematic concern of good versus evil, but instead the specifics of the narrative conflict and the outcomes of such struggles. What links the films discussed in this chapter specifically are the ways in which *The Brotherhood of Satan, The Witches* and *Race with the Devil* equally challenge a cultural phenomenon prevalent in this moment in history: a youthful counterculture. Stereotypically, the young have indeed been affiliated with the counterculture movement, one which rejects traditionalism while instead privileging the new and modern. The old, alternatively, are usually regarded as being more stalwart and conservative in their affiliations. Both *Rosemary's Baby* and *The Omen*, as was discussed in the first two chapters of this section, problematize this notion by offering protagonists who, on the one hand, are youthful couples who come to embrace modernity. Both the Woodhouses and the Thorns equally reject affiliation with any organized religion and are also unfettered by active engagement with extended family. On the other hand, however, both are identified by conservative gender roles and traditional nuclear family positioning. The antagonists in both narratives adhere to religious doctrine (even though they practice an alternative faith), and the Satanists in both narratives are efficacious in being grounded by community and an acknowledgment of familial legacy. Thus, the elderly Castevets and the Satanic acolytes of the Antichrist also question ideological alignment in being faithful to a belief system that is at once alternative and yet is also connected to orthodoxy. The same problem occurs with *The Witches*, *The Brotherhood of Satan*, and *Race with the Devil*. In the case of these three texts, modernity is once again pitted against orthodoxy; however, no single character stands as a representation of one side of this cultural dichotomy. In other words, this battle between traditionalism and modernity is not only fought within the larger narratives themselves, but also within each of the individual protagonists offered up in these works. In the case of the texts specifically discussed in this chapter, to be modern is not to be involved with consumer culture per se, or to debate free will, but instead to enter into a debate with the cult of youth. It is this self-same debate that forms the essential conflict of these narratives, as well as the internal conflict of each leading character as they navigate the struggles inherent to this contemporaneous culture.

Modernity and the Cult of Youth

In order to understand how this problematic plays out in the three texts discussed in this chapter, it is first important to diverge away from a focus on the films and their adaptive novels and turn to a larger concern with contemporaneous debates regarding the old versus the new and the concomitant struggle between traditionalism and modernity. As is reiterated throughout this section, one of the characteristics of modernity involves a tendency to look forward rather than to look back—to privilege the new over the old as a means of achieving a degree of individual freedom from tradition. The modern world indeed promised an inexhaustible variety of things and ideas which the human subject was called to experience. For this reason, the culture at this time glorified self-exploration and a certain radical individualism over what was perceived to be restrictive, outdated historical alliances, such as religion and family legacy.

As historical continuity became increasingly maligned, those who were at one time seen to possess desirable qualities that were associated with age, namely wisdom and maturity, were regarded as a threat because identity instead became intrinsically tied to a newly prized status symbol, that of youth. Cultural historian Christopher Lasch asserts:

> In a society that dreads old age and death, aging holds a special terror for those who fear dependence and whose self-esteem requires the admiration usually reserved for youth, beauty, celebrity or charm.[3]

In addition to this focus on a cult of youth, as traditional religion was rent from culture by the self-same mechanism, the potential for a life beyond the grave, the promise of heaven to those who lived a good life, was also precluded. This forced individuals to live for the moment because, as the old adage goes, "it's later than you think." Instead of establishing a legacy and accumulating wealth and respectability whereby one's progeny would benefit, the resounding ethos was to throw all caution to the wind and live for today.[4]

Marshall Berman suggests that this narcissistic drive may be regarded as an endemic element of the modern condition. For example, in Goethe's *Faust*, a work considered by Berman to be the original and ultimate modernist text, these very debates regarding a privileging of the new over the old and youth over age are signified through the characters of Philemon and Baucus. This elderly pair is invested not only with distinctive traditional Christian values such as innocence, generosity, selfless devotion and humility, but according to Berman, they equally may be seen to be archetypes for those who, because of their ties to tradition, will come to be classified as obsolete:

> [Philemon and Baucus share] a distinctly modern pathos in being the first literary figures of what will become a popular modern trope, people who are in the way of history, progress, and development.[5]

This chapter will argue that it is, in fact, these debates surrounding the formation of the cult of youth, and the concomitant rejection of history, tradition, and the elderly that seem to be articulated and equally problematized in a group of films born out of this culture.

The Witches and the Dichotomy of the Old and the New

Both as a film and a novel, *The Witches* (aka *The Devil's Own*) is a work that debates the privileging of the new over the old through the presentation of an antagonist who becomes increasingly obsessed with remaining young, and who relies on the rites and practices of Satanism to achieve this end. Equally, in presenting the efficacy of Satanic practices over more traditional forms of religion such as Christianity, this work seems to reject orthodoxy, and thus seems to speak directly to the debates described above.

In the film version of *The Witches*, the efficacy of belief systems is clearly debated from the outset. In what amounts to a narrative prologue, set before the primary narrative arc, protagonist Gwen Mayfield is introduced as being a teacher for a missionary school in Africa.[6] The surrounding community, at the time of this scene, is in uprise and the school, now in danger of attack, is being vacated by the teacher and her staff of villagers. As Mayfield gathers her belongings, she attempts to calm the men who are assisting her, reassuring them that the local prevalent practice of Vodun, the spiritual antecedent of Voodoo, has no real power. Her rational skepticism is, however, exploded when a man wearing a traditional native mask, beads and grass woven loincloth enters and confronts the teacher. Horribly afraid of this "witchdoctor" and his potential to inflict not only bodily but indeed spiritual harm, the teacher faints and must be transported away in an unconscious state of mental breakdown. The film continues with this conflict of faith within the primary narrative setting, the village of Heddaby. This is signaled before Mayfield even arrives to this rural hamlet. During her interview for a teaching position, she first meets Alan Bax, an apparent man of the cloth, who meets her in his priestly vestments. They discuss not only her qualifications, but also her breakdown upon returning from Africa. Gwen attempts to reassure her potential employer that she has completely recovered, and that she has returned to her former state of rationality. She suggests that the people's rebellion was not really the fault of the villages, but instead instigated by the local witchdoctor who was fighting to retain power in light of an increasingly educated population. Bax seems to accept her explanation and thus offers her the position, even as he looks sadly reflective. This unconsciously conveyed sentiment, as will be explained later, is a foreshadowing of the fact that the very situation as experienced by Gwen in Africa is equally facing the village that he supposedly governs. The people of Heddaby are indeed also being led by a powerful leader who manipulates and controls the ignorant local community; however, this leader is not Alan Bax.

As is revealed upon arrival in Heddaby, the Christian Church, both as an edifice and as a congregation, is in a state of absolute ruin.[7] Bax explains to Gwen that the physical church has been in this state for over two hundred years. The people did not bother to repair it, and as a result of their lack of interest, it was "let go." However, while the locations of faith are shown to be destroyed, Bax at least offers an apparent representation of traditional faith. Not only is the man dressed in priestly vestments, but equally his study, a room to which he absconds throughout this narrative, is shown to be filled with visual and auditory symbols of Christianity: triptychs, crosses, and religious music. While the icons are singularly positioned and remain enclosed within the Bax estate as the sole visual representations of traditional religion, the music, alternatively, succeeds in emanating throughout the community. These hymns and chants are, in fact, the one element of traditional faith that is successfully disseminated within Heddaby itself.

Indeed, in this isolated rural village, traditional faith is neither venerated nor celebrated congregationally. While Bax seems to be a man of the cloth, he has no church physically or congregationally, and thus must celebrate his faith individually in isolation. However, as is the case with most of the characters in the films discussed in this book, this allegiance is troubled. It is revealed that Bax himself is not a priest or even a man of the cloth, having failed to be ordained (a characterization that differs from the literary version that will be explored later). It is thus suggested in the film that the Christian symbols, music and garb with which this character surrounds himself are used in the service of offering "a feeling of security,"[8] of holding the forces of evil at bay. However, in being wielded by a man who does not have the power to use them efficiently, since he is not an official representative of God on earth, these evil forces are allowed to flourish. In other words, rather than being able to wield objects that are made holy through his influence, these Christian symbols are only that—symbols, which are, like the man, impotent secular objects alone. In turn, rather than exorcising evil practices, or even consolidating the community around a traditional system of belief, because there is no one who authentically represents the Christian Church, the village becomes overrun by Witchcraft and Satanism, the only religion, in fact, that is truly believed and practiced. In turn, Satanism becomes more efficacious as a practice, possibly for the very reason that a powerful figurehead exists to guide and nurture belief, one who seems to use the faith for that which it was formulated: hedonistic pleasure. However, this too is problematized as is revealed when the tenets of Satanism are compared with their practice within the film version of *The Witches*.

Satanism as an Alternative Traditional Religion in *The Satanic Bible* and *The Witches*

In the prologue to *The Satanic Bible*, written by Anton LaVey, the "Black Pope" asserts:

This is the age of Satan! Satan rules the Earth! The gods of the unjust are dead. This is the morning of magic, and undefiled wisdom. The FLESH prevaileth and a great Church shall be builded [sic], consecrated in its name. No longer shall man's salvation be dependent on self-denial. And it will be known that the world of the flesh and the living shall be the greatest preparation for any and all eternal delights![9]

Indeed, in founding a belief system that is based upon the fulfillment of the hedonistic pleasures of the flesh and a rejection of the necessity of self-denial, the Church of Satan seems to support the ethos of the era in its celebrating the self and rejecting the traditional faiths of restraint such as Protestantism. In fact, when analyzing this "bible" further, it would appear as if this whole system of faith is set up as the antithesis to traditional Christianity overall, which LaVey perceives to be antiquated and obsolete. The religious tract begins with the Nine Satanic Statements, which, like the Ten Commandments of traditional religion, sets out the dictums of the faith. In these statements, indulgence, vengeance, instinctual action, and physical, emotional and mental gratification are all praised over abstinence and denial. The *Infernal Diatribe* goes on to suggest that as traditional religious faith has waned, man has become farther from God and, as LaVey suggests, closer to himself: "Closer to the Devil."[10] He continues:

Times have changed. Religious leaders no longer preach that all our natural actions are sinful. We no longer think sex is dirty—or that taking pride in ourselves is shameful—or that wanting something someone else has is vicious. Of course not, times have changed![11]

Satanism calls itself the modern faith, while at the same time acknowledging that man needs something in which to believe that appeals to his emotional/spiritual nature. Overall, the text and its founder concede the fact that man requires ritual and ceremony—that something is needed to bridge the gap left by modernity between the scientific and the religious. It is this structuring absence, according to LaVey, that will be filled with Satanism. Interestingly, even as traditional religions were shedding such supernatural connections, especially with regard to sacraments, accouterments and liturgy, Satanism was embracing them. During the Reformation and continuing thereafter, sacraments such as baptism, confession and communion were stripped of their supernatural power. In many Protestant faiths, the personal relationship established between God and man made the confessing of sin to the clergy unnecessary, as one could now confess directly without the need of an intermediary. Beliefs regarding communion and baptism were also stripped of supernatural power, as Protestantism increasingly denied that transubstantiation was occurring, that the wine and bread were literally transformed into the body and blood of Christ, and the water literally filled with his presence. Instead, communion, like baptism, became a show-and-tell device wherein one merely affirms and reaffirms their religion. Additional reforms to tradition came later in the twentieth century in the service of aggiornamento, or bringing together factions of Christianity. The Second Vatican Council equally called for sweeping reforms in the Catholic Church. One of these reforms involved the language of the liturgy. In changing from Latin to colloquial languages, the Church attempted to make the faith more inclusive by allowing for everyone to understand what was being said during mass.

Ironically, while traditional religion was becoming less ritualistic, the church founded by Anton LaVey aligned itself to more antiquated forms of spiritualism that pre-existed not only the Second Vatican Council, but the Reformation as well. Indeed, Satanism might well consider itself to be modern, but, in fact, when looking more closely, it might well be even more rooted in antiquity than the more traditional forms of religion that it rejected for this self-same reason of being out of step with the times. It is only in the focus of its practice, based upon individual gratification, and not the practice itself that this faith could be considered to embrace its contemporaneous culture.

In the film version of *The Witches*, a similar element of contradiction comes into play between the practice and its intended outcomes. In this adaptation, Satanism may be seen to offer up symbols that act to inhibit rather than bolster freedom, identity and the self. One example of this is in the form of a black cat, the archetypal witch's familiar, which lurks around the cottage that protagonist Gwen Mayfield inhabits. The creature, sent by one of the members of the Heddaby witches' coven, watches over and reports on the activities of the newly appointed teacher. The other diabolic object is a voodoo doll stuck full of pins, which possesses the power to sicken, weaken and kill its intended victim. Indeed, rather than representing the power of the individual, these items hold a malevolent force that is bent solely on the destruction of agency. The voodoo doll murders, literally destroying the self, while the cat, as an instrument of surveillance, inhibits action by disallowing private freedoms. When viewed in this way, this use of Satanism becomes diametrically opposed to radical individualism, the primary tenet of the faith as expressed by LaVey. However, while individual symbols of this alternative religion have the effect of actively robbing the victim, the intended outcomes of the rituals perpetrated by the coven seem to rest more solidly in line with a hedonist agenda.

While at the outset and on the surface, it appears that Alan Bax acts as the spiritual leader of Heddaby, it is in fact his sister, Stephanie Bax, who is the head of the village spiritual community: not a traditional church, but instead a Satanic witches' coven. However, like Bax, her representation as being a woman of faith is equally troubled. If Bax initially possessed and projected the outward attributes of faith, Stephanie, alternatively, appears to be a skeptical rationalist. She is introduced as an internationally famed investigative journalist who uses her deductive and unbiased powers of reasoning to get to the heart of her subject. When speaking of Heddaby, she denigrates its rurality. Characterizing the village as being restful and good for the soul, she regards her fellow villagers as simple people. It is this very nature of her location and its people that she manipulates in the film version of this text. The horror of *The Witches*, like all the works in this book, lies in the way in which appearances are, in fact, deceptive. In other words, while Alan appears spiritual, he is ineffectual; alternatively, Stephanie, who appears to be a skeptic, has successfully formed an alternative religious congregation. Likewise, as the head of this coven, she is about to manipulate the rites and rituals of Satanism so as to invade the body of a young village girl for hedonistic ends. Indeed, appearances are faulty, and in the case of *The Witches*, this middle-aged woman will take on the physical attributes of youth.

Stephanie is a powerful sorceress who, like Gwen, is aware of the efficacy of the practice of ancient supernatural rites for those who believe in their power. With this in mind, she manipulates the collective power of the coven for her own ends. The film suggests that Stephanie has studied witchcraft as a science[12] with the expressed desire to extend her life. She confesses to Mayfield, "I have tried to push my brain to the limit to help mankind. Only now at the end of my life I am only beginning to learn. If I could live for another fifty years, think of all the things I could accomplish."[13]

Unbeknownst to the villagers, who are expecting a sabot orgy, Stephanie will use the collective power of the coven to release a force that will "give [her] a skin for dancing in."[14]

Unlike the other films in this book, at the conclusion of *The Witches*, it appears as if good overcomes evil as Gwen manages to defile the evil ritual and thus defeat the sorceress. However, even given the defeat of the Satanists, the fact of the protagonist's unique victory is one that does not entirely fall in line with those of classical horror, making such alliances yet another problematic element. This is because rather than using the forces of good (and in the case of classical horror, these forces are decidedly Christian), Gwen Mayfield uses her own individual power to vanquish Stephanie. In other words, rather than using the symbols and beliefs of Christianity in the service of defeating the devil, as Alan Bax unsuccessfully attempts to do, the protagonist defeats the Satanists using secular powers: Gwen is victorious, yet remains an outsider to the faith. She is aware of the powers afforded to those who faithfully engage in ritualistic practice, but chooses not to adhere to these systems of belief.

In the penultimate scene of the film, the protagonist overthrows the Satanic ceremony, first in following the coven to the ruined church and then in subverting the proceedings involving a ritualistic dance and the sacrifice of a young girl, whom Stephanie will come to possess. However, not only does Gwen finally succeed in her quest to defeat the evil that was robbing her and others of agency, she does so through the volition of her own individual altruistic action alone. She defeats the coven not because she has faith in God, but instead because she desires a restoration of order wherein the old get older and die, and the young are preserved and protected. This subversion and defeat suggest that collective will is ineffective, possibly because it is not collective at all. One must ask what benefits the villagers who join the coven hope to attain. What reasons are given for the community to sacrifice their own children? One possible benefit lies in their being allowed to engage in orgiastic rites that would otherwise be prohibited. Another possible reason to follow might lie in their desire for ritual and faith.

Rather than the coven of *Rosemary's Baby*, or the Satanic apostles of *The Omen*, the Satanists of *The Witches* and their leader are not acting for a common purpose. Together they do not want to bring about the rise of the Antichrist. They do not want to usher in the end of days, wherein Satan will rule supreme. They do not even act due to a unified desire to revere the devil. They are instead a group of individuals acting based upon a desire for hedonistic pleasure, and when they are brought against the strong will of a committed individual who acts with integrity, they are defeated. It is this privileging of the individual that Howard Thompson notes in his review of the film published in the *New York Times*.[15] Written at the time of the film's release, the critic dedicates the majority of his analysis to the performance of Joan Fontaine, linking her choice of film to the career decisions of Bette Davis, Olivia de Havilland and Joan Crawford, all of whom not only accepted roles in horror/thriller pieces late in their careers, but in some cases assisted in orchestrating the making of these films to revitalize their careers later in life. This was true of Bette Davis in *What Ever Happened to Baby Jane*, who worked with and supported Robert Aldrich, not to mention using her celebrity to promote this film. It was equally true of Joan Fontaine, who initially obtained the rights to the novel by Norah Lofts. This engagement between older actresses and horror/thriller films was so prevalent that these works were even given a genre distinction, albeit a negative one: hagsploitation. Following from this pretense, in suggesting that the film was star driven, Thompson's analysis falls in line with a reading wherein the individual character assumes precedence as a fore-grounded narrative concern.

It is, in fact, only in the final scene of the film that this privileging of the individual is subverted, ultimately making this film harder to pin-point in terms of ideology. In what amounts to a narrative epilogue, Gwen Mayfield and Alan Bax, for the first time appearing without his religious vestments, are pictured together, and it is suggested that if they have not already, they will soon become romantically involved. In classical Hollywood style, all of the narrative ends are thus tied, including Bax's insecurity and Mayfield's spinsterhood, and it is with this conclusion that the film ultimately suggests that just as Satanic congregations may be effectual to a point, altruistic individuals who fight for what they truly believe is right may also succeed. However, traditional familial bonds, such as those that exist between husband and wife, are what is really necessary for the restoration of order and thus a "happy ending."

Academic Debates Involving *The Witches*

While much has been written about *Rosemary's Baby* and *The Omen* from an academic perspective, little consideration has been paid to *The Witches*, even given its potential status as a piece of Hammer Horror. When it is mentioned, it is usually as part of a larger film cycle. Adam Scovell in *Folk Horror: Hours Dreadful and Things Strange*, for example, characterizes this film as a representative of the Folk Horror Chain in regard to the skewing of beliefs and morality as presented in this work. Once again, as is the case with all of the films discussed in this book, religious connectivity is not taken seriously as a thematic concern on its own, but instead as a symbol for something else. For Scovell, the belief system in *The Witches* takes on a Saidian "Orientalist hue"[16] in its invoking an aura of paranoia wherein the middle class is endangered by a malicious foreign other. This concern with imperialism is also discussed in an article published in the Canadian academic horror journal *Monstrum*, wherein author Michael Wood argues:

> The larger argument of the film [*The Witches*], not an uncommon one at the time, is that despite its best efforts and best intentions, the British Empire is unable to control its subject peoples, who are easily manipulated by sinister leaders, whether tribal chiefs, practitioners of ancient religions or modern nationalists.[17]

This fear of the other is not only common to Orientalist theory, wherein the East is portrayed contemptuously by the West, the mainstream marginalizing the other, but also in feminist theory, which focuses upon patriarchal devaluation of the feminine. This latter form of othering is addressed in another film cycle into which *The Witches* has been incorporated: Hagsploitation, Psychobiddy or Grande Dame Guignol. This female-centric 1960s subgenre of horror film relies on the presentation of once iconic Hollywood femme fatales who, though past their prime in a sexualized sense, were nonetheless accomplished actresses still very capable of great performances. Peter Shelley explains of the characters portrayed by the likes of Joan Crawford, Bette Davis and, in the case of *The Witches*, Joan Fontaine: "[This character] may pine for a lost youth and glory, or she may be trapped by idealized memories of childhood, with a trauma that haunts her past."[18] Like many Gothic heroines, the characters of the Grande Dame Guignol must overcome past trauma that results in isolation from the external world. In this way, the Grande Dame Guignol presents a similar motif to the Folk Horror Chain in the sense that a belief has led to a separation from the everyday rational world of modernity. Also, as is the case with Hagsploitation, the old comes into conflict with the new. This conflict is an element equally noted by Wood, who suggests:

> Although it is not explicitly stated, *The Witches* equates ... ancient evil with Britain's "Old Religion," which at the time of the film's release was being reinvented as a legitimate form of religious expression: modern pagan witchcraft, otherwise known as Wicca. Britain is simply the continuation of an ancient rural tradition, [as] are the film's crude dolls poked with pins and the wild, perhaps drug-fueled dance that was to culminate in a human sacrifice. The former also seems to be a reference to Eurocentric stereotypes of the Afro-Caribbean religion of voodoo (Vodou), while the latter seems a call out to medieval descriptions, or fantasies, of witch's Sabbats.[19]

However, while, as Wood suggests, this theme is merely alluded to, while not being specifically stated, it is a concern that is made manifest in the novel upon which this film was based.

Returning to the Old: The Literary Version of *The Witches*

Just as the film may be read as being ideologically unsettled, the novel may be seen to be equally contradictory in presenting a traditional approach and conclusion, while at the same time being thematically subversive in its depiction of religion. In the novel, Thorby, the village patriarch and school benefactor, is a legitimate canon, not a character who remains unordained and simply uses religious vestments as a form of safety net. Equally, in the novel as opposed to the film, Gwen herself is presented as a traditionally religious figure whose faith is strong and humble. This is evidenced in her belief in the sanctity of marriage, as the character suggests, "Any woman who makes a home and brings up a child is doing the job God created her for."[20] Also, a product of her religious devotion is her guilt toward the pleasure that she takes in the material world:

> Wrong perhaps, ... to take such pleasure in nice surroundings, to set such value on what was, after all, mere material. One must remember, always, how little such things really mattered.... But even that Puritanical thought could not diminish her pleasure. God had put beauty into this world—even a snowdrop was meticulously designed—and He had given his skill to make beautiful things, so, if by chance one were fortunate enough to encounter lovely surroundings, one should be appreciative and grateful.[21]

Indeed, unlike the film, traditional religious affiliation plays a much more significant role in the narrative overall—a traditional horror conflict between characters that represent good, who are religious and God-fearing, and those who practice the "dark arts" of Witchcraft, and who are thus seen as being evil through defaming God and his church.

An example of this moral struggle is addressed in one local family's battle with Granny Rigby, the chief antagonist and main purveyor of Witchcraft within the world of the novel. The power exacted by this Satanic figure is seen in a wholly negative light and becomes conflated with the practice of evil within the narrative: "Would God put such power into any mortal hands?"[22] One young boy, Sydney Baines, who becomes prey to the village witches seems to be the primary victim as he becomes caught within this interplay of innocence and malevolence. Gwen describes him as a "Methodist ... [who] had probably been reared to believe that little boys who told lies went straight to Hell."[23] The God-fearing Baines family is the first victim of the evils of the village, as Sydney falls into a coma at the hands of Rigby.

When Gwen speaks to Emily, the boy's mother, following this incident, this once religious woman is distant and reluctant to admit that her son was a victim of foul play, causing Gwen to discern, "Mrs. Baines has changed sides."[24] Mr. Wesley Baines suggests of his wife's transition, "Em's took against me, and against you, and against chapel, and took up with *owd* Mrs. Rigby."[25] In fact, later in the narrative, like in the film, once cured, Emily disappears with Sydney, while Wesley, choosing to stay in his ancestral home, is killed during a sabot on Midsummer's Eve. Later in the novel, Gwen seeks Emily and Sydney out in their new home in London, where, after a brief interview with Mrs. Baines, her suspicions of Emily's complicity in the Heddaby coven are confirmed:

> I was right about her. She changed sides to save Sydney; she brought the intelligence and teachability which had enabled her to pass her professional examinations to bear upon the learning of the Black Arts. She has been disgusted by the filth. She wasn't the convert they thought they had made.[26]

Gwen Mayfield is in many ways an example of an active and morally conscious protagonist, while Canon Thorby's sister, Isabel (Stephanie in the film), acts as a character foil, not only in being morally ambiguous, but also in lacking a certain strong self-agency.[27] The text describes the character as follows: "Her manner was gracious, her words well chosen, her smile sweet and frequent, but it all added up to nothing. She was not there, and she somehow reduced you to nothing too."[28] Rather than the chief purveyor of evil, as she is portrayed in the film, this character is instead presented as being merely possessed by the evil powers of Witchcraft. The novel suggests that after having died as a child, Isabel was taken to Granny Rigby, who administered certain herbs that brought her back to life—a turn of events for which she will be forced to pay throughout her newly restored existence:

> When Isabel was—shall we say moribund, Mrs. Thorby, who was alive then and a bit of a crank, insisted on calling Phoebe Rigby who brewed some nettle tea or something horrid and got her breathing again.[29]

In other words, rather than being a willing and active participant, Isabel is presented as a character who is beholden to practice witchcraft in order to pay restitution for being saved from death. In this way, Witchcraft is conceived of as being evil and agency robbing, rather than a source of power—a depiction that will be radically challenged in texts such as *Rosemary's Baby* and *The Omen*.

The Old and the New: *The Witches* and the Efficacy of Traditionalism

Nonetheless the novel and the film agree on many plot points. They both clearly regard the practices of the coven as being hedonistic, and they both end with the defeat of the antagonists at the hands of the protagonist. However, although akin to the film in many ways, the novel differs widely in terms of theme when it comes to the efficacy of religion. In the film, in fact, traditional religion does not play a strong role and seems to have already been obliterated at the start, while in the novel it is religious conviction, rather than individual conviction, that leads

Gwen to discern the true nature of Granny Rigby and Isabel, and thus overcome the evil in the village, thereby functioning more as a classical horror text.

Like in all the texts presented throughout this book, alternative religion, whether it be Paganism, Satanism or Witchcraft, is characterized as an old religion, predating all others, even traditional Christianity. Usually, in terms of these other alternative religion texts, this connection to history is used to bestow an element of power and authenticity to this non-traditional faith, thus making it even more orthodox than orthodoxy. In the case of the literary version of *The Witches*, however, the reason for this articulation has more to do with establishing Witchcraft as being outdated and uncivilized rather than historically grounded. Also, in suggesting its being an ancient faith, it can be easily dismissed by skeptics as having no connection to the present day, its contemporary practice an impossibility.

In the novel, Gwen suspects witchcraft, but soon dismisses it as being a nightmarish impossibility, regarded more a fantasy than fact: "His mother's strange almost distraught accusations against Mrs. Rigby seemed like some detail from a nightmare, remembered in bright sunlight."[30] However, as Gwen comes across an effigy of the young Baines boy, her suspicions, unlikely as they are, seem to be confirmed:

> What madness is this? This is the year nineteen hundred and fifty-nine. Nobody has believed in witchcraft for at least two hundred years; the laws against it have been repealed; and here I stand an ordinary God-fearing village school teacher.... With evidence in *my hand*.[31]

When Gwen tries to go to Canon Thorby, the village patriarch, she is discredited: "If I gave one moment's credence to such superstition, I should be utterly unfit for the vocation I follow."[32] As she pursues the matter, increasingly convinced of her conclusions, she is silenced ostensibly by the very powers that she seeks to vanquish. She, like young Sydney, is incapacitated, hospitalized, and awakens from a coma with no memory of what had happened before.

Convinced that the key to her memory lies in returning to Heddaby, she returns to her cottage. Once there, not only does her memory return, but she also becomes aware of the reason behind its loss:

> She had thought that her loss of memory was due to a blow on the head, but apparently, it had another cause, something not very far from a form of mental illness. Having cried herself out, she knelt by her bed and prayed for courage, and for faith, and for help.[33]

However, even though the practice of witchcraft is seen to be not only possible, but indeed powerful, it is still not a modern belief, not of the here and now. Thus, when it is used, it is confined to small villages in remote locations like Heddaby. Much like Folk Horror—narratives that will be explored in the next section of this book, once the characters escape the rural setting (in this case, the English village of Heddaby), they escape the threat of being prey to the spells cast by the coven. This is why in the novel the Baines flee to London, a modern metropolis where the threat of witchcraft is alleviated.[34]

The novel suggests that in addition to being perceptually antiquated, the nature of the sabot rituals are uncivilized and thus an abomination before God. It is for this reason that during the rites and rituals of Witchcraft, the use of Christian dogma and its icons sink into obscenity and the profane. The final scene of the novel, like the film, involves the attempted sacrifice of a young village girl. As opposed to the ceremonies presented in the novel version of *The Witches*, those portrayed in the film are not sexually or violently graphic. Neither do they in any way suggest that these practices are a form of religious desecration, as is evidenced in the novel. In the literary version, the ceremony is held in the local church that is desecrated with ceremonial orgies, overindulgent feasting and drinking, and the partaking of a Satanic communion. This inverted sacrament involves not the incorporation of bread and wine, the body and blood of Jesus, but instead the ingestion of fecal matter and viscera. When these vile elements are spilled into the chalice designed for more traditional religious practices and then placed on the altar used for the traditional sacraments, their use as an object of desecration becomes even clearer. This is redoubled with the foregrounding of the bodily over the spiritual, as these rites are not only enacted without any vestments at all, religious or otherwise, but are concluded with an orgy. Of these practices, Gwen observes:

> The books had said "sexual orgies" and "debauchery" and "perversion," but to her these had been mere arrangements of certain letters which formed certain words. They had no more prepared her for what, on this Hallowse'en, was following the feasting and the drinking…. Even to look upon this scene was to be soiled for this was deliberate obscenity.[35]

Indeed, another characteristic of alternative religion texts produced from the mid–1960s onward is an increased use of bestial sexuality and overindulgence as a rite versus the sabot rituals that involve human sacrifice that characterize the earlier classical horror films. This suggests that whereas the concerns of the earlier works rest with the protection of human agency enabled through religious orthodoxy, the texts of the later period concern themselves more with the expression of human desire, a trope that will come to characterize not only the works produced in the 1970s, but, as discussed above, the concerns of the era as a whole.

The second way in which the film version of *The Witches* differs from the novel has to do with the purpose behind religious ceremony. As discussed above, the rituals in the novel are enacted by the coven as a desecration to the Church. It is through this inversion that they gain their power and achieve their collective ends. However, in the film, the rites depicted are much more personally motivated. In her desire to possess the body of the young village girl, and thus achieve everlasting youth, Stephanie Bax falls in line with the contemporaneous cult of youth, the fear of old age and death, and the undesirability of posterity. Indeed, in the film, Stephanie, as the antagonist and head of the coven, is seen to be affiliated with Satanism not as a method of achieving power from collective agency, but instead wields the dark forces under her control for wholly selfish reasons. In other words, unbeknownst to her followers, who appear to be faithful to her more than to a higher power, Bax seeks to enact the ritualistic sacrifice in homage to the cult of youth over an homage to Satan himself.

Race with the Devil, the Counterculture versus Tradition

Race with the Devil, according to one review, "seems to be trying ... for an archetypal confrontation between middle–American values, and the bizarre counterculture elements embodied by the Satanists."[36] This analysis will follow such an argument by suggesting that it is, in fact, this very conflict that links *Race with the Devil* to the cult of youth as detailed above. Indeed, as the sixties era progressed, the countercultural movement became increasingly aligned with the youth movement, to the point where the two became almost indistinguishable. Not only did its leaders like Abbie Hoffman (ironically twenty-nine himself at the time) warn not to trust anyone over thirty, the young people of the late 1960s and 1970s had come to adopt many of the tropes and tenets reserved for countercultural adherents. According to cultural historian Beth Bailey in *Sex in the Heartland:*

> By the late 1960s America's youth culture had come to look very much like the counterculture. Long-haired boys and braless girls. Psychedelic music. Pot. Sex. The counterculture and its style became mainstream youth culture, the styles and behavior that challenged the notion of respectability became increasingly widespread.[37]

to both spiritual and physical death. Although the ending is an open one, and thus the viewer can draw their own conclusions with regard to the outcome of this last stand, the situation facing the protagonists is a dire one and escape seems unlikely at best. The narrative thus seems to privilege the unification offered by faith. Although an alternative spirituality, this belief system still possesses ties to the traditional more than the modern, making the ideological alignment of the narrative rather unsettled in terms of contemporaneous debate.

If the alignment of this text is narratively undecided with regard to the characters and themes, then this conclusion further complicates things when it comes to a connection to tradition in terms of narrative. In other words, not only is the conflict not one of the standard good versus evil, but also the protagonists may or may not be seen to be wholly on the side of the just, and the antagonists are firmly aligned with wickedness, making empathy problematic. Finally, the open end precludes narrative closure, potentially denying receptive satisfaction. These devices all suggest a structure that is as unsettled as the themes and characters that it presents.

As suggested above, these narrative signals, when combined with a consideration of the filmic extratextuality, render this work even more unsettled. The film indeed provides significant links to an earlier film directed, produced and starring Peter Fonda, *Easy Rider.* From the opening shot of a motorcycle to an early scene featuring Fonda racing a Datsun motorbike, to a later race between Fonda and Oates on Kawasakis, the connection between *Race with the Devil* and *Easy Rider* is made manifest when considering that the earlier film presented Fonda and Hopper on motorcycles. However, as has been the case with all of these works, this connection is troubled. Fonda rides a motorcycle, but it is not the quintessential Harley Davidson. The Harley or HOG (Harley Owners Group) in its 1960s and 1970s advertising set itself up in contrast to more mass-produced motorcycles such as Honda and other companies based in Japan. Honda's advertising motto, "You meet the nicest people on a Honda," was contrasted with Harley Davidson, which appealed to a working class, macho, antisocial attitude. Associated with motorcycling's dark side, manufacturing in the late 1960s and 1970s adopted the look of the renegade chopper, characteristic of those used in *Easy Rider*. It is, thus, somewhat ironic that in *Race with the Devil* Fonda is riding the very type of motorbike that was devalued by the HOG community—the Japanese import. Equally, while both films are located in the southwest, the ways in which this terrain is navigated are altogether different. Rather than traveling with a chopper between his legs, Fonda travels in a motorhome, the arguable bastion of middle-class family life. When he is pictured riding, it is on a track, going in circles, and not on the open road. It would thus ironically appear that the titular race with Satan will take Fonda, Oates, and their wives equally in circles, traveling to nowhere after all. *Race with the Devil* may in fact be considered to be *Easy Rider* commodified, given the fact that Fonda and Oates sell bikes to be tinkered with and sold. Rather than a means of escape from the middle-class status quo, motorbiking is thus linked to issues of commodification. Indeed, the mobile home, it must be remembered, has a color television, whose antenna might well pick up Guy Woodhouse's ad for the "Swingin' World" of Yamaha. The fact of the wives being portrayed by television stars (*MASH*'s Loretta Swit and *Dark Shadows*'s Lara Parker) furthers this connection between *Race with the Devil* and television.

While *Race with the Devil* and *Easy Rider* are aligned, the later film in many ways presents almost an antithesis of the earlier film, a reversal made manifest when comparing the ending of these two works. The final scene of *Easy Rider* involves Fonda and Hopper riding on a deserted desert highway, on which they are confronted by local "good ol' boys" who shoot at them with shotguns while passing in a pickup truck. In the penultimate scene of *Race with the Devil*, Fonda and Oates shoot at their pursuers with the self-same weapon, a shotgun. Finally, while Fonda is associated with the counterculture movement, and the minor characters associated with television, Warren Oates and R.G. Armstrong, who plays the sheriff, are both associated with New Hollywood cinema, equally being featured in the work of Sam Peckinpah, a leader in this cinematic movement who is famous for his scenes of violence.

It could thus be argued that this very narrative construction, when combined with a consideration of extratextual elements, provides a contradictory ideology. This troubled articulation of contemporaneous cultural debates may be the reason for the negative way that the film was received. Indeed, like *The Witches*, reviews regard the film as incomprehensible. For example, according to the *New York Times*, this film was criticized as a:

> Ridiculous mishmash of a movie for people who never grew up, which is not to say it's for children. One would think that Mr. Fonda and Mr. Oates had better things to do, but perhaps not. American movie production is in a bad state.[46]

Significantly, a reference to the childlike narrative structure further alludes to the dichotomy between the old and the new, the youthful and the aged, the modern and the traditional. While, undoubtedly, this film does engage with these self-same debates, it seems to fail to take sides.

Moreover, potentially controversial articulations regarding sexuality, sacrifice and alternative religious practice may be the cause for its overall negative reception in a culture that was increasingly fracturing along these same fault lines.

Academic Concerns in *Race with the Devil*

Even given strong textual and extratextual indicators suggesting an alignment of this film to issues with a cult of youth and an occult sensibility, academic debate thus far has yet to regard this film in light of these issues. Much as is the case with *The Witches*, little has been written about this film, even given its obvious alignment with New Hollywood and the counterculture movement. When it is mentioned, as is the case with a review of the film published in *Jump Cut*, a journal focusing on contemporary media, *Race with the Devil* is seen as being concerned with a breakdown of the family and middle-class values more than being aligned with the occult, or even the counterculture overall:

> The film's major metaphor is that of the mobile camper, which is portrayed as having all the luxuries and conveniences of the modern U.S. home.... The motorhome is the physical embodiment of the fundamental yet paradoxical desire of the protagonists. The U.S. conception of vacation implies a basic dissatisfaction with the American way of life. The very notion of "vacation," as it has developed into a modern national institution, has become more an escape from one's daily condition, the routine of work, rather than a coming to a new experience with which one might enrich one's daily life.[47]

When the focus is taken off of the cult of youth and the occult threat that, as has been suggested above, is of primary concern not only to this work, but indeed to a significant number of horror films from this period, then the malevolent satanists depicted in this film can equally be interpreted as a projection, an incarnation, of the fears of the protagonists—threats that are always lurking just outside, threatening to invade and evade the character's sense of security and stability. According to this author, the home is transformed into a nomadic fortress, always seeking safety, always fighting off the terrible demons which threaten to invade it and indeed invade all individuals existing in this era at the crux of the age of modernity.

However, if this reading is once again reinterpolated into a concern of the dominance of the cult of youth and the debate of the efficacy of communal spiritual alignment, then the motorhome driven by Peter Fonda and his companions might indeed be seeking refuge not from the threat of a breakdown of middle-class values, but of a breakdown of rational modernity itself under the threat of an efficacious system of belief in the powers that exist outside of the self altogether. While these characters are offered the open highway as a means of escape, those existing in the last film to be discussed in this chapter, *The Brotherhood of Satan*, are denied even this figurative and/or literal road to salvation.

The Brotherhood of Satan and the Reversal of the Cult of Youth

In a scene that opens *The Brotherhood of Satan*, a family drives their midsize sedan on a deserted country road. As they progress on their journey, the first horrific event of the film occurs as the car is first pursued and then crushed by a large military tank.[48] This unlikely weapon kills all inside save for a young boy who, completely unharmed, walks away from the devastating crash in a trance-like state. While the child turns his back upon this scene of grisly violence, the camera focuses on the blood and gore. In a zoom shot, the bloody car itself comes into focus, containing not only disembodied limbs, a standard trope of the horror film, but also a rosary which rests on the dashboard, an inclusion of a less common nature. In this scene, two things are established. First is the fact that this will indeed be a horror film, and second that the families depicted within this piece of low-budget cinema will be depicted as being aligned with the Catholic faith, the oldest and arguably most traditional ecumenicisms of all Christian faiths. A second scene early in the film confirms this, when a young mother and father are seen scolding their two children for leaving the protective environs of the home. The concerned father draws his offspring inside, wherein the mother has set the dining room table for dinner. The family sits down and prays for forgiveness and deliverance from evil, and then they all begin to eat. Thus, right from the very opening the film articulates the primacy of home and hearth as a source of safety and stability, and religion as a tool for further unification and protection. In many ways, in fact, *The Brotherhood of Satan* engages with similar debates to those films discussed throughout this section: arguments surrounding the modern versus the traditional, and the efficacy of spiritual affiliation for social, cultural and individual stability. Equally, as will be noted in the following analysis, *The Brotherhood of Satan* likewise reveals a narrative concern with the countercultural cult of youth, as do all of the films in this discussion. However, as alluded to in the introduction of this chapter, this low-budget film, while falling in line with this contemporaneous concern, is also unique in providing an interesting point for analysis. This is so for two reasons.

First, the film presents, for the first time in this section, a true dichotomy of belief. Both Christianity and Satanism are equally represented, thus establishing a conflict similar to that of *The Wicker Man,* a work that will be discussed in detail in the subsequent section of this book. In other words, rather than engaging in a battle between skepticism and faith, such as occurs in *Rosemary's Baby, The Omen,* the film version of *The Witches,* and *Race with the Devil,* in this film the local villagers are depicted as being as unified in their faith as their Satanic counterparts. Secondly, because it is the young who are seen as being more traditional while the old are seen as being radicals, this work offers up a reversal of contemporaneous cultural debates regarding the establishment of the counterculture youth movement. In fact, ironically, it is the young who believe in the sanctity of the family and the power of traditional Christianity to protect such traditional kinship formations against any evil that poses a threat.

This privileging of the traditional is depicted in the private realm, the homestead, in which individual families gathered around the dining room table bow their heads in prayer before eating their supper:

> Oh Lord, we thank thee for the bounty we are about to receive for the blessings that will come our way in the future. Oh Lord, we thank thee with a full and humble heart, Amen.[49]

These traditions are, however, not unique to a single family. Indeed, as is suggested by the inclusion of the rosary in the car that opens the film, this embrace of Catholicism unites every family in the village of Hillsboro, under the guidance of a local parish priest. Likewise, the elderly members of the town practice an alternative faith that is guided by a religious leader, demands allegiance to a higher power, and requires familial connectivity. It is not wholly ironic that this group, although collectively worshiping the devil, are labeled nepotists and not Satanists in the ending credits of the film. The reasons for this favoring of relatives, however, as will be seen later in this analysis, are not those commonly associated with the traditional nepotist.

This religious mode of life, regardless of whether traditional or alternative, is equally steeped in the devotional and thus stands apart from its increasingly secular cultural milieu. This conflict is literalized by the way in which the village is set in a remote and isolated location, thereby cut off from external influences such as the radio, and by the way in which this village is contrasted by the outsider protagonist family.[50] Indeed, from the moment the protagonists are introduced, they are presented as character foils to the village inhabitants. While engaging in secular rituals, such as a children's birthday party, a gathering doubled by the Satanists at the end of the film, they do not observe any religious traditions. While the families in the town are dressed conservatively, Nikki, the protagonist mother figure, wears a skimpy bikini. While the nuclear families in the town are joined by a traditional marriage, Nikki and her partner, Ben, are merely dating. While the children of the Hillsboro families are the product of these married parents, Nikki and Ben are not the parents of K.T. Ben is her father, but her mother has died prior to the start of the narrative. When this blended family arrives in Hillsboro, they are surrounded by the villagers who accost them violently. The sheriff, as he removes Ben from behind the wheel at gunpoint, accuses him of having a child out of wedlock more than of any other crime. Although the reason for this reaction is later revealed to be the result of the family being the only outsiders to enter this community in several days, there is also an ideological reason for this admittedly overblown reaction. In other words, the outsider family stands apart, and is reacted to as such, not only because they are strangers within a closed, tightly knit community, but also because they are not representative of tradition in the same way as the locals themselves are seen to be.

Just as the strangers are "other" and divorced from conservative traditionalism, so too, ironically, are the elderly of the community. The coven engages in well-established rites that have been handed down through the generations, as is evidenced by the ritualistic promise that for their devotion they will receive yet another lifetime in the brotherhood of Satan. Even given the elderly coven's promise of selfless devotion by uttering a statement using the traditional biblical vernacular, "I have nothing that is not thine," this faith is not presented as being a traditional belief mechanism, as was the case with the other works in this section, making this film a novel articulation within the alternative-faith horror cycle. Further, the fact of the elderly engaging in such a radical religion breaks from stereotypes offered within contemporaneous cultural discourse overall. Finally, the way in which this film ends, with a blackout and an intertitle reading, "Come in Children," which is how all of the coven and the sacrificial victims were welcomed, implicates all who watch this film in its aberration.

Indeed, while at this moment in history, it became common for the young to adopt an alternative lifestyle, in presenting an aged group that does the same, *The Brotherhood of Satan* seems to provide a contrast not only to the discourses of the films discussed in this book, but indeed to the modern ethos overall. Although both the old and the young seem to hold faith in the power of religion, the choice of faith and the reasons guiding their choice are almost diametrically opposed.

If the young families of Hillsboro hold on to their faith as a means of protection for the family unit, then the older inhabitants worship for the narcissistic gains they will receive. Operating from a more hedonistic perspective common to the modern culture, the belief system held by the elderly members of Hillsboro will lead to personal reward, in this instance being made young again by inhabiting the bodies of the children they abduct. In this way, *The Brotherhood of Satan* articulates a thematic concern that is almost diametrically opposed to texts such as *Rosemary's Baby*, the latter film presenting a youthful couple, the husband of which is willing to sacrifice his family for personal success, while the elderly Satanists, although on the surface alternative, seem to adhere to a religion that in many ways is figured as being traditional in nature, as discussed in chapter one. Indeed, while the members of the Satanic coven in *Rosemary's Baby* are, admittedly, all elderly, they practice their faith to bring about the rise of the God that they worship. In other words, the result of their devotion will benefit the deity, and if they in turn are rewarded, it will be offered tangentially; the reward is not the reason for the devotion but its by-product. Likewise, whereas Rosemary fears that the Satanists want her baby for a sacrificial ritual, this turns out not to be the case. The Satanists want the baby not to sacrifice but to revere. However, these fears are, in fact, realized in *The Brotherhood of Satan* wherein, as with *The Witches*, the elderly will kill the children so as to provide an embodied vehicle for eternal youth.

What sets this work apart from other classical horror narratives is not in the battle of good versus evil, for as is the case with most of the works of horror produced after "the death of God," the "nepotists" are set up as being evil, while the Catholic families are configured as being decidedly good victims. It is instead the outcome of this struggle that makes this work wholly unique and possibly even revolutionary. *The Brotherhood of Satan* pits two equally reverential communities against each other and, once the battle is fought, it is hedonistic Satanism and not traditional Christianity that emerges victorious. Although the priest in the community fervently prays for the souls of his parish, sprinkling holy water, and admonishing sins, he is not able to save the children of Hillsboro. Even though he researches into the possibility of these abductions being the result of Satanic worship and tries to warn his parishioners of this potentiality, upon witnessing the enactment of this "nepotism," he is rendered mad. The geriatric worshippers of the devil, on the other hand, achieve their desire in taking over the bodies of the children.

When researching the reception of *The Brotherhood of Satan*, it is the outcome of this self-same dichotomy that is rendered incomprehensible.

Roger Greenspun of the *New York Times* while overall giving this film a positive review, suggests of the coven:

> The actual brotherhood is a pretty dismal affair, a kind of black magic golden age club to whom hooded figures serve cocktails before they settle down to do their blood and witchcraft. Much of the latter involves a parody of religious rituals ... that only disrupts the mood at hand.[51]

Further, when Greenspun speaks of religious parody, questions arise as to which religion is derided, Christianity or Satanism. For indeed, Satanism, existing as an inversion of traditional religion, could be considered a parody, especially when the rituals enacted rely upon accouterments that align its practice with more traditional forms. At the same time, in presenting old age pensioners as worshippers of the devil, a practice that, at least in terms of the media has been reserved for the likes of Mick Jagger, Kenneth Anger and Jayne Mansfield, this wholly oppositional representation can equally be said to parody this radically alternative form of spiritual belief in terms of practitioners. Likewise, Christianity is mocked due to its ultimate lack of efficacy. The young traditional adherents fervently believe yet fail.

Conclusion

Thus, while regarded as a Catholic other in *Rosemary's Baby* and *The Omen*, Satanism is alternatively articulated as a hedonistic sacrilege in *The Witches* and *The Brotherhood of Satan*. The reasons for this dual alignment include several factors. First, all the films discussed in this section require the older members of the coven to be subservient to their god, a commonality of all religions. Also, as with traditional religion, the members of the congregation must show subservience, bowing to their god, making restitution for sinning against him, and pledging to follow the will of their deity above all else. Finally, like in traditional religion, there is the promise of rebirth. However, in *Rosemary's Baby* and *The Omen*, this rebirth comes in the form of a supernatural incarnation, producing the Antichrist. For the Satanism presented in *The Brotherhood of Satan* and *The Witches*, however, this rebirth is merely physical and not a spiritual renewal. The elderly keep their identities, which are inserted into youthful bodies. There is also an element of propitiation, but this sacrifice, in the form of the children of the township, is not meant as a form of reverence or as a mechanism for the forgiveness of sin, but instead as a means for personal gain: to enact a return to youth. Finally, this religious practice, as is the case with *The Witches* and

The Brotherhood of Satan, also involves the use of the accouterments of Christianity: candles, chalices, robes and Latin liturgy; however, because such rituals are enacted in the service of individual hedonism, they are wielded not in deistic worship, but instead as sacrilege.

As the narrative progresses, it is discovered that Heddaby and Hillsboro are not only geographically isolated and willfully cut off, but more importantly philosophically apart. This alignment is, admittedly, not wholly unprecedented within the culture at this time. Even as the counterculture brought about an opening up of religious affiliation, this was also a time when ultra-conservative faiths, such as the church led by the Rev. Billy Graham, were on the rise in the United States, a powerful vocal force in the religious community amongst the young and old alike. However, in terms of popular discourse, it is predominantly modernity that seems to characterize this time frame, and possibly because of media portrayals, the cult of youth seems to take precedence when looking back at the 1960s and 1970s. As discussed in the introduction to this book, rock music, popular film, and television all seemed to foreground this idea, and standout texts such as this work, and the film and novel *Carrie*, wherein a young mother tries to raise her daughter as a fundamentalist, are fairly uncommon. Alternatively, the negation of historical imperatives, including familial connectivity and religious traditionalism so as to bring about drives toward hedonism, appear much more widespread, at least when it comes to articulations of Satanism. This, however, appears not to be the case when it comes to representations of another popular horror-faith, that of Paganism, as will be revealed in the next section of this book.

SECTION II

Paganism as an Alternative Culture

FOUR

Ritual and the Rural in Anglo-American Co-Productions

John Bowen ... takes Norah's uncertain point of view, echoing *Rosemary's Baby* while looking forward to ... *The Wicker Man*. Rarely has the dark side of British folk legend been portrayed with such fearsome precision.[1]—DAVID THOMPSON's review of *Robin Redbreast*

People growing up in communities of memory not only hear the stories that how the community came to be, what its hopes and fears are and how its ideals are exemplified in outstanding men and women; they also participate in the practices—ritual, aesthetic, ethical—that define the community as a way of life.[2]—ROBERT BELLAH, *Habits of the Heart*

Introduction

In the penultimate shot in *Robin Redbreast*, an installment from the BBC series *Play for Today*, Norah Palmer, who up until this moment has been held as a veritable prisoner in her cottage by the local residents, turns around and gazes at her rural retreat for the last time before enacting what she believes will be her long-awaited escape. In a moment of true insight while regarding the scene behind her, she witnesses her maid, her handyman and the village patriarch alter in appearance, divulging their true natures. The maid is revealed to be a witch, the handyman a magus, and the patriarch Herne the Hunter, the horned god of the English forest. This revelation acts as confirmation of what she had come to believe throughout the teleplay. This truth, lurking just below the surface of a perceived reality now made manifest, is that the community in which she briefly made her home is in fact Pagan.

111

Moreover, it is thus confirmed that she was indeed made prey to secret propitiatory and fertility rituals, rites hidden from anyone outside of this closed community. As the rural residents are revealed in their true colors,[3] their outward appearances are now commensurate with their inner beliefs. Likewise does Palmer outwardly reflect her inner being. Garbed in a mini dress, behind the wheel of her expensive sports car, pregnant but unmarried, the protagonist of this narrative herself becomes an exemplar of the modern woman. However, now that her eyes have been opened, the inexplicable momentarily revealed, she is no longer the same Norah Palmer. Even as she both literally and figuratively turns her back on this isolated and isolating rural world and the religious affiliation with which it is inexorably associated, she herself has also been transformed. She has looked back not only through space but also through time. She has paid witness to an ancient Pagan past, an antiquity steeped in ritual and supernatural belief heretofore obscured from the outside world. In doing so, she must now wrestle with an internal conflict. This battle is one between belief and skepticism, between an acceptance of the power of the supernatural and the rational world of modernity, and finally between a potentially deceptive, superficial perception and a more deeply accurate discernment. She also must live with the baby that grows inside of her, a confirmation of her brush with forces both beyond her understanding and outside her control.

Adam Scovell, one of the key authors to link these works within a cycle termed "Folk Horror," equally refers to these themes of perception and retrospection when he argues:

> [These works] often mimic this idea of looking back, where the past and the present mix and create horror through anachronisms and uncomfortable tautologies between eras. Folk Horror, the horror of folk, is out of time and within time with strangers within the landscape who have survived the ravages of modernity.[4]

Harkening back to the past in observing Pagan rituals, both the rural village of *Robin Redbreast* and the folk of Bellenac/Bellac in *Eye of the Devil* and *Day of the Arrow*, as will be discussed below, also mask not only themselves but also their religious practice and their spiritual belief. Hidden behind the garb of more traditional faith mechanisms (more specifically, Anglicanism in the former and Catholicism in the latter), the Pagan lurks undetected to the eye of the interloper. This obscuring was also the case in *The Omen*, discussed in chapter two of this book, wherein Satanism masked itself as Catholicism. Even while sharing certain characteristics with *The Omen* in obscuring the true nature of worship, and whilst aligning with *Rosemary's Baby*, *Race with the Devil* and *The*

Brotherhood of Satan in hiding the Satanic cabal behind the guise of respectability and benignity, *Eye of the Devil, Day of the Arrow* and *Robin Redbreast*, as Pagan Horror films, more significantly diverge from those works discussed previously. Although not practiced out in the open for all to see, neither is Paganism maligned as being evil, as was the case of the films analyzed earlier, works wherein Witchcraft is aligned with Satanism. The Pagan faith instead is offered up as a distinct and efficacious belief in its own right not to be conflated into a Satanic melting pot (or cauldron, as the case may be). This religious delineation was

Top left and below: Christian de Caray (David Hemmings), Odile de Caray (Sharon Tate), and bottom right Philippe de Montfaucon (David Niven) from *Eye of the Devil*. Right inset: Mr. Fisher (Bernard Hepton) as the watcher and Herne the Hunter from *Robin Redbreast*.

noted in the reception of the novel *Day of the Arrow*, written by Philip Loraine,[5] upon which the film *Eye of the Devil* was based. In this book review published contemporaneously in the *New York Times*, the literary critic notes this thematic concern with Paganism when he states, "The answer [to the riddle of Bellac] will come as no surprise to anyone who has ever leafed through *The Golden Bough*; but its obviousness in no way diminishes its power."[6] The way in which this review appears to support rather than malign this film might very well speak to an increasing acceptance of alternative faith communities, as suggested in the introduction to this book. More specifically, in enacting a return to nature, engaging in a reverence of Mother Earth and desiring to live communally among like-minded believers, these texts seem to align, at least on the surface, with a countercultural group known as the hippies. Common to other groups that made up the variegated counterculture, the hippies searched for a more authentic existence through which the individual could rediscover the self, reestablish meaningful interpersonal relationships and reconnect to the world. However, the hippies were also ideologically divergent to their counterculture milieu in seeking this self-actualization through a rejection not only of all things traditional, but also of the modern world and its trappings. In other words, this movement not only saw conservative orthodoxy as being confining, but equally renounced the primary mechanism whereby tradition was usually rejected: modernity itself. Indeed, the hippies argued that it was only by rejecting the urban world of forward-focused commerce, enacting a physical return to nature, and spiritually communing with the natural world that man could once again achieve happiness and a sense of fulfillment. Thus, they searched for answers by looking back to an archaic time: a time long before the Enlightenment and the Reformation, long before even the birth of Christianity itself. They embraced a time in the distant past when man was inexorably tied to the agrarian landscape and thus not only figuratively but also literally closer to his roots. As a result of this connectivity, hippies came to worship the source of the bounty by which their lives were bound: the gods of Mother Earth.

As suggested above, even given the way in which the adaptive book superficially aligns with the neo–Pagan hippie, even with the way it was received at the time of its release as a Pagan film, and even though academic debate interpolated this work into a Pagan cycle of films known as Folk Horror, certain film scholars still regard this work as presenting devil worship and Satanic rites. In his book, *Raising the Devil: Satanism, New Religions and the Media*, Bill Ellis notes:

> Those who wished to see what a black mass was like, however, needed only to head to the nearest cinema where a number of British studios were producing sensational B films on satanic themes. Among the first of these was a film variously titled *Thirteen* or *Eye of the Devil*, a *Wheatleyesque* story of an evil black magic ring.[7]

However, rather than following Ellis in relying upon a potentially oversimplified conflation, characteristic of films like *The Omen* and *Rosemary's Baby*, this chapter will analyze *Day of the Arrow*, *Eye of the Devil* and *Robin Redbreast* so as to open up debates concerning the representation of alternative faiths during this period. This will be achieved beginning with a textual analysis of *The Eye of the Devil*, then continuing on to an interpretation of the film's literary antecedent *Day of the*

Arrow, and finally concluding with a consideration of the teleplay *Robin Redbreast.* To focus on a novel, a film and a teleplay, all of which equally foreground a thematic concern with Paganism, as opposed to Paganism-cum-Satanism, might very well suggest the extent to which this contemporaneous culture adopted an increased acceptance of viable alternative religions across media. Jonathan Rigby also seems to foreground this concern when he argues:

> With interest in esoteric religions at an all-time high at the turn of the 1970s, *Robin Redbreast* occupied a pivotal position, thematically as well as chronologically, between the urban folksiness of *Rosemary's Baby* and the offshore paganism of *The Wicker Man.*[8]

However, to focus on these three works that likewise mask this faith behind more traditional religions might equally allude to how far the culture still had to go in terms of tolerance. Indeed, this was not only a time that was characterized as being a period of opening up, it has also been regarded as a "treacherous moral landscape"[9] of skeptical modernity and conservative backlash.[10] In other words, while Paganism was indeed presented as a faith in and of itself, its rites were also hidden from those who, in learning the truth of this ancient propitiatory religion, would see it stopped and its adherents punished. Arguably, modern skeptics and traditional Christians alike would regard the sacrificial rituals presented in these works as being murderous, even though the latter faith, ironically, once incorporated animal not to mention human sacrifice within its practice. Likewise, the hippie would regard this return to nature not as a form of "getting loose," to borrow a phrase manipulated by Sam Binkley, or even as a method of finding oneself, but instead see the communities presented in these works as being highly stratified. The Paganism of *Eye of the Devil, Day of the Arrow* and *Robin Redbreast* offers up a system under which historical imperatives and inescapable duty are paramount even to the death. This is something that Scovell discusses specifically in relation to *Eye of the Devil.* He suggests, "The English landscape is the site of numerous struggles between the forces of power and privilege and those who thought to resist them."[11] As is the case in *Eye of the Devil, Day of the Arrow* and *The Wicker Man,* which will be discussed later, the head priest is also the lord of the manor. As a society in which everyone therein is placed in a rigid hierarchy, the Pagan village is more commensurate with conservative traditional culture than a progressive counterculture.

Likewise, in terms of past connections and spiritual articulations, Paganism can equally be seen as not in conflict with tradition, but instead seeking to underpin it, as this archaic religion actually becomes a foundation upon which traditional religion—both Catholicism and Christianity—is overlaid. More specifically, as suggested above, both Christianity and Paganism rely upon the rites of sacrifice, burial rituals and the belief in the persistence of life after death, martyr rituals and reverence, even Christian holidays are superimposed upon Pagan sabbats.[12] These religions are thus not at odds, but instead form a continuum: the Christian laid atop the Pagan as a veneer. It is indeed not the Pagan and the Christian that are at odds, but instead the faith community and skeptical modernity, the latter not only denying historic faith, but also generational legacy. However, even given this foundational basis, the modern Christian looks upon the spiritual journey from Paganism to Christianity not as a continuum but instead as a palimpsest, as indeed does Sir James Frazer in *The Golden Bough*, a foundational text for all these works. In this seminal work, as will be discussed further in a discussion of *The Wicker Man*, Frazer, possibly as the result of his own historical and cultural influences, related to religion as did Darwin to biology, seeing spiritual belief as a process of evolution. For Frazer, the Pagan reliance on supernatural ritual was thus rendered inferior to the more modern Protestant faiths that eradicated irrational such beliefs from their worship.

Thus, *Eye of the Devil*, *Day of the Arrow* and *Robin Redbreast* stand at odds not only to the neo–Pagan, back-to-earth hippie movement, but also to Christian doctrine, whether Protestant or Catholic, and finally to modernity, which holds orthodox faith communities to be folly. It is for this very reason that this faith must be masked, or it would indeed be eradicated as an arcane atrocity. The people of these communities are bound to each other, for it is only through a collective reverence that this faith (or indeed any faith) might continue. Their safety is in secrecy; their efficacy is in community.

However, while acknowledging this representation of Pagan belief as one that out of necessity must be hidden, Scovell seems more concerned with the ways in which these characters are connected to the rural landscape than to the Paganism that maintains their way of life, even as it threatens to end it. For the Folk Horror Chain, the landscape becomes a focal point through the way in which the rural topography is aesthetically represented, making works like *Robin Redbreast*, in the words of Scovell, a "virtually perfect example of [the Folk Horror's] landscape mechanism."[13] Rigby, much like Scovell, regards the primary concern to be centered around location over spiritual belief, grouping these works as being part of Britain's long-standing tradition of "rural horror." Thus, academic debate figures these films as being more engaged with a conflict of the rural and the urban than that of faith versus skepticism, as will be revealed further in relationship to *Eye of the Devil, Day of the Arrow* and *Robin Redbreast*. The project of this chapter, and indeed this book overall, is to reinterpolate the debates surrounding faith and spiritual alignment back into these works, for indeed it is this concern with spirituality that grounds these communities through connecting the individuals living within them to a force outside of themselves to which homage must be paid. Likewise, it is this faith that must be hidden from outsiders who might fail to believe in the efficacy of these rituals, regarding them not as reverential but instead as reprehensible, even as those who do believe are willing to give their very lives for these rites that they firmly believe will both literally and figuratively bear fruit.

Enacting a Return to Nature and Tradition as a Rejection of Modernist Fragmentation in the Film Version of *Eye of the Devil*

As discussed throughout this book, the late 1960s and early 1970s culture recoiled from the destabilizing forces that modernity had unleashed as a result of rejecting stifling traditionalism. Desiring reentrenchment through new objects of devotion, individuals sought to fill the void left by the disintegration of old systems of belief and authority. Many within the youth generation sought both a physical and psychological space where things could be done differently—where individual and social stability could be achieved without being stultified in the process. According to an article published in *Time* magazine, the hippie movement provided one road to these aforementioned ends through self-reflection and communal living. The article suggests:

> [The hippie movement] hoped to generate an entirely new society, one rich in spiritual grace that will revive the old virtues of agape and reverence. Its disciples, who have little use for definitions, are mostly young and generally thoughtful Americans who are unable to reconcile themselves to the stated values and implicit contradictions of contemporary Western society, and have become internal emigres, seeking individual liberation through means as various as drug use, total withdrawal from the economy and the quest for individual identity. They [thus] reveal ... the exhaustion of a tradition: Western, production-directed, problem-solving, goal-oriented and compulsive in its way of thinking. Hippie millennialism is purely Arcadian: pastoral and primordial, emphasizing oneness with physical and psychic nature.... Historically, the hippies go all the way back to the days of Diogenes and the Cynics.[14]

Challenging the social norms of the period by engaging not only in acts of free love as a means of social connection, but also in Eucharistic drug use so as to connect to a spiritual realm beyond common human experience, this youth movement sought nirvana, a place which they believed could not be found in contemporaneous modernity. Thus, adherents chose to drop out, either figuratively through the taking of drugs, or literally by establishing idealistic societies outside society. Rather than rushing off to the cities, as many had done previously in a search for freedom, many youths during this era absconded off to the rural countryside, a locale once the "very old and very new."[15] Communities such as the famed Morning Star[16] Commune drew nature-loving hippie tribesmen who sought to escape the commercialization of the city. The agrarian commune could provide roots and open up the opportunity for a meaningful, connected existence. Here, one could be grounded and free at the same time—to have one's vegan oatcakes and eat them, too. As cultural historian Sam Binkley suggests in *Getting Loose: Lifestyle Consumption in the 1970s*, "One could release oneself into the loving spirit of a replenishing earth and all of its interdependent systems, if one could sufficiently open one's mind and reform one's habits."[17] Marshall Berman supports Binkley's assertion regarding this return to nature and the importance of this move when he argues:

> The country seemed the place where experiments in social change could be practiced differently, on a smaller, more intimate scale, directly upon one's self and on one's style of life. Pastoral life, for many counter-culturals, promised radical self-fulfilment in an arena sheltered from the turbulent upheavals of modern social life.[18]

It is precisely this return to a more authentic, purposeful and meaningful existence that becomes the focus of *Eye of the Devil*, a British/American co-production made in 1966, one year before the publication of the *Time* article quoted above. Like with the scene from *Robin Redbreast*, discussed above, the characters of *Eye of the Devil* must look back to a time and place rooted in the past. In returning to a place from his childhood, a place steeped in the arcane, the protagonist of this film answers the primal call of the rural. However, as will be suggested below, this siren song takes on a very different, indeed an antithetical, form from the nature-loving hippie ethos of "dropping out" that drove the counterculture to the country.

The first scene of the film opens with a party at the home of protagonist, Philippe de Montfaucon. This sequence reveals the privileged and successful lifestyle adopted by the Montfaucon family within their Parisienne urban penthouse. This city, an external locus of European modernity,[19] is redoubled within the apartment itself, furnished with contemporary panache, and set off with large picture windows which highlight the locale. During this party, the Montfaucon family—father, mother, and son—are together, sitting enrapt by a harpist's performance.[20] This familial unity is disrupted as Philippe is summarily called to return to his ancestral home from which he has long been absent. He is informed that the reason for the request has to do with the surrounding vineyards which have not been yielding fruit. This has been causing havoc not only for the village, but also for the family business which sustains it. Even though the plot does not make clear exactly what will be required of the landlord, Montfaucon seems to know. As he contemplates the necessity of this return and what it will entail, he begins to doodle on a notepad emblazoned with his familial crest. As he draws an arrow through the dove on this historic genealogical signifier, his role as sacrificial victim of an ancient Pagan ritual is foreshadowed. While the protagonist is quite aware of what will be required in order to reinvigorate the crops, his wife and children, like the audience, are completely unaware of the reason for the summons. Also, in being products of modernity, they are not invited to accompany Philippe. Indeed, they would be completely out of place in a world that Philippe's wife likens to being straight out of the Middle Ages.[21] In returning to Bellenac, Philippe is thus effecting a return to the past, to historic traditions that have lain dormant in his unconscious as he assumed his modern life.

Even as he speeds through the village in his modern sports car, signaling the divide that has grown between Philippe and the village, the villagers nonetheless greet Philippe with respectful awe, embracing him as their lord. Each takes off his hat as the marquis passes in sign of respect for their master upon whom their lives depend. This village is thus represented as being highly stratified, the pecking order made manifest right from the start. At the culmination of what amounts to a welcoming procession, Father Dominique, the local priest, bestows upon the landlord a pendant, an heirloom which Philippe bows down and kisses. The trinket, like the class system and the religion to which all adhere, has been handed down from generation to generation and therefore must equally be revered. The opening of the film also signals the conflict of the film: tradition versus modernity. While Paris seems to represent modernity, it is also populated with a harp song, signaling a Pagan influence that is redoubled by the arrow that Philippe draws through his family crest. Likewise, the land presents a conflict, for in enacting a return to the country and to the Pagan connectivity with nature, Philippe will become divided from his modern nuclear family, and instead become engulfed in the deeply rooted tradition that binds him to the legacy of his extended family. This legacy will culminate in a loss of self rather than assertion of individuality and free will, a further conflict between tradition and modernity.

This schism increases with the arrival of Catherine de Montfaucon and Philippe's two children to Bellenac, against the wishes of her husband. As she awaits a reunion with her husband, she observes a second and more private ceremony to that of the public welcoming. In this ritual, enacted behind closed doors, the further complicity of the landlord in the events that will follow is marked. In a room lit by candles and presided over by twelve men garbed in dark robes, a small dove shot through with an arrow is presented, a sign hearkening back to the drawing that opened the film.[22] When Catherine confronts her husband about these rites and his involvement therein, Philippe answers that Bellenac is steeped in "strange rituals that have been practiced by his family for a thousand years."[23] He goes on to suggest that once again he has begun to think in terms of generations, and to embrace tradition. Much like Norah Palmer, he will continue to look back.

This unhinging from the modern is evidenced further when Catherine finds Philippe praying with the local priest, the last ritualistic preparation for his final sacrifice. She inquires as to why he is engaged in such an act of reverence. Father Dominique, rather than Philippe, retorts that it is a strange and secular world that demands what it means for a man to pray.[24] This final sentiment directly alludes to the protagonist's increasing loss of connection with what it means to be modern. Indeed, not only is he engaged in ritualistic practices, steeped in faith and tradition, and willing to give his life over to these, he has also now relinquished his voice, allowing the Church to speak on his behalf. Thus, the return to nature that is presented in this film is not a loosening of ties that bind and a bolstering of opportunities for personal freedom, but instead a radical return to a deeply rooted tradition that engulfs the individual within a generational imperative. It is for this reason that this text (and equally *Robin Redbreast*, as will be discussed later) negates the ethos of the era in which it was created. In many ways, it foregrounds a return not to the earth per se, but instead to stratified, ancient propitiatory traditions to which all are beholden, inasmuch as they are bound to the religion that reveres the gods of nature that sustains this agrarian community.

Thus, the acceptance of spirituality becomes a thematic imperative of *Eye of the Devil*, an imperative that links the villagers to each other and to history. However, rather than openly embracing Paganism, the faith that has come to dominate Bellenac and the surrounding village is one that is masked as being Catholic. However, upon closer inspection, the Catholic Church is in fact merely a veneer, a coating that masks but does not dominate over the Pagan roots that undergird it.

This religious obfuscation is made manifest in a local festival known as "The Treize Jours," or "The Thirteen Days" when translated into English. The name of the festival is in many ways overdetermined and thus the meaning behind the title potentially significant for both Catholic and Pagan beliefs. The "Treize Jours" could, on the one hand, easily be a mispronunciation of the thirteen performers/dancers, or the "Treize Jouers." Ritual dance, according to Yale University theology professor Ramsay McCullen, is significantly shared by both the Pagan and the early Christian as familiar to Augustine in the first century as it was before. McCullen argues:

> It was to be seen both at martyr tombs and throughout city precincts and squares. It spared neither the close vicinity of the churches nor the saints' days themselves ... offering the equivalent of a prayer in the language of gestures ... but dancing was also a practice the bishops recognized for what it was, or what it had been in unreformed days for their congregation: a rite performed in the sanctuary before the temple in traditional pagan fashion.[25]

Even as the practice of dancing could equally apply to either the Pagan or the Christian, the number of dancers being thirteen is more directly connected to the Church in representing the Twelve Apostles plus the sacrificial lamb of Christ, who must die to bring about new life. In this context, those who dance may equally be interpreted as those who follow the steps of the Savior, as the apostles followed in the way of Christ. Likewise, the dance is not only used in early Christian ritual as described above; it is also presented specifically in the *Apocrypha*[26] which talks of the "twelve dancing on high." There is no longer a biblical referent for this connection between followers of Christ and dancers in the modern faith, however. The only remaining substantial tie between Christ and the act of dancing can, however, be found in a popular contemporary Christian hymn entitled "Lord of the Dance":

Dance then wherever you may be; For I am the Lord of the dance, said He,
And I'll lead you all, wherever you may be; And I'll lead you all in the dance said He.[27]

What is interesting about the hymn, written by Englishman Sydney Carter,[28] is the fact that, whereas the tune was taken from an American Shaker song, the words have a decidedly Pagan element, as was noted in the obituary of the songwriter published in *The Telegraph* newspaper. Of the song, Carter admits:

> I did not think the churches would like it at all. I thought many people would find it pretty far flown, probably heretical and anyway dubiously Christian. But in fact people did sing it and, unknown to me, it touched a chord.[29]

The fact that this hymn is modern, penned in 1963, and went on to become, according to the same article, one of the most popular and celebrated religious songs of the twentieth century, potentially suggests another popular cultural connection between this film and its milieu.

The Pagan influence within an apparently Catholic celebration like the Thirteen Days is derided by Montfaucon's wife who, upon witnessing but not comprehending the significance of these rituals, describes the celebration of "The Treize Jours" as "primitive nonsense."[30] Yet, Philippe, now wholly subsumed in these religious traditions, retorts, "It is our belief in something that makes it for a moment, or forever divine."[31] This, again, is a signal of the dichotomy and increasing division between not only the beliefs of husband and wife, but indeed between what these individuals represent: Catherine, the urban world of skeptical modernity, and Philippe, the ancient, pre-modern propitiatory world of Pagan tradition.

The roots of the festival of the Thirteen Days can be linked, like etymology of the name itself, to many historic religious roots. On the surface, the obvious connection is to the Christian celebration of Pentecost. During this festivity, the gift of the Holy Spirit is bestowed to all mankind, signaling the birth of the Church and the ministry of the apostles in spreading the message of Christ. However, as with "Lord of the Dance," there is also a deeper significance to this ritual. Indeed, it is suggested within the film that this divine belief system, practiced in the local church and presided over by Father Dominique, is not reducible to a traditional Catholic mass held in Latin, but instead a service invoking the "older gods," the thirteenth member of the dancers being a living deity, but not necessarily a Christian one. Significantly, it was during this time that the Second Vatican Council allowed for the Catholic mass to be conducted in local vernacular and not in the traditional Latin in order to make the meaning of the services more accessible to the celebrants. In this case, the use of Latin not only evokes a return to a traditional mass, but also masks the significance of the celebration and the focus of the worship.

At this point in the narrative, when Philippe is led away to meet his fate, several questions come to the fore. At the end, will he fully submit to this rite, even though it means the sacrifice of his life? If he does submit, what will become of his family: his wife and young son? Finally, once sacrificed, will the ceremony result in a renewal of the crops and a stabilization of the community? The film indeed answers the first of these questions when it concludes with the sacrifice of Philippe amidst the grapevines of Bellenac. During this climax, the protagonist is mortally wounded by the titular arrow from the novel *Day of the Arrow*, from which the film was adapted. The second question is also addressed. Catherine looks on but is powerless to stop the proceedings as the body of her dead husband is carried on horseback to the manor, a bookend to his arrival. As he rides through the community once again, this time he travels by ancient means. The villagers likewise bow their heads and remove their hats. In awe of their savior, they cross themselves, suggesting a connectivity to the Catholic, and to the Pagan, both of which are revered and for which sacrifice becomes necessary as a propitiation to God. Just as Philippe had arrived as a modern man, he leaves as an ancient sacrificial victim. His role has been fulfilled. In turn, it is Catherine's role (and the community's) to act as a witness.

In the final scene of the film, the fate of Philippe's son is also indicated. As the family (minus the paternal sacrificial victim) is about to drive away, Jacques delays the departure, claiming to have left his watch behind. He returns to the manor house, seeking not his watch, however, but instead a final audience with Pere Dominique. As the priest and the new lord of the manor meet, the boy is bestowed with the same medal awarded to his father. He returns to the car. His mother asks if he has found what he had forgotten, to which Jacques replies in the affirmative. This final scene, like the opening, suggests two things. The first is that the son has accepted his legacy—that what has been visited upon by the father, and indeed all the fathers of the Montfaucon family, will also be visited upon the son. The second thing that is revealed (or more properly masked) is this very acceptance, which will remain hidden until he, like his father, will be called to remember. Even though the final question, as to the efficacy of this ceremony, is left open, regardless of the outcome, the import of such rituals rests in their acceptance and continuance. And indeed, the continuation of the secret rituals from generation to generation is ensured by the son accepting the symbolic medallion and all that it entails. This gift and its resultant promise are, however, hidden from Catherine, suggesting that while a Montfaucon in name, she is not of the family by blood and thus will always remain an outsider.

This ending in many ways presents an analytical challenge. Is good restored with the return to the traditional ways of the village, the prospering of the land, and the rites that keep this connectivity intact, or does evil win out as both the father, Philippe, and son, Jacques, were and will be sacrificed for the land? If the former is true, then the film uniquely challenges the ethos of modernity, wherein the self increasingly assumes precedence over all else. It is this contemporaneous disconnect that renders this film, like the others discussed in this book, quite controversial. Indeed, in the exceedingly short review published in the *New York Times, Eye of the Devil* is panned as being a text that is rendered incomprehensible for its sacrificial ending. Bosley Crowther argues:

> David Niven, a wealthy vineyard owner ... gets himself hopelessly involved with his peasants in some black magic rituals in order to restore the health of his grapes. In order to bring his vines back into condition, he has to allow himself to be destroyed by a silver arrow, which is enough to mystify anybody.[32]

Thus, even though complicit in cultural debates by enacting a return to nature, the film's insistence on providing a focus on something greater than the self through foregrounding the importance of a link to history and a connectivity between the community ultimately renders this film culturally incomprehensible. Alternatively, it might very well be that the significance of this ritual is not incomprehensible, but its meaning merely hidden for us as members of a more properly rational landscape of modernity.

Day of the Arrow and *Eye of the Devil* as a Discursive Continuum

The novel on which the film *Eye of the Devil* was based, entitled *Day of the Arrow*, written by the screenwriter Robin Estridge under the alias Philip Loraine,[33] articulates many of the same themes as that of its adaptive text. Indeed, as in the film, the necessity of belief, the acceptance of historical imperatives and the inescapable need to embrace tradition are all pitted against the ethos of modernity, making the original and adaptive texts appear as a continuum.

In terms of organization and thematic concern, both the film and its literary antecedent do equally establish a dichotomy, in which the modern city life and the pre-modern, Pagan, pastoral environment come into direct conflict. Equally foregrounded in both versions of this text is a discussion of what can be gained from making such a choice when it comes to accepting the necessity of spirituality and historical connectivity. Indeed, as this textual constellation progresses, there is an obvious connection, on the one hand, between certain characters and the tenets of modernity, while on the other, characters who symbolize the pre-modern. Also, like the film, these characters embody the central conflict of the narrative. This is revealed from the outset of the novel, as Philippe Montfaucon seems to abandon his patrilineal duties to his ancestral home, thus initially setting him up to be a modern man similar not only to his wife Françoise (Catherine in the film), but also his room-mate James Lindsay.[34] The book reveals that Lindsay and Montfaucon once not only shared a friendship, but also accommodations in Paris. Philippe, the text suggests, relocated to this urban mecca to deny his provincial roots and ancestral legacy, while Lindsay, a poor Scottish[35] painter, moved to hone his skills and establish himself as an artist. However, like in the film, those characters that are aligned with modernity and those that are more connected with the pre-modern begin to differentiate themselves as the narrative progresses.

For the novel, this process of dichotomization begins with a geographical dislocation, as Lindsay remains in Paris, while Montfaucon ends up marrying "the girl" and embarking upon a blissful journey of self-discovery with his new wife. Even as the protagonist and his character foil seem to share a modern sensibility at the beginning, this ideological connection likewise begins to break down, just as it does between Montfaucon and his wife in the film. Upon reconnecting with Lindsay in Paris, Françoise de Montfaucon, who is found to be engaged in an extramarital affair, speaks of a newly acquired attitude in her husband, which has had the effect of driving them apart. Lindsay learns that the marquis, in the interim, has not only returned to Bellac (Bellenac in the film), but has also begun to embrace his agrarian roots. The novel suggests that as Philippe has come closer to his thirtieth birthday, a time of transition from young adulthood[36] to adulthood proper, another metamorphosis has begun to take hold. Françoise explains of her husband, "He used to laugh about it [Bellac]; he said he'd rather die than live there; he used to do wicked imitations of the people and the dialect."[37] Now, however, this derision toward the Montfaucon legacy has completely abated, as has the physical and psychological dissociation. The marquise goes on to say, "He hasn't left the valley in two years. He isn't living in Bellac, he *is* Bellac."[38] This entanglement is further made manifest during a conversation between the old roommates once they are reunited upon the request of Françoise. While Lindsay is seen to be a bit sentimental for his somewhat misspent youth, Philippe, by contrast, now regards his past with the same disdain that he once felt for Bellac. The marquis suggests:

> Never envy those people [modern individuals], James. Living as we did: a month here, three months there—Rome, New York, Lisbon, London, Rio— it's like ... a chain of caves; one progresses ever deeper into absolute nothingness, absolute darkness, a kind of living extinction.[39]

This observation, given the climax and conclusion of the narrative, admittedly, is somewhat ironic, not only because of the way in which the perceived countercultural thread is severed in choosing tradition over freedom, but equally because in embracing tradition and a connectivity to history, only a promise of death and sacrifice ensues. However, when given insight into what Philippe has come to believe, accept and enact, this sentiment has specific and profound resonance. Indeed, in offering himself through the spilling of blood to rejuvenate the crops, his life is transferred to the grapes that sustain the family and the surrounding villages, and thus his spirit will be extended, worshipped and glorified.

In this way, the groundless condition of disbelief cannot but culminate in a spiritual death, while the act of sacrifice that will bring about death in a literal sense becomes life affirming. Arguably, Montfaucon is made authentic by being grounded in something bigger, more significant and more real than the individual alone could ever provide. Philippe goes on:

> I stood there looking at it [Bellac] in the moonlight, listening to the owls, and dogs barking miles away, and the ducks on the lake making a fuss about something. And you know.... I could feel.... I could *feel* all those wasted years peeling off me.... I lay down on the grass. I felt.... I felt suddenly that I had become myself.[40]

This connection to family, heritage and an historical imperative is equally foregrounded when, in describing the Marquis de Bellac, Lindsay suggests:

> [His self-assurance] came, he always imagined, from a youth spent in a world where the family was still the pivotal point, the centre of the universe, a fortress of love, all protecting—instead of the kind of incompetently run youth hostel it had become in America and England.[41]

The legacy and historical connection of "old families" is also clearly meant to bolster a sense of belonging to something larger than the individual self, while equally acting to assuage loss or feelings of being alone. This represents an ethos that, like the geographical dislocation, stands apart from the ethos of modernity.

Significantly, this sense of belonging is signified by the presence not only of the familial estate itself, a physical locus, but also the adornment of the castle walls with portraits of the Montfaucon lineage, a genealogical connectivity there to support or scorn accordingly. Even though apparently "incomprehensible," to quote the words of Crowther, these ties that bind nonetheless hold a certain allure for the more modern nonbelievers such as Françoise, who goes on to suggest of her husband and his beliefs:

> He wouldn't be the first frightened man to ... to fall back on old superstitions.... More than that ... is our century so robust—is our way of life so secure—that we have no need of ... reassurance about things of the spirit?[42]

In fact, as is suggested in the film as well as the novel, the role of the Montfaucon male is more than that of a landlord. The marquis is a spiritual figurehead to be cherished and adored for the very reason of the imminent sacrifice that each will ultimately make. While the film visually alludes to this, the novel makes this relationship between lord and villager manifest: "Lindsay was watching the nursemaid, transfixed by the look which she had turned on her master—a look of blind adoration."[43] The people of Bellac, it would seem, do not look upon the Marquis de Bellac as a mere mortal man, but instead as a god, a being imbued with supernatural powers and magic.

The Pagan as a Traditional Faith

The Day of the Arrow, like *Eye of the Devil*, foregrounds this supernatural element by linking the practice of Paganism to that of Witchcraft, and also to that of Catholicism.[44] While all the films in this book foreground alternative religion as another traditional faith mechanism, the films discussed in the previous section clearly diverge from the works of Pagan Horror discussed in this section. Even though *The Omen* and *Rosemary's Baby* present rituals and representations that link Satanism to its Catholic other (as is also the case with *The Witches*), these religions are set up as antagonists to Christianity; indeed, in two of the three texts, the desire of the believers is to usurp Christ's dominion on earth by bringing about the apocalypse. *The Day of the Arrow* and *Eye of the Devil*, alternatively, seem to obscure the earlier faith by masking it as a more traditional, supernaturally rooted, propitiatory ecumenicism. One example of this can be found in the form of the sacrificial dove. As suggested in the scene described above, the dove is a signifier for Philippe, one he acknowledges by drawing an arrow through its breast in much the same way as he himself will be pierced. Like the film, the novel regards this act with reverence, as being akin to "some kind of Eucharist."[45] Also, while the vast majority of the members of the inner circle of thirteen are male, there is one female, Odile, portrayed in both the novel and the film as having unexplained powers that alter perception. In a scene that appears in both the novel and the film, she changes toads into doves, and almost lures Catherine/Françoise to her death by making her perceive that she is safely away from harm, even as she almost steps from the parapet of the manor house. This power results in Odile being called a witch, like so many females before her. The novel suggests, "Oh yes ... she is a witch, all right. Never underestimate the knowledge of a witch; mankind has forgotten more things, than he will ever learn."[46] However, unlike *The Witches* and *Rosemary's Baby*, it is not Witchcraft-cum-Satanism that drives the beliefs of the village of Bellac, but instead a worship that is decidedly Paganism masked as Catholicism, as is later suggested in the novel:

> But witchcraft isn't the answer; that isn't what drives Philippe. A man who spends hours ... on his knees in front of the altar isn't pagan; just the opposite—he's almost too much of a Christian.[47]

This faith that hides its Pagan roots within Catholic window dressing is directly evidenced by the celebration of the Thirteen Days, represented in both versions of the text, and which the novel describes in the following way:

> There were processions, fancy dress, masks; the beautiful crucifix was taken down from the church and carried around the village. Even Lindsay, with his slight knowledge of things, could see that much which happened on Bellac's day of the Thirteen Days had its roots in the religions that flourished before Christ, but then everybody knew that the early Church had been much too wise of try to eradicate the ancient beliefs, preferring to incorporate them into her own ritual.[48]

Although both the novel and the film present this celebration and allude to its Pagan roots, thus aligning the two texts overall in terms of theme, the novel, in making the history manifest, directly links these belief systems, and thus their similarities likewise become more durable.

In fact, the literary version goes into more detail than the filmic adaptation with regard to the basis of the celebration of the Thirteen Days. The book makes clear that this feast is offered as a dedication to Mithra, the Persian god brought to France by the Romans. This deity, who in the novel is described as reigning over both light and darkness—protecting cattle and guarding rivers, in fact may be seen to rule over the Pagan natural world. Equally, however, Mithra has connections to Judeo-Christianity when he is described as a god who preached of good overcoming evil in the same way as Christ had done much later in history. In offering this description, the reason for the masking of one faith behind its more conservative other makes more sense. The aforementioned dance carried out by the thirteen dancers, represented in both the film and the novel, is thus revealed to have significance as a fertility ritual enacted to make the earth fruitful, as Mithra himself did when he sacrificed a bull from whose wound sprang not blood, but instead ears of corn.

Also, like the film, the connection between the observance of the Thirteen Days and the concept of the performance/dance (Jours/Jouers) is made manifest. The ritual involves not only a celebration alone, but may be regarded as divisive, as is suggested in a poem that is used as an epitaph and grave marker:

> I would be saved, and I would save, Amen
> The Twelve dance on high, Amen
> The Whole on high hath part in our dancing, Amen
> Whoso danceth not, knoweth not what cometh to pass,
> Amen.[49]

Herein, not only is there a reference to the significance of the dance, it is made using the traditional language of the Church, once again over-laying the Pagan with the Catholic. It is this obfuscation that is common not only to this textual constellation, but also to the teleplay *Robin Redbreast*. For indeed, like in the village of Belenac/Bellac, the village relies upon burying the Pagan beneath the Christian so as to ensure the continuation of a ritual practice that, if made manifest, might be in danger of eliciting retribution from the public at large.

Configurations of the Rural Community: The Pagan versus Skeptical Modernity in *Robin Redbreast*

Robin Redbreast was a BBC teleplay produced and aired as part of a larger series entitled *Play for Today* during the traditional British super-natural programming season leading up to Christmas. Within this work, a fictional Pagan community is configured as one side of an essential dichotomy. As has been regarded to be the norm with these works, this world of ancient belief is pitted against the modern world of spiritual incertitude and cultural skepticism. Also, like in the aforementioned *Eye of the Devil/Day of the Arrow*, this archaic agrarian society, though isolated from external influence, is internally highly communal, which allows for a sense of purpose and meaning outside of self-interested individual action. This is contrasted with the urban world, which, even while being apparently open and unfettered, is seen to have, ironically, an isolating effect by privileging the individual over all else. Finally, as is the case with *Eye of the Devil* and *Day of the Arrow*, this belief is concealed from outsiders.

To begin, the conflict between ancient spirituality and modernity is established from the outset of the narrative. In the opening scene, before leaving London, Norah Palmer attends a party with her longtime and indeed only friends. She uses this occasion to inform those close to her of her imminent temporary relocation from this urban mecca.

She suggests that her motivation to leave is not a result of a desire to relinquish her connection with the contemporary world altogether, as was the case with many in her contemporaneous culture, but instead due to a drive to escape an environment that she has come to associate with the failure of her ten-year relationship.[50] As a result of her breakup, Palmer feels that she needs a change—some time to reflect and a bit of isolation to regroup. With these goals in mind, she plans to establish residence in an isolated, rustic country cottage purchased by the protagonist and her former lover as a getaway retreat. Her friends voice their misgivings. They are dubious of such a radical prospect whereby she will eschew her modern environs, comforts which she has heretofore relied upon to such an extent that she has now come to take them for granted. To assuage their doubts, Palmer shows the couple quaint "before" snapshots of her newly renovated domicile. However, this does little to allay their reservations, for the cottage appears to be in grave disrepair. They ask to see the "after" shots, but Palmer admits that there are none to offer. She explains that it was her former partner who possessed the camera. Thus, from the outset, it is the antiquated that is privileged over the modern, the latter literally hidden from view. In other words, if photos are the way in which modern man remembers his past, then the cottage will be evoked in memory as it was before modernization, its modern other buried. The landscape of the narrative proper will thus be recalled and regarded as antiquated, part of an archaic landscape, even given the costly renovations that have taken place since, almost as if they had never occurred at all.

This resurgence of the past and its conflict with modernity is further addressed once Norah arrives in the village. While in the process of moving into the cottage, the protagonist is met by one of the locals, Fisher. This man, who arguably acts as the community's religious leader, orchestrates the events that will entangle Norah within the village's spiritual web, although doing so behind the scenes, ruling the community from underneath, as it were. He is presented by Auntie Vigo, Norah's maid, as an aesthete, a man of learning, a student of and expert on many things including local history, ancient religions, and archaeology. Fisher requests entrance into the fenced garden so that he may look for "sherds," or fragments of ancient pottery, more accurately "potsherds." He suggests that he has a gift for finding such artifacts. He has, as the teleplay suggests "a nose for it."[51] Norah grants him permission,[52] but suggests that she has never seen any such antiquities, even after the dirt and landscape have been disturbed and uprooted in the process of renovating the cottage. Indeed, she argues, the only things that he might find amongst the underbrush are broken bottles and old beer cans left by the workers. These expectations of what lies beneath the earth are significant and representative of the ways in which the characters may be defined in relationship to their environs. Fisher's expectation is one of buried ancient treasures of religious and historic significance, as a result of the world of ubiquitous spirituality over which he reigns likewise below the surface. Alternatively, Norah's world is one of rubbish and the disposable relics of modern commercialism based on her experience of modern London life. Thus, the landscapes by which the individuals themselves are defined become sites in this war between the traditional pre-modern world and the contemporary world of modernity. Likewise, the essential natures of these characters are hidden, literally and figuratively buried beneath the surface. It is this very theme that is noted in the reception of this work. According to one review by Vic Pratt, Fisher and his community, like the sherds he seeks, may be seen as being aligned, fragments of an antiquated past long buried. Pratt suggests:

> Such sherds [are] fragments of ancient, rural tradition, pieces of cultural, folklorish pottery that Fisher and his mischievous associates gather together and strive to preserve amidst ... a time of great change, pessimism and uncertainty.[53]

If Fisher can be read as a symbol of the old ways through being the hidden religious leader of the community, then Norah Palmer, like Françoise Montfaucon, may be equally regarded as a thoroughly modern woman, at least on the surface. This is evidenced not only by the aforementioned connections between character and location, but also (and potentially more significantly) by the actions that are normalized as a result of the mores (or lack thereof) that are established and encouraged within these environs. In fact, the world of modernity is revealed to be a universe of sexual freedom and inherent cultural skepticism, a condition that was also expressed in the novel version *Day of the Arrow* by Françoise Montfaucon. Even though married, and defined by this union,[54] she is also engaged in an extramarital affair, possibly made feasible by her connection to the quintessential urban mecca, Paris, the "City of Love." If Françoise Montfaucon may be regarded as a product of modernity, then in turn Norah might be defined as being even more so as the narrative progresses. Indeed, the protagonist of *Robin Redbreast* is, in many ways, not merely a product of modernity, but in fact an ultra-modern woman herself. She has lived with a man openly, outside of wedlock, she engages freely and regularly in sexual intercourse, as suggested by her possession of a diaphragm, and she is involved in the seduction of a partner almost ten years her junior. Not only this, but as a result of this fleeting physical union, she has become pregnant and thus must make an equally modern decision: to either have an abortion, or to raise the baby as a single mother. However, she also desires a stable relationship, admitting that she remained with her former partner long after she should have, refusing to "cut her losses." She equally refuses to have an abortion, a decision that she confesses to Rob as being troubling to her ideologically speaking, making this alignment less secure.

Another apparent connection between Palmer and an ethos of modernity is her choice of profession. She is a scriptwriter for television and thus aligned with all that is contemporary: the world of the media overall and, more specifically, the world of television—the most modern media of them all. As a result of her métier, she has become financially independent. It is a remarkable feat for an individual, not to mention a single woman,[55] to possess a London flat and a country cottage. This is unlike Catherine/Françoise, who is solvent—wealthy in fact, but as a result of her marriage and not by independent means.

However, like the Marquise de Montfaucon, this way of life, this privileged ultra-modern existence, leaves her feeling at a loss, empty in a way that those who hold belief and a sense of community do not. Lost to her is not only the ability to form lasting relationships, but also the ability to believe in anything greater than herself. If it could be argued, as Daniel Bell does throughout *The Cultural Contradictions of Capitalism*, that the problem with modernity is a problem of belief,[56] then indeed, both Norah Palmer and Catherine/Françoise seem to be its chief spokespersons. Like Catherine/Françoise, Norah holds no belief in tradition, as can be evidenced by her lifestyle, and equally she holds no belief in traditional religion. This latter alignment (or indeed lack of alignment) is made evident in a scene about halfway through the teleplay. Norah is at her cottage, channel surfing. She comments that she can find nothing suitable to watch, it being Easter Sunday, aside from the typical British faith-based television program, *Songs of Praise*. In disgust, she turns off the television. Her lack of belief and her connection to the world of the media provide an antithesis to all those who live in the village surrounding her country retreat, save one.

Similar to the formerly discussed textual constellation this narrative is in fact organized around character foils. Norah is set up in contrast to the only other significant female character in the village, Auntie Vigo. If Norah can be considered a young, beautiful, modern woman who is concerned and connected to no one apart from herself and her self-interest, then Vigo is represented as a village matriarch and a crone. She is indeed presented as being a disagreeable old woman who, as will be suggested below, is not only verbally abusive to Norah, but also culpable in the physical abuse of her own adopted son. She is sinister in manner, with magical or supernatural associations that, as occurred with the antagonists of *The Witches*, can make her either helpful or obstructive. As will be seen, her alliances are to the village and her desires are to further the rites enacted therein, whereas she also furthers the obfuscation of these very rites from all outsiders. These rituals in which she takes part are ancient and have been carried out for centuries, and this connection to old ways also binds her to the community, even as it divorces her totally from modernity. Even as Norah and Auntie Vigo are diametrically opposed, not all the characters are antithetical in *Robin Redbreast*. If Norah's foil is Vigo, then Norah's apparent counterpart is the gamekeeper, Robin (née Edgar). Although having grown up in the countryside, Robin, or Rob for short, is nonetheless set apart from his environment. To begin, Rob does not share any familial connections to the rural community; he was not born into it, but instead adopted by Auntie Vigo. The only element suggesting a genealogical connection between Rob and his "family" is his name. This is not only his family name, which is a common familial indicator, but also his given birth name, which was changed from Edgar to Robin by Vigo. Rob is not told of this renaming, but only comes across the hidden evidence of this when he uncovers his birth certificate with his birth name recorded thereon. Vigo insists that this change was not a choice, but instead born out of necessity. There has always been a Robin in the village. Although not her son by birthright, Vigo took it upon herself to raise Rob, treating him as one of her own. Actually, she has treated him far better than her own, offering him the opportunity to attend grammar school and then an agricultural college. This preference has nothing to do with Rob's aptitude, however. On the contrary, he does not appear to have a great deal of intelligence at all. Instead, the privileging afforded Rob is as a result of the role he will come to perform. Although unaware of the reason behind this status, Rob nonetheless is affected by it, viewing his education as a sign of elevation.

If the pre-modern man judges his worth as a birthright, either in terms of nobility or birth order, the first son assuming dominance, Rob, considers himself above his community as a result of his knowledge. Ironically, it is this that in Rob's eyes establishes a commonality between himself and his modern female counterpart, who is also not really from "around here" and is most certainly educated. It is, however, a sentiment that is not shared by Norah, who perceives Rob not as her equal, but instead as a means whereby she can, in effect, scratch an itch using someone she considers dull and dumb, but nonetheless "dishy." Indeed, the one thing that Rob does seem to have going for him is his outward form. His face is as attractive, as is his body, which he chooses to keep in peak condition, more for the opportunity of attracting a mate from outside than for anything else. However, even as he, like Norah, engages in actions that he feels are products of his freedom of choice, it turns out that his personal maintenance (like Norah's promiscuity) allows him to be even more suitable for the unwitting part he has been chosen to carry out—a role that, like Norah's, is at the very heart of this rural community's spiritual belief system. Robin is revealed to be the titular *Robin Redbreast*, a Christ-like figure whose breast has turned red as a result of spilled sacrificial blood. The connection to the robin and a sacrificial victim has not only to do with the fact that they are one of the few birds seen during mid-winter and into spring, signaling first the re-birth of the land, and then later the re-birth of the spirit, a sign of the birth of Christ, but also to the bird's appearance: the coloring of the bird's plumage, a bloody stain that links the bird to the Christ who was the ultimate sacrificial victim bringing about new life.

Equally, Norah Palmer's appearance and conduct make her an ideal representative of the Pagan goddess Diana. First, Norah, not unlike Rosemary of *Rosemary's Baby*, sports a short haircut as a sign of being "with the times." However, possessing shorn locks was also, historically speaking, a symbol of allegiance to this ancient fertility goddess. In ancient times, women would sacrifice their hair to Diana, for this offering provided both an outward sign of their complicity and a sacrifice toward a successful harvest—the self-same shorn golden locks standing for the reaped golden crops come autumn. Further, the terms of conduct under the guise of sacrifice were to give of one's virginity and to engage in sexual intercourse, mimicking the desired fecundity of the harvest. Sir James Frazer, in his seminal discussion of comparative spirituality, *The Golden Bough*, suggests of the fertility maiden and her worshippers:

> They were expected to fecundate themselves by contact with the divine source of fecundity. And it is probable that a similar motive underlay the sacrifice of their chastity as well as the sacrifice of their hair ... to strengthen the divine beings to whom it is offered by feeding or fertilising them.[57]

Thus, although not purposely so, Palmer's actions as a modern woman open to the whims offered by a complete freedom of choice also make her an ideal Diana figure, and her getting pregnant from a man other than a husband seals the deal. Indeed, as is suggested by Frazer and reiterated by Fisher in the teleplay, while assuming the role as a representative of a goddess, this character is chosen to bestow the village with a new Robin: her son, who Vigo suspects will be given up by Norah and then adopted by the community as Rob himself was.

If embodying an ethos of modernity makes Norah an ideal representative fertility goddess, then, in turn, Rob is also made into an ideal harvest king. Not only is his physique one that seems appropriate to his station, he also gives of himself what is required, although like Norah, unwittingly. Frazer suggests that if the woman must sacrifice her chastity and her hair, the male must sacrifice his flesh—both his seed through the sex act and his blood through the sacrificial rite. This is exactly what Rob does, although again not of his own volition. Following their coupling and Norah's return to the country in the final stages of her pregnancy, Rob comes to the cottage. This time it is not out of amorous intent, or even an intent to kill rodents,[58] but instead out of fear. Norah, who is equally unsteady after firmly coming to believe that she has been trapped in the village and must remain until Eastertide, does not let him in at first. He remains locked outside and is only permitted entrance when he admits that he is unaware of any plot the village has concocted against Norah or himself. Also, like Rob, Norah is scared, ironically the basis for letting him "in" the first time, both literally and metaphorically speaking. During this second meeting, the cottage is infiltrated. Fisher leads the handyman down, both facing off with Norah and Rob. Norah passes out from fright, and Rob is killed off-camera, as is evidenced by his scream, a sound to which Norah is not privy. Since the next morning is Easter and the sacrifice was accomplished the night before, Norah is allowed to leave. Although told that Rob has left for his long-awaited journey to Canada, she is aware (more unconsciously than consciously) that he has become a victim of the village, a sacrifice for the fertility of the crops, for, as Vigo suggests, the spilling of blood is man's work, a task not meant for women.

Indeed, Diana, according to Frazer, could only be appeased by a blood offering. He goes on to suggest that the gods needed worshippers as much as the worshippers needed the gods. Without followers, the gods would cease to exist, and without the gods, those who lived off of the fruits of the land that the gods provided would also die.[59] Vic Pratt alludes to this reciprocity in his review of the teleplay when he argues, "Bacchae ... in my reading represents the conflict between the Apollonian and Dionysian ways of living more than the mere tearing to pieces of a Sacred King."[60]

In fact, as was suggested at the beginning of this chapter and alluded to throughout, while the ethos and the religious affiliation of the village become a foil to the world to which the protagonists align themselves, the machinations of this world are nonetheless hidden, an obscured occult. In being aligned with modernity, Norah, as discussed above, at first refuses to accept the possibility of the supernatural, holding firmly to her connectivity to the modern world of the rational. However, incrementally this ignorance and denial begin to breakdown.

The first indication of this process of awakening is the half marble that she brings into the cottage and then transports home with her, hidden in her luggage, again without her knowing. Upon seeing it, Vigo comments that it looks like an eye, and indeed, the name for this type of marble is a "tiger's eye" or "cat's eye." Equally, white marble amulets were used by the druids as symbols of power throughout the Celtic world. Even though Norah brings this eye, this symbol of Pagan power, indoors, she is unaware of its meaning. It is only half an eye, and in being inherently incomplete, becomes a symbol for Palmer's own lack of vision, or an inability to see beyond the surface to what is really taking place regarding the actions of the villagers, even though they make their intentions manifest.

Indeed, this figurative blindness actually becomes a trope with regard to Norah's character throughout the text overall as the villagers continually challenge Norah to awareness by directly stating their intentions and referring to what has happened just out of her field of vision. For example, after the night of her coupling with Rob, she notices that the drainpipe on the outside of her cottage has been dislodged. Norah comments upon it to Fisher and Vigo, and Fisher responds, "I should say it was somebody on your roof,"[61] as Vigo retorts, "Careless."[62] This exchange confirms what was suspected all along, namely, the chain of events leading to the impregnation is confirmed as being a setup, beginning with a bird that was forced into her house via the fireplace, causing Palmer to scream, in turn leading Rob to the rescue and the ultimate seduction. It also further suggests that Fisher has orchestrated these events behind the scenes—happenings that appear random, but in fact have been carefully planned. Later, there is a similar occurrence when Norah's car is mysteriously rendered out of service. Again, when Palmer questions the means whereby the car has ceased to function, Fisher responds by intimating a design to this accident. He states, "One would be bound to notice. To crack the rotor from the outside, as it were. With scissors, say." It appears as if Fisher knows all too well what has happened to the car, because he was likely also behind its "breakdown." However, as a modern woman, Norah is blinded to that which lurks right beneath the surface. Unlike in *Eye of the Devil* and *Day of the Arrow*, the arrow of meaning flies right over Norah's head. It is, in fact, this very unseeing skepticism that leaves her open to being used by the villagers as she not only completely rejects even the possibility of a plot based on spiritual connectivity, but equally the prospect of ritualized sacrifice, which rests as the culmination of these actions. This blindness continues until the very end of the narrative, as discussed in the introduction to this chapter, when her eyes are effectively opened.

Finally, as was the case with *Eye of the Devil* and *Day of the Arrow*, *Robin Redbreast* also hides the Pagan behind its Christian other, much as it hides its leader like a sherd below the surface. In the case of *Robin Redbreast*, this more traditional faith is not Catholic, but instead Anglican Christianity. As was suggested earlier, the rites performed by Vigo, Fisher and their rural community are performed during times which are equally revered in the Christian Church: the harvest festival and Easter Sunday. The Harvest Festival is celebrated more prominently in Anglicanism than in other Protestant faiths such as Lutheranism, Methodism or even Episcopalianism, the American Anglican Church. In British Anglicanism, thanks have been given for successful harvests since Pagan times. The harvest festival is traditionally held on the Sunday near or on the harvest moon. This is the full moon that occurs closest to the autumn equinox. The celebrations on this day usually include singing hymns, prayer, and decorating churches with baskets of food. This festival, known as Harvest Festival, Harvest Home, Harvest Thanksgiving or Harvest Festival of Thanksgiving, is depicted in *Robin Redbreast* specifically. Following the scene in which Robin plants his seed, Auntie Vigo comes to collect Norah and take her to church. This is the first time that the church has been mentioned, and indeed the first of only two instances that Vigo accompanies Norah to services. Unlike Easter Sunday, the second time Norah is led to worship, the Harvest Festival is depicted in montage with images of baskets being heaped upon the altar. Easter Sunday is the day after Robin is sacrificed so as to be reborn into the crops during a time wherein resurrection is also celebrated in the Christian faith. Norah is trapped in the village, as suggested above, until Easter, and after attending church, she is released.

When combined with dialogue, these visual signifiers make manifest not only the fact that the rites that are alluded to are religious in nature, but, more specifically, Pagan in the sense defined by Sir James Frazer in *The Golden Bough*. Thus, like the larger textual constellation discussed above, *Robin Redbreast* offers this belief system not as an offshoot of Satanism, as is suggested in the classical horror texts discussed in earlier chapters, but instead as a unique and distinct spiritual practice. As reviewer Vic Pratt suggests of Fisher and his community of believers:

> [H]is beliefs are not quite as unusual as all that. *Robin Redbreast* reflects a cultural moment when witchcraft and the occult were no longer ludicrous. Increasingly, it would seem, people were turning back to the old ways. In the face of a modernity devoid of authenticity and meaning, ancient superstitions were ... a viable alternative.[63]

This representation as alternative versus merely evil and wrong-minded aligns these spiritual paradigms to the culture out of which they arise— one in which there was an opening up of spiritual affiliation to extend beyond the realm of monotheistic representations of good (i.e., Christian) versus evil (i.e., any other faith). However, this alignment may not be as clear as it might first appear. This is due to the fact that, while represented, the practices of these communities are hidden from outsiders, thus challenging, in some ways, this apparent increased cultural acceptance.

Day of the Arrow, Robin Redbreast and the Extratextual

The theme of Paganism and alternative religion was a serious one not only for the screenwriter of *Robin Redbreast*, but also for Robin Estridge in his penning of *Eye of the Devil*. He was indeed serious enough about the authenticity of his representation of these practices to hire occult guru Alex Sanders as a consultant. Sanders, also known by his craft name[64] Verbius, was an English Occultist and Wiccan High Priest. He was not only a practitioner, but also the founder of a sect known as Alexandrian Wicca, a neo–Pagan faith that relies upon gender division in the reverence of the gods and goddesses, skyclad (or, ritual nudity), and a belief in Hermetic Qabalah, the basis for many contemporaneous occult traditions including Aleister Crowley's Thelema. Rumors at the time of production suggested that during the filming, Sanders took the opportunity to introduce actress Sharon Tate to the occult. Although never substantiated, the actress might be connected to cults in another way. Tate's celebrity is arguably more as a result of her connections to famous filmmaker husband Roman Polanski and her tragic end than her career as an actress. From an extratextual perspective, this connection proves interesting not only because it links this film to another in this cycle of alternative religion narratives (namely *Rosemary's Baby*, which was directed by Polanski), but also because it links this work to the pervasiveness of the spiritual and the religious cult during this time period. Indeed, the fact that Tate was killed by the infamous "Manson Family" indelibly ties this work to the import and influence of a contemporaneous desire for community and spiritual connection that is discussed throughout this book. According to cult theorists, the key to Manson's control hinged on ensuring that his followers saw him as an all-powerful messiah and thus to follow him would ensure their membership among the saved, the cherished, and the elect.[65] At a time of unparalleled acceptance of spiritual alternatives, the pseudo-religious cult, like the hippie movement, the neo–Pagan Wiccan coven and the Satanic cabal became defining mechanisms of the mid–1960s and 1970s.

Even when pinpointed as being culturally contiguous, in retrospect, much like *Eye of the Devil*, *Robin Redbreast*, possibly as the result of being televised as opposed to theatrically released, experienced even more controversy than the film at the time of its release. For example, when John Bowen first submitted the script to *Play for Today*, he was told that the thematic connection between ancient Pagan fertility rites and the celebration of traditional Anglican Church observances such as the Harvest Festival would be "too much for the powers that be." Whilst being televised (entering the domestic space of the home, as it were, and therefore more prone to issues of censorship), it is still surprising that this teleplay received so much criticism for its content. One cannot fail to take into account that, firstly, the 1970s offered an abundance of films dealing with Paganism and the occult, as discussed throughout this book. Also, the culture at this time appears to have had a fascination with this alternative religious practice. Finally, the episode was to be screened in the weeks leading up to Christmas, a time during which the BBC commonly aired supernatural programming like the annual British television event, *A Ghost Story for Christmas*, for example. However, even given these considerations, it would appear that cultural connectivity and televised and filmic precedence were not enough to assuage censor doubts. To continue with the theme of regarding this work within the context of other works of media, as was alluded to earlier, *Robin Redbreast* is often denoted as being a precursor to *The Wicker Man*, both of which share an interest in the esoteric belief systems and culture during the period. However, for Scovell, the former is in fact far ahead of that film in terms of its script. He argues that whereas Hardy and Shaffer merely reference *The Golden Bough*, Bowen's script seems to be interested in the genuine details of the past and its folklore, as opposed to only the elements that would be dramatically effective. In many ways, it benefits from its mixing of these more questionable forms of historical folklore, such as the controversial work by Sir James Frazer, with genuine events, namely the Warwickshire murder of farm laborer Charles Walton in 1945.

Walton, like the fictional Robin, was an outsider to the small civil parish in which he lived. In the case of Walton, this was the agricultural community of Quinton in the Stratford-on-Avon district. Also, like Robin, Walton had a special gift for which he was renowned. Whilst Robin was known for killing vermin, Walton was a notorious horse whisperer. On February 14, the laborer began the day by castrating two calves and then went off to clip the hedgerows surrounding the pasture. He was found later that afternoon, bludgeoned, stabbed, and castrated. The murder was quite similar to an earlier crime—the killing of the elderly Ann Tennant, a distant relative of Walton, who was in a neighboring village. At the time of her death in the late 1900s, Tennant was thought to be a witch; likewise, her relation Charles Walton was accused of having familiars, of being able to cast spells and cursing those who offended him with the evil eye. It was further claimed that it was these suspicions that led to his and Ann's ritualistic murders, which involved their blood soaking into the ground to replenish the soil's fertility. Locals held a belief in the folkloric black shuck, a phantom black dog who roamed the area as a harbinger of death. It was claimed that, soon after Walton's murder, a black dog was found hanging from a tree close to the murder scene, and that witnesses and police investigators had encountered a black dog while walking at dusk while investigating the crime perpetrated on Meon Hill. Later accounts claimed that the man had been killed by a reproduction of a druidical ceremony on St. Valentine's Eve. The police took numerous statements from individuals, but admitted that, overall, most of the local residents were secretive, closed-lipped and reticent to discuss the case.

Lastly, and possibly even ironically, teleplay director James Mac-Taggart, who wrote and directed over one hundred television plays and episodes over his twenty-year career working for the BBC, was himself famous for instilling fantasy and expressionistic elements into his work. Alongside fellow writer Troy Kennedy Martin, whom MacTaggart joined in London specifically to pursue non-naturalistic drama, the duo vowed to "destroy naturalism … if possible, before Christmas."[66] It would thus appear that if foregrounding the depiction of natural landscapes and including direct historical references made this episode of *Play for Today* more viable realistically, this outcome was not altogether intentional.

Thus, while on the one hand, *Robin Redbreast, Eye of the Devil* and *Day of the Arrow* align with each other and their contemporaneous culture in presenting the viability of Paganism as a belief that bolsters the community while connecting the individual to a higher purpose outside of the self, it also challenges the sixties and seventies ethos by interpolating this connection into a religion that is equally imbued with a sense of historical legacy and hierarchy. To be Pagan is to join oneself to a tradition whose very practices of propitiation might very well result not in the freeing of life, but the loss of it. This theme will be explored again in a film that, if not at its contemporaneous time, is today regarded as a cult classic in its own right: *The Wicker Man.*

FIVE

A Clash of Convictions
in *The Wicker Man*

I look forward to a time when we are all pagans again. I think we would have a much better time of it. We would have a lot more faith, a lot more belief.[1]—ANTHONY SHAFFER, author of *The Wicker Man*

There is a touch of paganism in all of us in so far as we do all of us depend on the elements which have been there since the dawn of time and without which we could not exist.[2] —CHRISTOPHER LEE

The Wicker Man presents a view of good and evil so evolved that the film removes itself from the horror genre and becomes an essay on moral philosophy. In going back to the Old Religion, Anthony Shaffer may have been attempting to replenish the horror genre's vocabulary, to find a relatively novel type of terror. He ended up drawing a line back to humanity's earliest origins and to the furthest point in its future.[3]—ALLAN BROWN

Introduction

In the final scene from *The Wicker Man*, written by Anthony Shaffer and directed by Robin Hardy, it is revealed that the apparent abduction and murder of a young resident of an isolated island in the Scottish Hebrides was part of an elaborate plot designed to lure the film's narrative protagonist like a literal and figurative lamb to the slaughter. Village patriarch Lord Summerisle, along with the members of his community, ensnare Sergeant Neil Howie, painstakingly prepare him for his role as sacrificial victim, and then lead him to his fate—as Summerisle puts it, "His date with the wicker man."[4] As Howie witnesses the structure, a gigantic wicker edifice shaped like a man into which animals such as goats, lambs and pigs have been trapped, he realizes what will

141

be required of him. He will be made a martyr to the crops, burned along with the other sacrificial animals as a form of propitiation to ensure a successful harvest come autumn. As this dawning awareness washes over him, he cries out, "Oh Lord, Oh Jesus Christ."[5] This utterance may at first be regarded as an explicative—a curse commonly used in modern times. However, this is not the case in this instance. Howie is not merely taking the Lord's name in vain. He is not sinning, drawing away from God by breaking one of his commandments, but instead calling upon his savior, as a righteous man would call upon a god whom he firmly believes has the power to grant salvation. Howie goes on, "I am a Christian and as a Christian I hope for resurrection and even if you kill me now, it is I who will live again, not your damned apples."[6] Lord Summerisle retorts further, confirming the extent of the belief to which Howie prescribes, "That is good, for believing what you do, we confer upon you a rare gift these days, a martyr's death."[7]

In this scene, two things become clear. First is the thematic concern of this film, one not related to a conflict of modernity versus traditionalism, as are the majority of texts discussed within this book, but instead a struggle between two equally efficacious systems of belief. Secondly, the outcome of this narrative conflict will remain unclear as to who is finally vanquished and who remains the victor. Indeed, as was the case with the narratives discussed previously including *Rosemary's Baby, The Omen, Eye of the Devil, Day of the Arrow* and *Robin Redbreast*, to name a few, the ending remains open. Will Rosemary care for her son and thus potentially bring about the apocalypse? Will Damien rise as predicted in biblical prophecy? Will Philippe's sacrifice enact a restoration of the crops and, if so, will Philippe's son return to act as a sacrificial victim like his father should the crops once again fail? Will Norah raise her son, or will she give him up for adoption, thus offering up another Robin Redbreast for Fisher, Vigo and their heirs? And finally, will Howie's sacrifice result in his "resurrection" into heaven as an elite member of God's elect, or will his death enact a resurrection of the crops, or both, or neither? For all of these texts, however, the answers to these questions might, in fact, be irrelevant, for the primary active force that drives these narratives is the belief that what is destined will indeed occur. In other words, they all hinge upon a total acceptance that the actions of the group are manifestations of the will of the gods that are worshipped, reverenced and adored. As the Bible suggests in the book of Matthew, "Wherever two or three of you gather in my name, there I am with them."[8] In the case of *The Wicker Man*, it is not only the Christian faith to which Howie adheres that has power, but also the Pagan rites of Summerisle are equally and uniquely efficacious. This is because they both are firmly believed, even to the death. Likewise, as was the case with *Eye of the Devil, Day of the Arrow* and *Robin Redbreast*, this propitiatory faith relies upon an act of sacrifice to ensure that the gods will be pleased and the crops be fruitful. Considered an act of murder by outsiders, these rites must be kept separate from those who would seek to end them. If the way in which this is achieved is through obfuscation in the aforementioned works, as discussed in the previous chapter, then the way in which they are protected in *The Wicker Man* is through dis-

Visions of *The Wicker Man.*

tancing. The community of Summerisle must remain both spiritually and physically apart. This separation is an indicator that is equally discussed within the academic debate surrounding this film. The division of the rural and the urban is, indeed, an integral tenet of Folk Horror, for which *The Wicker Man* is theorized to be a key text.

The Wicker Man and Folk Horror

In the introduction to his text that outlines the formal tropes, aesthetics and themes of what he and Mark Gatiss have called "Folk Horror," Adam Scovell reveals the goals he has set out for his study. He states, "The book itself is akin to the plough from the opening of [Piers] Haggard's film [*The Blood on Satan's Claw*], churning up the various relics and summoning its previous inhabitants."[9] His study goes on to explore a range of film and television texts, which he then connects to what has come to be known as the unholy trilogy: *Blood on Satan's Claw, Witchfinder General* and *The Wicker Man.* All three of these works, like the larger conglomeration (what Scovell refers to as the "Folk Horror Chain") share a concern with a paranoid revisiting of past elements which conflict with modern, contemporary culture. This was the case with the texts discussed in the previous chapter, works to which Scovell refers in his book. The world offered up in *Eye of the Devil, Day of the Arrow, Robin Redbreast, The Wicker Man* and the like is a rural landscape set apart in space and time. Scovell connects this dissonance to the ancient realm of the Wyrd, an Old English term that references all that is antiquated, magical or legendary. This is also the case with the Gothic, another way in which horror texts are grouped based upon an anachronistic tendency, as discussed in the introduction of this book. The folk horror chain equally features isolated characters who are irrevocably connected with their detached environment. For the Gothic, and indeed the classical horror film that borrows much from this literary predecessor, this environment is the castle, an edifice set in a remote mountainous region of a country that holds to the power of superstition. For the Folk Horror Chain, this location is the rural landscape, which, like the castle, is set apart geographically and ideologically. In the three films mentioned above as comprising an "unholy trilogy," *The Blood on Satan's Claw, Witchfinder General* and *The Wicker Man,* the agrarian countryside breeds belief systems that will ensure its survival. Likewise, the country village, surrounded by miles of farmland and crops, becomes a locus for this potentially deviant spirituality, which remains unchecked as a result of this isolation. Not only is the worship of the gods of nature overall and Paganism more specifically regarded as being deviant due to its continued practice of propitiatory rites—this identity is equally troubled by being rooted in liminality. This faith, on the fringes between the old and the new, the rural and the urban, and the antiquated and the modern, conjures up a nostalgic drive. This results in an unsettled fragmentation of both memory and character, and it is here in this liminal space that the horror of Folk Horror rests. To return to Scovell:

> Folk Horror regularly builds its sense of the horrific around societies and groups of people that have very specific ways of life. This sense of divide between the accounts of what is called "skewed belief systems and ideologies," more ... than the allowing of pulp forms of paganism and occultism to grow ... uses the otherness that can be attributed to rural life to warp the very reality of its narrative worlds and often for its own explicit means.[10]

Within the diegetic world of these films, this spirituality provides both a literal and a figurative grounding for the inhabitants. Indeed, they are not only tied to each other, but more significantly to the land. However, even though it is, arguably, the belief more than the location that separates these communities from modernity, for Scovell specifically and for Folk Horror in general, the religious elements are not important in and of themselves, but instead seen as indicators of the contemporaneous debates overall. Thus, rather than taking a focus on religion seriously in and of itself, scholarship in this area, as has been discussed throughout this book, tends to regard spirituality as a symptom of and not a primary cause for isolation, deviation and disruption.

Spiritual Affiliation and the Role of Distanciation in *The Wicker Man*

The opening scene of the director's cut of *The Wicker Man* makes manifest the ways in which religion can result in distancing. The film commences with a tracking shot of a water plane as it lands in an urban harbor in the West Highlands of Scotland.[11] Upon deplaning, Howie, the protagonist of the film, meets his subordinate, and together they return to the station. As they walk, the latter notices some graffiti spray painted on a wall that says, "Jesus Saves." The officer, knowing his sergeant to be a religious man, makes note of this, to which Howie replies, surprisingly, that he wishes it to be painted over. He admonishes his underling: "There is a time and place for everything … get it removed."[12] Howie goes on to ask if anything significant happened when he was away, to which the officer replies that nothing unusual occurred. The normal incidences of rape, sodomy and sacrilege continued in the absence of the sergeant. This scene transitions to one of Howie in church. His hands are clasped in prayer. If the time and place for reverencing the Lord is not through graffiti on the urban street, this time in church is the very place for praising the Lord. In this way, a set of dichotomies are set up: the difference between locations of reverence, and the distance between Howie and his cultural milieu—a Scotland that is still, in theory, a law-abiding Christian country. This divide between theory and practice is personified in the police force itself. On the one hand, Howie is a lay preacher, a man of faith and undeterred principles, while on the other, his fellow constables are cynical non-believers who laugh at Howie behind his back for his faith and his resolve to uphold the law at all times. One makes a snide remark about the sergeant's choice to remain celibate, that he is not tickling anything but his fiancée's fancy.

The theatrical version of *The Wicker Man* further literalizes this divide not only spiritually, between faith and modernity, but also physically, between Summerisle and the mainland. More specifically, this is achieved through a foregrounding of the remoteness of Summerisle, fictionally presented as the most outlying island of the Scottish Hebrides. This scene, also depicted in the director's cut, involves Howie piloting a plane over a watery expanse. This shot runs for almost two minutes, and thus likewise makes manifest the apparent distance between the familiar world and the world that will come to inhabit the narrative. Summerisle is revealed to be beautiful, quaint and verdant, with no traffic—indeed, no cars to speak of. The difference between the urban mainland and the island is thus suggested through a visual comparison, at least in the director's cut, between the crime-ridden city and this apparent Eden.

Likewise, the island people uphold this significant division. The protagonist of *The Wicker Man* is an outsider and is treated as such. Unlike the procession welcoming Philippe de Montfaucon to Bellenac, the people of Summerisle react to Howie's presence not with reverence but with suspicion. The men working at the harbor and the harbormaster fail to send a dinghy and ask if he has permission to visit their island. They reprove his lack of propriety being that this is a closed community, the island a private property. Even as he gains entry, they remain in their homes and stare at him through the windows. He is on the island, but not a part of it. In the novelization of the film, the purposeful separation of the island is equally revealed in the form of two local "travel" posters decorating Summerisle port. Both of these public service announcements, while seeming to denote the modern desire to see other lands, have quite different connotations that actually warn against leaving. Indeed, when considering their written messages, "Want to travel to the world outside?"[13] and "Want to emigrate to the USA or Canada like your forefathers?",[14] in conjunction with the images that accompany these texts, the "travel" posters possess altogether opposing connotations. The "travel" picture is of a Glasgow slum on a rainy day, and the "immigration" poster depicts a particularly salacious section of the Bowery in New York City. In both cases, the subheading, "Consult Lord Summerisle for free advice,"[15] solidifies the message that leaving is greatly discouraged, if not prohibited. This apparent disconnect runs in both directions. On an island without a convenient and readily available means of traveling back and forth, which also lacks electricity, radio and television, communication between the outside world and the island is also effectively severed. Indeed, not only are the people dissuaded from leaving, but there is an equally strong desire to keep anyone from the outside from intruding into this isolated outpost as well. The threat of the outsider is expressed by Lord Summerisle in the novelization as follows: "I must say the mainland must be becoming more like a police state every day. When you're not interfering in education, you're poking your nose into religion. Sad that it has to be such an ignorant nose at that."[16]

It would thus appear that such isolation is maintained out of a perceived necessity. Further, at least on the surface, this separation seems to jibe with the hippie ethos of dropping out and returning to nature. In other words, like the hippie commune, Summerisle exists in seclusion, or else it would cease to exist at the hands of an external population that has come to vilify both the community and its practices. On a deeper level, this divide may be seen to exist not only between Summerisle and the ethos of modernity, and between Paganism and its Christian other, but also between Howie and his contemporaneous culture. In other words, if the island of Summerisle exists apart, so too does Sergeant Neil Howie. As the novelization directly suggests:

> Howie knew he was beaten. He'd seen English and American tourists standing baffled and angry on the quayside of Portocalie, with a fist full of money in their hands, trying to persuade a local fisherman to take them out on the Sabbath.... These people here might have a different religion, but they were of the same blood. His own blood. Stubborn, a bit hypocritical, and very proud.[17]

Indeed, what makes *The Wicker Man* unique is not the fact that it pits two opposing faiths against one another—one configured as evil and the other as good, as is common in classical horror cinema—but instead that it suggests that those who hold faith of any type, when pitted against a secular and unbelieving world, are equally devalued and denigrated. It is not an issue of good versus evil, but instead, as is the case with the narratives discussed throughout this book, one of belief versus skepticism. It is this dichotomy that is equally suggested in the reception of *The Wicker Man*. For example, in his review of the remake of the 1973 classic, Lucius Shepard points out the novelty in presenting a film dealing with the nature of belief at all: "One refreshing quality of the original film was that it preserved paganism as a religious choice ... and presented Christianity as an equally reasonable (or unreasonable) choice."[18]

When considering the way in which this film was received, *The Wicker Man* could be seen, on the surface, as addressing the popular debates of its cultural milieu with regard to freedom of belief and the opening up of choice vis-à-vis an adherence to traditional doctrine that had dominated the pre–modern world. However, as with *Eye of the Devil*, as discussed earlier, *The Dark Secret* and *Harvest Home*, which will be addressed in the subsequent chapter, the connections between these works and the ethos of the countercultural era are only valid until one scratches beneath the surface. Indeed, while choice became the byword for this generation, consolidation around a specific religion was found to be lacking, or at the very least waning. The quest of the religious seeker, which, according to Hugh McLeod, characterized members of the baby boom generation,[19] was to discover their own individual spiritual path, and while this may lead to the formation of organized groups and/or the practice of collective rites, the ethos of rejecting systematic rules for behavior often led away from rather than toward organized religion. McLeod suggests:

> There was a modest increase in the numbers of those professing other religions, such as Buddhism, Hinduism, or Islam, or stating that they had no religion. The main novelty was that those who rejected Christianity were increasingly ready to say so loudly and openly.[20]

This rejection of orthodoxy was characteristic of the eco-naturalist movement that brought about a revival of pseudo–Paganism and a worship of nature, while at the same time rejecting the age-old traditions inherent to this faith and its hierarchical system, both of which were challenged in the service of a desired "freeing up," as discussed previously. Indeed, the inspiration for *The Wicker Man*, as a film and later as a novel, was, for screenwriter Anthony Shaffer and the film's director, Robin Hardy, to get closer to the truth regarding the actual practices of Paganism,[21] which are far more grounded than the shopping-cart-style personal spiritualism so prevalent at this time. The importance of historical connectivity and rootedness was made manifest by the filmmakers through the choice of location, genre and inspiration through which the story is conveyed—all of which suggest that Paganism, like Christianity, is equally traditional.

The Role and Efficacy of Traditional Religion within the Novel and Film Versions of *The Wicker Man*

To begin, Scotland was selected as the site of the narrative because the Hebrides and, more specifically, the island of Iona have a specific and unique spiritual history as not only one of the oldest and most important religious centers, wherein the monastic tradition of Celtic Christianity was born and disseminated, but also, for Hardy, because Scotland harbored an ancient Celtic culture that has kept Pagan traditions alive, thus alluding to an apparent connectivity between these faiths, at least in terms of location. Further, in using horror as a vehicle, the authors wanted to explore and indeed explode the genre by undermining representations of the classic villains which were portrayed by Hollywood and Hammer Horror as maleficent Satanic witches, who, in the words of Hardy, "dance around pentacles with conical hats."[22]

This more authentic articulation of Paganism was then not only contrasted with but connected to traditional Christian beliefs in the film and novelization alike. Hardy goes on to suggest that by avoiding a reliance on generic stereotypes, *The Wicker Man* instead began to explore deeply religious issues with complexity. This argument was made not only by the director himself, but also by critic Allan Brown, who, in the introduction to the novelization, writes, "*The Wicker Man* was among the first mainstream features to use religious faith as subject matter."[23] In other words, while most classical horror films up until this time seem to articulate a conflict of good versus evil, this textual constellation instead acts to complicate this trope by suggesting that no brand of religious faith has a greater claim to authenticity than any other. This is to say, those who practice Christianity are not, for this alignment alone, wholly good, while those who follow Paganism, or any other non-traditional religion, cannot be defined as being evil merely as a result of their spiritual affiliation. Indeed, the narrative antihero, Lord Summerisle, and his people are not truly villains, while Sergeant Neil Howie, the protagonist, is not exclusively virtuous. In his analysis of *The Wicker Man*, Andy Boot seems to share this reading when he argues, "Woodward and Lee make fine sparring partners, one apoplectic and the other implacable, both as bigoted in their religious views."[24] Indeed, what makes *The Wicker Man* an interesting focus of study is the way in which (unlike the other films discussed in this book) there is no one who falls on the side of modernity. No one character strives to bolster the self by following the path of individualism. No character or group thus symbolizes the zeitgeist of the era, except for by extension the culture at large, a community that equally rejects both Howie and the people of Summerisle.

On one side of this spiritual divide of holistic belief, Protestant-affirming Sergeant Neil Howie is portrayed as being driven to follow Jesus and a Christian ethic above all else. Not only is his single-minded faith foregrounded in both the director's cut and the theatrical versions of the film, but this ethos is also more overtly articulated in the subsequent novel written by Hardy and Shaffer which further elucidates the totality of his spirituality. This is revealed from the outset of this text through the general actions and demeanor of this character, and more specifically through the way in which the protagonist's personal conduct affected his choice of profession, a role which assumes an identificatory prominence only second to his faith: "Knowing the law, in Christian Scotland, to be based on the teachings of Christ, he saw his work in the police as an opportunity to give a practical expression to his faith and convictions."[25] Indeed, his faith in the law, which underpins his role as a police officer and his religious faith, requires both an acceptance of a strict code of conduct and an adherence to a set of laws which cannot be broken without penalty. On the other side of the coin, the inhabitants of Summerisle, an isolated agrarian community, also exist within a cultural system of mores and customs strongly connected to their own form of religious belief, and which affects their chosen social roles as well. Because their livelihood is chiefly based upon the export of apples to the mainland, the practice of Paganism, in their eyes, ensures that the gods will be pleased, their crops fruitful, and thus their way of life preserved.

Although these two faiths come into conflict within the narrative construct, the efficacy of equal and total adherence to each respective system of belief cannot be denied. Further, so long as these religious practices are observed, there is a promise of reward versus punishment. Surprisingly, even given direct statements with regard to authorial intentionality, coupled with an apparent focus within the narrative itself, this complex thematic concern with religion seems to be downplayed in the secular press at the time of the film's release. *New York Times* reviewer Janet Maslin argues: "They [Robin Hardy and Anthony Shaffer] seem to have meant this as a tale pitting Christian values against pagan ones, concluding on a note of terrible irony. Is God Dead? Is God wearing antlers? Ask yourself. See how far you get."[26]

However, while the secular press devalues the reliance on faith and belief, this approach was not taken by the religious press at the time, and *The Wicker Man* was indeed rated offensive by the United States Conference of Catholic Bishops (USCCB) for exhibiting what was perceived as blasphemous concerns by the Catholic Church. However, in concluding the review with a discussion as to the film's depiction of excessive nudity, the review makes it unclear as to whether the offence chiefly rests in the depiction of religion, or in a perceived appeal to spectatorial prurient interests.

The Role of Sexuality in Textual Articulations of Paganism

One cannot dispute the fact that sexuality plays a substantial role in the film and in the novelization when it comes to depictions of Pagan practice. Indeed, while Howie's passion for Christ and justice results in an adherence to an incredibly ascetic existence, Lord Summerisle and his people revere the gods of nature and fertility. It is this focus on fecundity that comes to underpin the beliefs of the inhabitants of Summerisle, for, according to the novel, "sex seemed to be the ruling passion of this strangely fecund island ... his mind was suddenly obsessed with the idea of earth being the conduit of seed to the womb."[27] While this depiction of sexuality can, admittedly, render this text controversial, such representations nonetheless extend beyond the merely salacious. Characteristic to the Hammer Horror films of this period, which equally embraced exploitative images as a means of garnering audiences, the filmmakers admit that such films as *Lust for a Vampire, Countess Dracula* and *Twins of Evil* were created to be not simply works of horror, but equally softcore pornographic films. Rather than being narratively motivated, nudity and sexual imagery in these films were wholly gratuitous, added only to bring in audiences. However, while nonetheless potentially titillating, sexuality, within *The Wicker Man* is in fact directly linked with representations of Paganism, the sex act a fertility rite enacted to ensure Summerisle's verdant landscape.

One such ritual involves the youthful members of the community engaging in sexual intercourse out in the open, upon the earth. This scene not only appears in the film, witnessed by Howie with a lack of understanding bordering on disgust, but is also depicted in the novelization in the following way: "A dozen pairs of young lovers were coupling on the grass.... In every case the girl sat astride her young man, who lay on his back. Their sexual rhythm was unfaltering."[28] This portrayal of the primacy of ritualized sexuality is further articulated in two scenes involving Willow, the "landlord's daughter." In the first scene, which was later excised from the theatrical version of *The Wicker Man*, Lord Summerisle leads a young male islander to the Green Man Pub, where Willow resides. After a ceremonial exchange, the young man is bid to enter and engage in his first sexual encounter in Willow's second-floor bedroom. The villagers in the pub, in the meantime, look up toward the ceiling and sing in unison a ballad meant to commemorate this occasion, a song entitled "Gently Johnny." Given the ritualistic and routinized manner in which these events occur, it is suggested that this is a common occurrence, a rite of passage for the young males as they enter into adulthood. Another scene mimics the first and involves Neil Howie, a man who is later revealed to also be a virgin.

This scene of attempted seduction, arguably taken from a novel by David Pinner entitled *Ritual*,[29] once again alludes to the strength of belief that Howie possesses and his resolve not to give into actions that he believes would be sinful. This challenge is thus a pivotal moment of the narrative as these two-belief systems clash. In what some regard to be the originating text, *Ritual*, David Pinner writes:

> David [Howie] listened with his groin. Nothing moved in her room. He felt himself drawn towards the wall. He refused to be magnetised. He knew her hot body demanded through the stale mortar.... She amused herself, knowing David was stroking the wall. David slid his hands over his side of the wall, lingering where the subtle incline of her navel would be.... Her left breast was Anna's favourite. She flexed it towards the wall. With disgust David found that he was licking a faded dancer off the wallpaper. She whispered his name over and over, but he did not come.[30]

In both the film and novel versions of *The Wicker Man*, Willow, attempts to "initiate" Howie by performing a ritualistic dance. Willow is naked. As she sings her siren song, she writhes and drums against the wall of their adjoining bedrooms. Under the influence of this lure, the sergeant is almost driven to broach the space that separates them. With prayer and fortitude, Howie finally manages to resist the young and vivacious Willow. He does not copulate with her, as have all the other male villagers before him.[31] In the novelization of *The Wicker Man*, this act is further revealed to awaken not only sexual longing in Howie, but also panic, as he questions whether his desire for acquiescence is not in fact a sign of God's abandonment of his soul:

> Panic was not an emotion that Sergeant Howie had suffered much before. But now the thought that there might, just possibly be, coursing through his veins an agent that could twist or bend his will, turn what he regarded as the base desires that he shared with every other man, but with God's grace had learned to control, into a lust that he would be powerless to deny ... that thought was the stuff of panic for Howie.[32]

However, this is finally denied as the faith that Howie cherishes above all else reasserts itself, allowing him to resist this sexual attraction and keep true to his virtue: "God, he felt suddenly, was with him and all at once he was able to shut out the song and fell to kneeling by his bedside as he had done every night since he was a child."[33] This is the only time, ostensibly, where Howie acts based upon his own initiative, and is thus a narrative turning point, however brief, as will be discussed below.

The Lure of Sacrifice and the Connectivity of Traditional and Alternative Belief

As suggested in the introduction to this chapter, although unbeknownst to the protagonist until the end of the film, Lord Summerisle and his people have specifically lured Howie to the island by concocting a story relating to a young island girl, Rowan Martin, who has been reported missing and is suspected to have been abducted by someone on the island. Howie arrives and begins his investigation, whereupon he becomes increasingly certain that the girl has been hidden by the community. As the "Spring Maiden," he is made to believe that she must fulfill her calling and be offered in sacrifice to the gods to ensure the fertility of the crops, which, for the first time in the history of the island, have failed. However, in the final scene, it is revealed that it is not the young girl who was the desired sacrifice, but Howie himself. As Lord Summerisle suggests, Howie is indeed an ideal propitiatory victim. First, he has come to Summerisle of his own free will as a representative of the king. As a police officer, he is not only a symbol of authority, but also an individual acting to uphold the laws of the land as decreed by the sovereign. However, even though ordered to do so, he remains and seeks Rowan based upon his volition more than for the sake of his service to the police force. He has also come as a virgin. Finally, he willingly plays the part of the fool. In order to infiltrate the May Day festivities, Howie renders the village publican unconscious and steals his costume, a Punch figure, the ceremonial "King for a Day." Of his unwitting complicity in this plot, Lord Summerisle suggests:

> You see our research had told us that you were just the man we wanted and we were determined to get you here. Of course we were equally determined to control your every action and thought once you had arrived.[34]

Indeed, the hunter becomes the hunted in this textual constellation as Howie is first made to believe that he will succeed in leading the vulnerable young girl to safety, foiling what he believes to be Summerisle's evil plot, while in fact his actions from the start were controlled by the village under Lord Summerisle to keep him on the island until the May Day festival, when he would inevitably "Keep his date with the wicker man."[35]

According to Sir James George Frazer's *The Golden Bough*, which, unlike *Ritual*, was a key influence for *The Wicker Man* in all its forms, the Pagan belief system is indeed based on propitiation, culminating in the carrying out of a sacrifice designed to mollify the gods to bestow upon the agrarian community continued agricultural success. In articulating a thematic concern with sacrifice, Anthony Shaffer suggests that the film presents something unique to the thematic concerns of the English films of the period.[36] Sacrifice is, however, not a uniquely Pagan concept, but instead is also common to Christianity in both the Old Testament and the New. In the Old Testament, sacrifices and burnt offerings were made to God for mercy and forgiveness, while in the New Testament, Christ negated the need for these rituals by his own sacrificial death and resurrection, a freeing of sin which is bestowed upon the Christian at baptism and which is celebrated in the sacramental feast of Holy Communion.

This connection between the Pagan and Christian belief in the power and necessity of sacrifice is articulated in both the film and the novel. The Pagan rituals celebrated in *The Wicker Man* as part of May Day are seen to be akin to those of the Christian celebration of Easter. Island schoolteacher Miss Rose explains:

> [May Day] is a feast of fecundity, celebrated in the form of an ancient dance-drama…. There is the sacrifice whose death and resurrection, or course, is the climax of the dance…. The victim is as symbolic or not as the Christian's bread and wine. You eat it at communion, do you not? And the Roman Catholic Christians believe it is turned miraculously to the real thing in their mouths. Others believe it is symbolic … a matter of taste, if you'll forgive the pun.[37]

Thus, the first scenes of the director's cut wherein the protagonist, Sergeant Howie, is seen taking communion, a rite that is enacted to remind Christians of this sacrifice of God's son, bookend the final scene, wherein Howie becomes a burnt offering. Both ceremonies foreground the customs that are shared by these two spiritualties. *The Golden Bough* further makes this connection between the Pagan spirit of the corn and Jesus:

> If Adonis was indeed the spirit of the corn, a more suitable name for his dwelling place could hardly be found than Bethlehem, "The House of Bread" and he may well have been worshipped there at his House of Bread long before the birth of Him who said "I am the bread of life."[38]

However, whereas sacrifices are no longer made in the name of Christianity, as Jesus, for modern Christians, became the perfect sacrifice to atone for all sin, this is not the case for the Pagans on Summerisle. To ensure strength, fertile crops and health, sacrifices of animals were first made to the most holy of all objects on the island, the mistletoe covered oak tree:

> The bones of long since decomposed "victim" sacrificial animals lay everywhere, but among them were something more unexpected. Close to the tree, upon the side that faced the lake, were hundreds of crudely carved hands and feet, hearts and ears, et cetera. Some were made of wood and others of clay. Scratched upon them were names like Jonquil, Maize, Peony, Yew, Poplar, and Sycamore. People's names, as Howie had learned to recognise them. Howie had read somewhere that the Roman Catholics went in for something like this at shrines where saints were supposed to preside over miracles. But where they simply placed candles to burn—exactly as he made offerings as a sideman at Saint Andrew's to support the church—these Summerisle people, if you could grace them with that human name, clearly offered up the suffering animals so that the goddess would grant their requests.[39]

Further, according to *The Golden Bough*, the oak was revered among the Pagan worshippers due to its essential utility. The wood of the oak could be used for the lighting of fires, the construction of buildings, roads and canoes, as well as a source of acorns for feeding livestock. Frazer argues: "No wonder then, if the tree from which they received so many benefits should play an important part in their religion and should have been invested with sacred character."[40] While all oaks were revered, those upon which mistletoe grew were particularly sacred, because it was believed that whatever grows on these trees is sent from heaven, signaling that the tree was chosen by the gods. For this reason, mistletoe and the tree on which it grows is regarded as a universal healer, effectual for almost any ailment, and hence it was to this tree that the sacrifices and prayers for healing were made in the novel *Ritual*. Later, in the novelization of *The Wicker Man*, the connectivity between Christianity and Paganism is further alluded to through the symbol of the tree:

> He [Howie] contented himself with gazing up at the great Gothic arches the trees made above them and imagined himself in some vast cathedral in a golden age, sometime before the "fall" of Eden.[41]

This connection between the Christian edifice and the forest is one that is suggested equally in *The Golden Bough*, which makes the connection more manifest by tracing the etymology of the term sanctuary, which is commonly used to refer to the purposes and ultimate mission of the traditional Christian Church: "Amongst the Celts, the oak worship of the Druids is familiar to everyone, and their old word for sanctuary seems to be identical in origin and meaning with the Latin *nemus*, a grove or woodland glade."[42] Like their representative religions, there are also additional connections to be found between faiths, as their textual representatives, Lord Summerisle and Howie, share an apparent reverence for nature.

In the novelization, Howie is revealed to be an ardent bird watcher, and the opening of this text is devoted to his pastime. For Howie, this love supports his spirituality, the beauty of nature grounding his belief in the goodness and beauty of God as revealed in His creation. For Lord Summerisle, spirituality is equally tied to a reverence of nature, only more directly. As a Pagan, it is his belief that nature is animate and sentient, each element having a being and a soul to which propitiation must be made. The successful result of his piety is revealed in the landscape, the verdant crops, and the diversity of nature. However, for Howie, this belief is seen as being antiquated and misguided, and while the connections between faiths are registered, they are not fully recognized or appreciated, as Howie observes of Lord Summerisle in the textual version of *The Wicker Man*:

God sometimes chose the most mysterious vessels for His Divine will, he thought. Any family that could have guarded such a secret for four generations [as to the presence of the great auks, who were considered extinct] received at least some of Howie's respect. But he could not help the somewhat ungenerous reflection that the Lord Summerisle and the great auks of this world had a certain amount in common. Evolution was against them.[43]

Ironically, this could also be said of Howie himself, a relic of an age that was based on tradition and religion in an increasingly secular age.

Modernity versus Traditionalism: The Pagan and the Skeptic in *The Wicker Man*

As Sir James Frazer suggests in *The Golden Bough*, magic and religion are both belief systems that, under the dual influences of the Enlightenment and the Reformation, have been eclipsed by rationality and an affinity to science, a condition that in fact exemplifies modernity overall. For Frazer, this supposed evolution of human thought has been one that initially embraced magic as part of a holistic worldview. This included not only the relationship of the individual to his physical environment, but also formed his or her connection to the spiritual realm. Over time, however, a theosophy was adopted that, under the guise of the more orthodox Protestant faiths, came to reject supernatural elements as an integral component of faith. The last step in Frazer's theorized evolution of belief wholly embraced the scientific, and furthermore used science as a means whereby the supernatural, the inexplicable, and the irrational could be either discerned, analyzed and understood, or rejected. For Frazer, this stage represents the culmination of human reason. According to *The Golden Bough*:

Magic is gradually superseded by religion, which explains the succession of natural phenomena as regulated by the will, the passion or the caprice of spiritual beings, like man in kind, though vastly superior to him in power.... Religion, regarded as an explanation of nature is displaced by science.... It is probably not too much to say that the hope of progress—moral and intellectual, as well as material—in the future is bound up with the fortunes of science, and that every obstacle placed in the way of scientific discovery is a wrong to humanity.... In the last analysis magic, religion, and science are nothing but theories of thought, but science has supplanted its predecessors.[44]

It is this "evolution" from superstitious to scientific belief that is revealed on the island of Summerisle, but ironically in reverse, as is suggested by Lord Summerisle's familial history. To return to the novelization:

And so you see, Lord Summerisle was saying, "with typical mid–Victorian zeal," my great-grandfather set to work. But of course, almost immediately, he met opposition from the fundamental ministers, who threw tons of his artificial fertilizer into the harbour on the grounds that if God had meant for us to use it, He'd have provided it. My great-grandfather took exactly the same view of ministers, and realised he had to find a way to get rid of them. The best method of accomplishing this, it seemed to him, was by giving them back their joyous old deities, so he encouraged, as it were, a retreat down memory lane; backwards from Christianity, through the Age of Reason and Belief to the Age of Mysticism.[45]

In this way, the people of Summerisle ostensibly underwent a process of regression, at least from the perspective of Frazer, from scientific method to supernatural religious ritual. Summerisle's grandfather, a "worshipper of science," realized the necessity of an agrarian lifestyle for the survival of the island and its residents, and thus adopted and furthered a religious doctrine, Paganism, to support the successful conversion of the villagers to this lifestyle choice. Interestingly, what began as a rationally and scientifically grounded decision became an ingrained spiritual system of belief, an example of *The Golden Bough* in reverse. In other words, what began as an expedient way of maintaining his experiment, a method for the furthering of scientific inquiry, became a more firmly rooted belief system not only for the people of the island, but for the first Lord Summerisle himself:

What my great-grandfather had started out of expedience, he continued because he truly believed it was far more spiritually nourishing than the life-denying God-terror of the kirk. And I might say, Sergeant, he brought me up the same way—to love music and the drama of the rituals of the old pantheism, and to love nature, and to fear it, and to rely on it, and appease it where necessary.[46]

The novel also reveals a connection between the history of the British Empire and the practices of Paganism on the island of Summerisle as Howie looks upon the face of Rowan Morrison for the first time:

It was a sunny, smiling face with the fair Scandinavian cast to the features that is often found in the outer isles where, in the dark ages, the Vikings raped and pillaged leaving little but their bloodlines and their place names behind.[47]

While in the film Rowan is mousy-haired with brown eyes, in the novel version, the connection to Viking roots is established both genetically as well as spiritually. In other words, the people do not only share a common ancestry, but also a common belief to the culture responsible for bringing the last onslaught of Paganism to Britain. It will be this long-standing historical connectivity to religious faith that will be pitted against Howie, who, as his plane flew over the island of Iona, historically the stronghold of Christianity, where the first monastic monks retreated so as to enact an isolated and austere communion with God, "could see below the restored monastery from which most of the Celtic west had been brought the news of Christ reborn. Howie was proud as a Scottish Celt, that this church had long preceded Rome in converting the heathen English."[48] This view of the Celts as being associated with the spread of Christianity is complicated by the views of the people of Summerisle, who seem equally connected to their Celtic forefathers as Pagans, for according to Lord Summerisle, "The tradition of the arcane and the mysterious cleaves to the people of this island with a tenacity that makes it seem an inherent and inalienable possession. They're Celts after all."[49] This supposed contradiction alludes to the historical war for religious dominance between Pagans and Catholics, which infiltrated the island until the eleventh century and was eventually resolved not by overtaking one belief system with another, but instead overlaying the former atop the latter. This configuration of faith, long since established on the mainland, was reversed on the isolated island of Summerisle with the Pagan dominating over its Christian other.

Extratextual Considerations of *The Wicker Man*

Much like the other texts considered in this book, *The Wicker Man*, when regarded in terms of the choices made during its production, is a text that is fraught in its overall social and political alliance. Additionally, its conception, realization and dissemination likewise rest upon a series of conflicts of belief.

When this work was first conceived, it was as a screen treatment entitled *Ritual*. David Pinner got the idea for the film after becoming interested in Witchcraft as a result of reading the novels of classical horror novelist Dennis Wheatley. This author not only informed the original screen treatment, but also the film screenplay, penned by Anthony Shaffer. According to Adam Brown, author of a definitive behind-the-scenes study of the film entitled *Inside the Wicker Man*:

> The film's general interest in paganism also no doubt owes something to Dennis Wheatley.... While Wheatley's books swam in the darker waters of the pure occult, they contained a charge of creeping evil deriving from the often isolated nature of their settings, which were heavy with rural mysticisms and cherished superstitions.[50]

However, Wheatley, whilst founding his novels upon well-researched depictions of Witchcraft and Satanism so as to be considered an expert on the occult, nonetheless took a hostile view toward these practices. For Wheatley, in many ways a traditional thinker, the foundation of his occult stories was a conflict of good versus evil. In one interview, conducted by the BBC in 1970, Wheatley argued that at this moment in history, there was a rise in uncertainty amongst contemporary youth. These young people, searching for something to hold onto, had, according to Wheatley, begun forming covens. Tempted by evil influences, the promise of hedonistic pleasure and the use of drugs (a practice which he also linked to Witchcraft), these individuals could at the very worst cause socio-political chaos, and at the very least lose their minds. The interviewer asked the author if, in publishing books that represented the occult, he himself was complicit in this struggle by aligning himself with evil over good. To this, Wheatley replied, "I can't believe that because in every book I write, I always give a warning: this is evil and no good can ever come to anybody who dabbles in it."[51]

Additionally, in keeping with a consideration of conservative alignment, whilst writing the treatment, screenplay writer Anthony Shaffer suggests that he had Michael Winner in mind to direct—a man who, during the same era, would become famous for *Death Wish*. This is not wholly a surprise given Shaffer's affinity for the allied mystery/thriller genre. Indeed, his initial artistic success occurred as the result of the Tony Award–winning stage play *Sleuth*, which shared a concern with crime detection. *Death Wish* and its sequels focused on vigilantism as a potential answer for inner-city violence. At the time of its release, Roger Ebert suggested of the film, "*Death Wish* is a quasi-fascist advertisement for urban vigilantes, done up in a slick ... action movie."[52]

When the film project failed to be realized, Pinner was encouraged to turn the screenplay into a novel, which was subsequently published under the same title. Ironically, there was more interest in adapting *Ritual* back into a screenplay following the novelization of his original treatment not only by the eventual production team of Anthony Shaffer, Robin Hardy and Christopher Lee, but also by David Warner. The latter of these optioned for the film rights so that he might assume the role of Sergeant Howie. Although this never came to fruition, Warner did go on to portray the role of Keith Jennings, thus forming an interesting connection between this work and *The Omen*. At the ripe age of 50, Christopher Lee, who, as discussed in his autobiography, had decided to "Draculate no more,"[53] was more interested in the role of Lord Summerisle. Even as he desired to break new ground and leave behind the role that had lent him notoriety even as it typecast him, his ability to garner the staid horror audience represented by Hammer is not something to be overlooked. Likewise, Ingrid Pitt, also known for her earlier horror cinema roles, added to the film's genre clout. However, such connections between the film and the infamous *Hammer House of Horror* were something that Shaffer wanted to downplay as he considered the film to be more of a work of art and less a genre piece. To cast Pitt was not only to connect the film to Hammer, but also to align the film to potential sources of distribution outside of the horror powerhouse. The actress herself was partnered with George Pinches, head of exhibition with the Rank Organisation, who, in turn, owned the Odeon film theater chain, making this decision not only beneficial artistically but commercially as well.

Speaking further to choices of cast, David Hemmings, a friend of Hardy and himself coming off of his role of executioner in *Day of the Arrow*, was ironically offered the role of the sacrificial victim, Howie. He declined, but not only agreed to assist in financing the picture, but also to let Hardy shoot some initial footage in his stately country estate, the gardens of which were fortuitously embellished with phallic topiaries that served as a fitting backdrop to the Pagan tale. Indeed, much of this footage was used in establishing shots. The part of Howie was eventually offered to and accepted by Edward Woodward after Shaffer became impressed by his work in the televisual series *Callan*, this forming another connection of the film to the crime thriller genre.

To further the alluring potential of this film, Swedish actress Britt Ekland was offered the part of the erotically charged landlord's daughter, Willow. This maneuver was common to the genre at the time: to tread the line between horror and a softcore porn. She was willing to strip down to her waist for the seduction scene described above, but did not agree to appear fully nude. The actress suggests that this decision was two-fold: first, she felt that the body below the waist was private and personal, and even if this was not a concern, she would not have agreed after discovering her pregnancy. Thus, and supposedly unbeknown to her, a body double was employed in Ekland's stead. To this day, and much to the actress's chagrin, she is still known for her dance of seduction, even though the posterior that waggles back and forth is not her own. Later, when the production concluded and on the verge of the film's distribution, a rumor circulated suggesting that Ekland's partner, rockstar Rod Stewart, was threatening to buy and destroy all of the negatives of the film to prevent audiences from feasting their eyes on her naked flesh.

In addition to garnering the aforementioned connections, *The Wicker Man* recruited veteran actress Diane Cilento, who, after training at the Royal Academy of Dramatic Art, went on to feature in films such as *Tom Jones* before becoming not only a screen Bond girl, but also the wife of Sean Connery. At the time, she had retired and was only convinced to return to the screen after reading the script. It was reported by Shaffer that at this moment in her life she was interested in receiving a spiritual education and to answer the essential questions we all ask ourselves: why we are here, what we are meant to be doing, and what happens to us later? Shaffer thought that she took on the role in order to learn and grow spiritually. Robin Hardy also notes the connection between the actress and alternative spirituality:

> Diane Cilento was very interested in the whole pagan white witch thing, so she did all the choreography for [the scene in which the girls of the village take part in a fertility ceremony by jumping over an open fire].[54]

The choreography for this and other ceremonies depicted throughout the film were further enhanced by the work of folk singer Paul Giovanni, who gave voice to the Pagan themes of communal gathering and submission to music. In writing the original soundtrack for the film, he tried to bring out the natural spiritual fecundity of *The Wicker Man*, the themes that drew Cilento to the project. Relying on ancient acoustic instruments, an eighteenth-century pub harlot ballad, which became the "Landlord's Daughter," produced a more authentic sound.[55] Equally historically relevant was the adoption of poetry from the ploughman's poet Robert Burns. The opening scene is set to "Corn Rigs Are Bonnie," the words for which were taken from a Burns poem. The first stanza states:

> It was upon a Lammas night,
> When corn rigs are bonnie,
> Beneath the moon's unclouded light,
> I held awa to Annie:
> The time flew by, wi' tentless heed,
> Till 'tween the late and early;
> Wi' sma' persuasion she agreed,
> To see me thro' the barley.

Lammas night, one of the Scottish "term" or "quarter" days, is a division of the liturgical and natural year. Along with Candlemas (celebrating the purification of Christ in winter), Whitsun (celebrating Pentecost in spring), Martinmas (celebrating the feast day of Saint Martin of Tours in autumn), the celebration of Lammas (the Harvest Festival of summer) is tied not only to Christian feast days, but also the Pagan festivals which likewise correspond to each of the seasons, Imbolc (winter), Beltane (spring), Samhain (autumn) and Lughnasadh (summer). This is yet another indicator of how Christianity might be aligned to older Pagan rites.

Not only was the score of the film specifically written to showcase such essential thematic elements of the film, so too were the characterizations devised to showcase certain members of the cast. Christopher Lee, who, as was discussed above, became instrumental in the film's production, says of *The Wicker Man*:

> [T]he part was specially written for me. Now that doesn't happen very often. And when you've got an author the calibre of Shaffer, what more can you ask for? So, *The Wicker Man* was the best part I've ever had ... the best performance I've ever given. What a part, what a wonderful, wonderful part.[56]

In fact, many involved in the production had similar feelings, including Edward Woodward. Although not the first choice for the role of Howie, he nonetheless experienced a strong connection not only to the role, but to the film overall. Woodward states, "What a unique and affecting experience my involvement with *The Wicker Man* has been. It just remains a terrible pity that such a superb film has been so blighted."[57] This blight is described fittingly by Woodward as a "strange evil," and specifically relates to the problems faced in the distribution of the film. At the time, British Lion Films, a company known for being in and out of financial distress since the 1950s, was undergoing a takeover by EMI, and as a result of this, the film's producer, Peter Snell, was fired and replaced by EMI producers Michael Deeley and Barry Spikings. Christopher Lee argues that Deeley hated the film and was responsible for re-editing it to run as a second feature in a double bill with a film of equally charged supernatural versus skepticism themes, *Don't Look Now*. When Lee went to the film's theatrical release, he remembers questioning the producer about this new edited version, and equally remembers being told that Deeley thought the film was one of the ten worst films he had ever seen, which may have resulted in the lack of support for the distribution of the film, and for the original negative of *The Wicker Man* being unaccountably lost, barring restoration to the full director's cut. When re-edited, certain background scenes were cut from the film, and only a few of them survived in the theatrical release. The removal of scenes including an opening wherein Howie is patrolling the streets of inner-city Scotland, and a scene where the protagonist not only receives but distributes communion bread and wine, acts to limit the efficacy of the narrative in revealing the nature of the main character as a highly religious outsider, turning this prominent character trait into mere subtext. Lee, Hardy and Shaffer considered the film to have been butchered, and as a result, the two writers ended up penning their own novel version, much like Pinner before them, wherein their characterizations, thematic concerns and imagery could be fully realized. Lee, on the other hand, spent significant time and resources in attempting to regain the original director's cut, finally finding a copy in the hands of American film director and producer Roger Corman, who was initially approached to re-edit and release the film in the United States.

Conclusion

Within the narrative structure of the textual constellation known as *The Wicker Man*, Paganism and a worship of the gods of the earth came to dominate an isolated fictional Hebridean Island known as Summerisle. Therein, as a result of an unwavering adherence to this spiritual affiliation by the local inhabitants, not only their religion, but by extension their way of life became efficacious, productive and harmonious. Likewise, through his steadfast belief in Christianity, Sergeant Neil Howie comes to uphold the enduring power of religion, which, in turn, renders his life and his work meaningful. While on the one hand, Christianity is regarded, culturally speaking, as being a faith that is inherently traditional in nature, and on the other, Paganism is equally located, socio-politically, as a radical alternative faith mechanism by the contemporaneous culture, within the world of *The Wicker Man* itself, these two faiths, while narratively oppositional, are shown to share many similarities. Both spiritualities are invested in the power of sacrifice, and the gods of both faiths are also revered by enacting a series of rituals and rites rooted in a strong historical imperative. This connectivity is revealed in the final shot of the film, as Howie, who has been given the uncommon honor of a martyr's death, calls to his God for strength and solace during a time of incredible adversity, as do the people of the island, who sing to their collective gods during a time of equal suffering and loss, thus intermingling these two religions in a unified voice. Indeed, while seemingly in conflict within this text, these two faiths are really not so different after all. The film concludes with the burning of the wicker man as the sun sets in the distance, rather than alluding to whether or not the Summerisle crops will be re-instilled with fecundity, or whether or not Howie will equally be reborn, for, as was seen in the case of *The Eye of the Devil, Day of the Arrow,* and *Robin Redbreast,* and as will be noted subsequently, those who hold on to religion as a defining mechanism firmly believe that this will be the case, which is ultimately all that is required for a faith to be rendered efficacious. Thus, just as Howie firmly believes he will be resurrected, the Pagans believe the same of their crops. Such unremitting acceptance of the power of the supernatural, however, holds no sway in the modern world of unbelief and skepticism, creating both a literal and figurative divide between these two realms. *The Wicker Man,* like the other texts within this alternative religion horror cycle, is thus received as a work that is rendered incomprehensible and/or unacceptable by its socio-political milieu, as is revealed by popular reviews of this text in the secular and religious press alike. In addition to critical reception, the way in which *The Wicker Man* was "butchered" by a production company that found it to be out of step with the times seems to suggest that whereas the battle for belief may be said to have been won within these narratives, the war for acceptance at the time of their release appears to have ultimately been lost within a modernist world that arguably fails to believe in anything outside the primacy of commercial self-interest.

Six

Paganism, Witchcraft and the Feminine in American Horror

I thought—jealously, perhaps—how much greater was the legacy of Cornwall Coombe than was ours, we who had lived half our lives in the city. Here, all around us was the richness of heritage ... what [the] forbearers had bestowed.—THOMAS TRYON from *Harvest Home*[1]

The Mother was the goddess. The goddess provided fertility. Fertility was needed. Without it, there would be no corn. Without corn no money for food. Without them, people died. Mother; fertility. Hope; belief. They all believed. All the village.—THOMAS TRYON from *Harvest Home*[2]

Introduction

At the conclusion of the 1970s horror film *Season of the Witch*, protagonist Joan Mitchell, an unhappy and unfulfilled suburban housewife, shoots her husband who has returned home unexpectedly from a business trip. Claiming that she believed him to be a burglar, Joan is not only ultimately exonerated of all criminal charges, but also becomes the recipient of a hefty insurance policy that will ensure her financial independence for the remainder of her years.[3] In the final scene of the film, the protagonist is shown at a cocktail party surrounded by friends from the local community. All attendees, the women especially, show support and sympathy for her newly widowed status. While most of the women seem to regard Joan's situation as one of loss and impending loneliness as the result of losing a life-long mate, one woman approaches Mitchell differently. This character, another *Jack's Wife*[4] who is now as equally repressed and unhappy as Joan once was, walks up to the protagonist

165

and inquires as to whether or not the rumors about her are true. Joan retorts, "Yes, they are. I am a witch."[5] The final static close-up shot frames Joan as she stares straight into the camera, apparently confronting the nameless housewife as she equally confronts the viewer. Much like ourselves, this unnamed everywoman is engaged as a privileged spectator called to witness, almost dared to pass judgment, almost dared not to follow her lead. It is through this final narrative exchange that the awakening process of this conservative suburban community is revealed. Once faced with the forcefulness of an empowered female, this allure acts as a guide toward fulfillment. This self-actualization will not be achieved by adopting a contemporaneous politically oriented feminist agenda, however, as was fairly common during this period. Instead, these women will be awakened through a less ordinary alternative. As is revealed in *Season of the Witch*, the protagonist comes to adhere to a radical alternative faith that is inherently female-centric, namely Wicca. Further, in establishing a link to community within a potentially isolating and male dominated universe, the privatized domestic world of these upper-middle-class American housewives is forever altered. Indeed, by the end of the film, Joan herself has become an emblem of the freedom to be gained through a self-realization that ostensibly could have never been achieved through traditional means within such a phallocentric culture. She is now a witch, and a member of a coven: a knowledgeable, learned woman, both powerful and connected.

As works that debate feminist concerns, these texts, produced within the United States, including the underground film *Season of the Witch*,[6] directed by George Romero, *The Dark Secret of Harvest Home*, a network television miniseries, and the adaptive novel *Harvest Home*, written by Thomas Tryon, all share similar thematic concerns. Unlike their Anglo-American[7] counterparts, *Eye of the Devil, Day of the Arrow*, and *The Wicker Man*, these works foreground female characters as figureheads for their respective religious communities rather than passive followers of aristocratic male leaders. Indeed, in relying on the work of Sir James Frazer as a basis for their understanding of Paganism, *Eye of the Devil, Day of the Arrow* and *The Wicker Man* come to privilege patriarchy, as did Frazer himself. *Season of the Witch, The Dark Secret of Harvest Home*, and *Harvest Home* are instead informed by the neo–Pagan Wicca movement. In other words, while the former works present male spiritual leaders within narratives that are on the whole dominated by male agency, the latter texts, as will be discussed in this chapter, foster feminist debates by positioning women in powerful key roles both textually and spiritually. Not only this, but by configuring the Pagan as pre–Christian, existing at a time arguably before religion became patriarchal,[8] active matriarchal agency can in fact be realized and potentially enacted.

This foregrounding of female agency ties not only into feminist debates and a demand for equal opportunity by women for women, but also to larger paradigmatic shifts related to the efficacy of historical traditionalism. This cultural awakening resulted in significant changes with regard to familial roles, gender positioning and religious affiliation both in the public and private realms, thus fostering a climate ripe for these discourses to come to the fore.[9]

While these works will be read as

(Clockwise) Joan Mitchell (Jan White) from *Season of the Witch*, and Missy Penrose (Tracey Gold, top right), Widow Fortune (Bette Davis), and Nick Constantine (David Ackroyd) from *The Dark Secret of Harvest Home.*

diverging from Frazer and thus opening up room for contemporaneous debate, literary reviews of *Harvest Home* nonetheless tend to group this book with other Pagan Horror. As *Time Magazine* critic John Skow suggests:

> It suits Tryon to imagine a great green heart beating slowly beneath the earth, with every rootlet and capillary in the village pulsing to it.... Where the author goes from there, though obvious enough in synopsis, is dark and intricate in the working out. The strangeness of Cornwall Coombe seems to center on the ritualistic way in which the town's corn is planted and harvested.... Ned Constantine, foolish male, has apparently never read *The Golden Bough.* He keeps poking into the secrets of Cornwall Coombe until the full moon at harvest time. He is in deeper trouble than he knows.[10]

To link this work with *The Golden Bough* at once recognizes a thematic concern with Paganism and reverence of the earth while equally negating the possibility of opening up a space for female agency and feminist debate. Given the socio-political climate, indicators provided by textual analysis, and research into the creative process of Romero in making *Season of the Witch*, such a confluence in many ways denies the potential of these works to address the concerns of their cultural climate and artistic inspiration, concerns that were at the fore in the inception of these texts.

Paganism, Witchcraft and the Role of Matriarchy

Historically speaking, Paganism and Witchcraft were overall objects of derision. Indeed, the very name "Pagan" was a derogatory term coined by early Christians to describe Roman polytheists taken from the Latin root *pāgānus*, meaning rural, rustic, or in more common nomenclature, a yokel. Thus, to be polytheistic was to be uncivilized, a member of the peasantry. According to historians such as Owen Davies:

> It is crucial to stress right from the start that until the 20th century, people did not call themselves pagans to describe the religion they practiced. The notion of paganism, as it is generally understood today, was created by the early Christian Church. It was a label that Christians applied to others, one of the antitheses that were central to the process of Christian self-definition. As such, throughout history it was generally used in a derogatory sense.[11]

The term "Pagan" was originally devoid of specific religious meaning, a purely secular term with pejorative overtones. Likewise, to be defined as a witch was to be negatively othered. In *America Bewitched: The Story of Witchcraft after Salem*, Davies goes on to argue that even before the founding of America, during the infamous Salem witch trials of 1692, not only were women executed under the suspicion of being practitioners of witchcraft, but a number of Native Americans (who, by practicing their polytheistic faiths, were also regarded as being in league with the devil) were executed on similar grounds. According to Davies:

> Catholic missionaries also instigated witch trials ... in the northern New Mexico settlement of Abiquito some fifty miles from Santa Fe ... that led to the most extensive and complex witch trials involving the Inquisition and secular authorities[12]

To be Pagan was to be condemned as being in league with the devil, whether the object of worship was Satan, gods and goddesses or Mother Earth herself. This conflation of non–Christian faiths was prevalent from the fourth century onwards, continuing at least until the 1960s, as is revealed in the way in which alternative faith is represented and reacted to in the films from the previous section including *Rosemary's Baby*. However, even though equally persecuted by Christians, Paganism could be considered to be, in many ways, the root that lies beneath orthodox faiths rather than an anathema to traditional religion.

Indeed, whereas Christianity and Satanism were configured as being coterminous monotheistic faiths existing within an us-versus-them relationship of respective right and wrong-mindedness, to be Pagan, in the common modern vernacular, was, in certain ways, to reject this essential dichotomization. Equally, to be right-minded, ironically for both Satanists and Christians, was to engage in the praise of a phallocentric god who either fathered the world, or alternatively fathered evil within the world. Both these faiths also relied upon the subjection of women: Christ being born of a woman "visited"[13] by the Holy Spirit, and Satan instigating original sin by seducing Eve to eat from the tree of the knowledge of good and evil. Witchcraft, on the other hand, as was suggested by Robin Hardy (not to mention Sir James Frazer), is more appropriately associated with polytheism. However, unlike either Hardy's or Frazer's understanding, what is revered by Wiccan practitioners is not a god who created and bestowed life upon the earth, or even a pantheon of gods (a hierarchy often headed by a male deity), but instead Mother Earth, who, with the maiden and the crone, forms the triple goddess. Following this argument, it could also be asserted that while Christianity and Frazerian Paganism are equally hierarchical and male-oriented, Wicca or Witchcraft may be regarded as being female-centered in not only allowing for the possibility of the worship of a triune goddess or series of both gods and goddesses, but equally the possibility of an active female religious agent, the witch.[14] Likewise, in being figured around a confluence of female deities, and worshipped by a group or coven of witches rather than in a traditional religious order, these faiths are configured not as a hierarchy, but instead as a faith based on equality. Contrasted against a potential subsumption within a spiritual linear model formed, according to the Catholic model, beginning with the Pope, then the cardinals, followed by the archbishops, bishops, priests, nuns and finally congregants, the Wiccans are organized circularly, like the seasons, making all those who worship equally bestowed with power. In this way, these films engage with second-wave feminist Hélène Cixous, who suggested that women write from their bodies: not linearly, but circularly. For *Season of the Witch*, *The Dark Secret of Harvest Home* and *Harvest Home*, women worship in a similar way.

Cultural Shifts, Feminist Debates and the Role of Traditionalism and Modernity in the 1960s and 1970s

According to cultural historian Beth Bailey in her study of gender in the 1960s entitled *Sex in the Heartland*, the post-war era was in a state of flux when it came to cultural conventions. She argues:

> As America mobilized for war, national goals often conflicted with "the way we do it here," and though local ways often triumphed, the needs of the war-time state frequently challenged local custom. Most of these challenges were unintentional.... [N]onetheless, they sometimes undermined existing social hierarchies. In spaces created for federal action, other Americans contested the status quo, whether by demanding civil rights, or by defying definitions of "respectability."[15]

Those affected by these paradigmatic shifts were, as Bailey alludes above, those who were in marginalized positions, including people of color and women, thus ostensibly eliciting a call for civil rights and socio-political equality.[16] For African Americans, this resulted in the formation of activist organizations under the leadership of congregational churches, which, alongside groups such as the NAACP, not only inspired cultural debate from within these communities on a private level, but equally enacted change on both local and federal levels, thus impacting the public sphere as well. For women, "second-wave" feminism, spearheaded within a more secular society by individuals such as Gloria Steinem and Betty Friedan as well as political organizations including the National Organization for Women, also brought into focus debates surrounding gender inequality in what was increasingly being defined as a society based not only on patriarchy, but more specifically a Caucasian patriarchal system.

With regard to enacting cultural change and socio-political equality, there seemed to be three choices. The first of these involved eliciting transformation from within by a process of personal awakening. Through education and the internalization of alternative methods of self-definition and stabilization, it was believed a cultural shift could be enacted one individual at a time. Texts including *I'm Okay—You're Okay*[17] and other such self-help manuals by authors like Nancy Friday, who focused on female sexuality over more general self-improvement, assisted in this road to awakening.

The second process also involved instigating change from within through the formulation of legislation. This was guided by activists and organizations including civil rights leaders like Martin Luther King, Jr.

and groups like the Southern Christian Leadership Conference, which fought for racial rights. This also included activists such as Betty Friedan and organizations like the National Organization for Women that fought for women's equality more specifically.

Whereas the aforementioned methodologies may be regarded as being more conservative due to their inspiring change from within, the final strategy may be considered to be more radical, involving not merely a call for equality, but in fact a holistic rejection of the system that was regarded as being unjust. Separatists saw the road to equality as not being paved by reforms to existing social norms, but instead through repudiating old, traditional ones and starting anew. This was a road forged by activists including Malcolm X (at least in his earlier years) and the Black Panthers, who would fight for African American rights by any means necessary. This also included Shulamith Firestone and the Women's Liberation Front, which, according to its website, was composed of:

> Unapologetically radical feminists. Dedicated to the total liberation of women. WoLF is a radical feminist organization dedicated to the total liberation of women. We fight to end male violence, regain reproductive sovereignty, and ultimately dismantle the gender-caste system.[18]

With these choices in mind, it would appear, at least on the surface, as if the first film to be discussed in this chapter, *Season of the Witch*, opts for change from within. The main character, Joan Mitchell, the titular *Jack's Wife*, attempts to enact personal change, and this transformation, in turn, is allowed to resonate within her middle-class suburban community, affecting all who come in contact with her. Through adopting a position of empowerment, achieved through an affiliation to a coven of witches, as was discussed above, she succeeds in changing perspectives one individual at a time. In other words, their enlightenment is not driven toward bringing down patriarchy and social order, but instead toward creating an enlightened place of equality from within this society.[19] The second text, *Harvest Home* and its adaptation *The Dark Secret of Harvest Home*, on the other hand, seeks solutions by forming an isolated community wherein, under the guise of literally and spiritually returning to nature, a more female-centric ethos could be adopted alongside and not within society. Likewise, this model involves destroying patriarchy by destroying any male who might gain power by witnessing what the narrative suggests to be "what no man may see nor woman tell."[20] Those who do witness in this narrative universe pay the ultimate price, castration: to be robbed of the male gaze and thus male power. Indeed, whether from an internal or external perspective, these two texts, like the larger civil rights movement in which feminism grew and flourished, appear to turn the traditional establishment on its head from within and from without. However, as will be discussed below, the transformative drive presented in *Season of the Witch*, *The Dark Secret of Harvest Home* and *Harvest Home* in all cases is more complex than it appears. In neither the film, the teleplay, nor the novel do these female-centric communities attempt a radical overthrow of contemporary culture, as is the case with *Rosemary's Baby* and *The Omen*. Rather than bringing about an apocalypse, *Season of the Witch* calls for a magnified personal transformation. Likewise, in [*The Dark Secret*] of *Harvest Home*, there is no desire to transform the community at large whatsoever, which is why they must live apart. In this way [*The Dark Secret*] of *Harvest Home*'s Cornwall Coombe and *The Wicker Man*'s Summerisle are alike, functioning as alternative societies established apart from the mainstream through the adoption of an alternative faith. Indeed, the only films that call for a radical overthrow of society are not the Pagan Horror films discussed in this section, but the Satanist films which are analyzed in the previous section. *Rosemary's Baby* and *The Omen* are set up, like the religion that they revere, in antagonism to social norms, while the Pagan Horror works, like Paganism itself, do not challenge their Christian other, but coexists alongside it or secretly within it as a more empowered separate but equal faith.

Season of the Witch and the Role of Spiritual Affiliation and Belief for Sustaining Self-Agency

In *Season of the Witch*, debates of the era regarding feminism, modernity, spiritual affiliation and a break from tradition are articulated as *Jack's Wife* undergoes a sexual and spiritual awakening that frees her from what is regarded by the film to be the confining and punitive socio-cultural conditions of her middle-class suburban milieu. This thematic concern is reiterated throughout the film as Jack Mitchell chides "his Joanie." Early on as he prepares for work, and then later when Joan wakes from a nightmare, Jack scolds her for her wakefulness, telling her repeatedly to go back to sleep. However, ironically, it is during this state of unconsciousness that Joan becomes aware of her hidden and repressed desires. In other words, Jack desires her to sleep, but it is through this sleep she is awakened.

As Freud suggests in *The Interpretation of Dreams*,[21] dreams act as manifestations of unconscious wish fulfillments, giving voice to latent desires that cannot be fulfilled during wakefulness. This lack of fulfillment usually derives from repression in the form of internalized social mores. Feminists would argue that one of the chief forms of repression comes from systems of socio-political patriarchy which deny women equality by forcing them into roles of privatized subservience: wife, mother, homemaker. It is of this subservience that Joan dreams. In turn, in becoming consciously aware of her dreams, she makes the repression manifest. In this way, she embarks on a journey to enlightenment.

The opening of *Season of the Witch* is an extended dream sequence. She is pictured walking behind her husband, following and serving him while he ignores her, completely focused instead upon his morning paper. She passes her daughter, a baby, and herself in a swing, suggesting that not only is she subsumed with the role of wife and mother, but that by adopting this role she has made herself powerless—childlike herself. As she continues to follow Jack, he passes a series of trees. In clearing the way for himself, he flicks the branches upon her. This switching of his wife acts as a reference to the rule of thumb. This law, which at one time was thought to exist, gave allowances for a man to beat his wife as long as the stick was not bigger than his thumb. Jack's inadvertent beating of his wife is, for the purposes of the film, culturally condoned as an allowable punitive measure and thus accepted by Joan. Bloodied, she continues to follow her husband quietly. The ubiquitous physical and psychological male domination of this character is solidified as her husband, upon becoming aware of her, attaches a leash around her neck and forces her into a kennel cage held open by her male psychoanalyst. Indeed, she is not viewed as a person, but instead as just another and potentially more useful "man's best friend," a role that is in fact encouraged by her psychotherapist. Her fears of getting old, ceasing to be able to serve her husband both sexually and otherwise, and of being ignored are all results of a lack of a strong sense of self-agency, a lack that is, apparently, not addressed in her therapy sessions. The dream ends with her looking into a mirror, wherein she appears as a crone. Like most dream symbols, this final image is overdetermined. On the one hand, the image of the crone suggests Joan's fear of age and of being rendered unattractive and thus no longer valuable as a cultural commodity. On the other hand, the crone stands for one of the three persons in the triune goddess, the foundation of the Wicca faith that she will come to adopt. The crone thus represents the best and worst outcomes presented to this character: complete worthlessness and complete dominance. Upon awakening and remembering the dream, Joan starts her journey toward empowerment, for recognizing repression is the first stage in its obliteration. The second stage, psychoanalytically speaking, involves working through, or bringing repressed unconscious material to the light of day through discussion.

The material revealed in this dream, insecurities about agency and value are indeed held not only by Joan, but also by her friends. As she speaks to her closest comrade, Shirley, Joan learns that she is not alone in her fear of growing old, but instead a member of a community of like-minded individuals who share this anxiety. Shirley admits that she dreads being past her prime, at a time when "she is not done yet." Once revealed, this enlargement of concern from personal to societal furthers the era's feminist debates with regard to female agency being isolated and confined to the private sphere. Their experience is beyond the knowledge and understanding of males, who live in the public sphere, who read newspapers, go to work and take their wives for granted. At the same time, their experiences are common to most women who are relegated to the domestic space, hidden from view, and beholden to the repressive mechanisms of patriarchy that keep them subjugated. Indeed, in a trailer for the film, at the time entitled *Hungry Wives*, the female narrator suggests of the narrative universe:

> On a diet of men, everything women would want out of a marriage, except the one thing they crave most: Joan, available; Shirley, drowning her problems in drink; Marion, dabbling in witchcraft. They are all hungry wives. With an appetite for diversion, gambling with life and death, hungry wives lead normal lives, or do they? What goes on while their husbands are at work?[22]

While facing these concerns regarding the demonization of an active female agency born out of a traditional view of women, Joan's teenage daughter, who comes of age in the late 1960s and early 1970s, acts as a character foil for the middle-aged women in the film. Unlike her mother, Nikki openly breaks moral boundaries not only through her overt sexual promiscuity, but equally in her desire to continue to fornicate while at the same time remaining unbound to obligatory matrimony. What is interesting within the narrative is that when Nikki disappears halfway through the film, Joan comes to assume her role as a foil to traditionalism.

Joan's quest to become, in the words of film director George Romero, a "complete member of society,"[23] is, in fact, finally achieved through her becoming affiliated to an alternative neo–Pagan Wicca religion, namely Witchcraft. In the world of the film, this seems to be a religion that aligns a concern with efficacious feminine subjectivity with an equal need for effective and female-centered spiritual connectivity. Although in one interview, Romero denies an overarching concern with religion, there are many indicators that suggest otherwise, especially as the director equally concedes that much of what happens in the film-making process is instinctual and/or unintentional. Indeed, elsewhere, Romero discusses how while he was working for public television in Pittsburgh, he not only became aware of the feminist movement, which challenged the efficacy of patriarchal social positioning, but also became interested in exploring the occult at a time when traditional spiritual affiliation was also involved in cultural debate. The filmmaker discusses his views on modern spiritual connectivity when he suggests in an interview with Tony Williams:

> What's the point of just going to church every Sunday? In our neighbour-hood, we live near this Presbyterian Church and I don't think there's any sort of mystical thought going through anybody's head. They're all out there looking at each other and seeing how they're dressed and doing what they need to do to get into heaven by showing up every Sunday.[24]

Within *Season of the Witch*, traditional religion is compared and contrasted with alternative faiths as Joan moves from an alignment with Catholicism to an embrace of Wicca.

Traditional versus Alternative Religion in *Season of the Witch*

After meeting a witch, Joan begins to question the efficacy of the faith to which she adheres in the same way that she has come to question the restrictive patriarchal roles to which she has been forced to abide. This internal struggle of faith is magnified by the community around her. First, it is presented through the actions of her daughter involving sexual awakening and the failure of traditionalism. Then it is revealed through conversations between Joan and her friend, Shirley, involving the necessity of a self-sustaining belief.

Although Joan and Jack Mitchell are both practicing Catholics (at least at the beginning of the film), their daughter is most assuredly not. This lack of belief is confirmed by her promiscuous sexuality. As suggested by Daniel Bell and Hugh McLeod, one of the failings of the Church in the age of modernity has been the inability to pass on belief between generations, and this is certainly the case in *Season of the Witch*. To follow religion means to follow its rules and strictures, and if the Ten Commandments set out the primary laws of Christianity, then Nikki Mitchell has sinned in spades by not honoring her mother and her father, and committing adultery, an action that involves sexual intercourse with anyone outside of the covenant of marriage. While practicing Christianity, Joan is forced to remain in an unfulfilling marriage and to be subservient to her husband. Nikki, however, feels free to gratify herself sexually. While also a product of a Catholic upbringing, its mores are not internalized by the daughter inasmuch as they were by the mother. However, while being actualized sextually, Nikki is still not fully realized as an empowered woman. This is due to her sense of isolation.

Throughout the film, Nikki is only pictured with her mother, a repressed middle-aged woman, and Gregg, her casual sexual partner. Although connected physically with both (her mother through lineage, and Gregg through the sexual act), she is equally emotionally divorced from both. She does not communicate with her mother, nor does she share her feelings with Gregg. This is evidenced by Joan and Gregg's incomprehension of her leaving. No one knows where she has gone or why. However, when she disappears, she creates a vacuum that is taken up by Joan, who does so only more successfully. In other words, Joan not only questions and eventually abandons her restrictive patriarchal positioning, but she does so amongst a community of women who strengthen and validate her new identity. It is through this collective engagement that Joan's quest is rendered efficacious.

Also unlike Nikki, Joan achieves awareness incrementally and with full knowledge. While Nikki is born into her role, Joan must fight to achieve it. The first step in this process involves thought. As Joan begins to question her subject position spiritually and socially, she does so clandestinely. Even though this questioning of faith and its tenets is conducted internally, in dreams and conversations, it is initially not acted upon. The second step toward actualization comes in her working though this internal struggle with discourse. When the protagonist finally does admit that she has considered engaging in sex outside her marriage to her friend Shirley, she veils this by equally suggesting that it is an interest that is merely academic and will not ever be actualized. Her friend retorts, "You're a Catholic, sweetie. Isn't *academic* just as bad as doing it for you people?"[25] Indeed, according to a Christian penitential prayer, sin takes place in thought, word and deed, by what one has done, or by what one has failed to do. In this way, traditional faith is articulated as being impossibly restrictive, and Joan only realizes this through an interaction with someone close to her. Once given a voice and thus made manifest, Joan moves on to the third step in her road to freedom: action. It is only after relinquishing her Catholic upbringing and beginning to practice a faith that emboldens her that Joan herself becomes free to explore her sexuality and her selfhood amongst a community of women who not only share her fears and desires but are not afraid to act upon them without guilt or the fear of retribution.

As Joan increasingly goes through this process of enlightenment, she breaks such constraints by opening herself up to Witchcraft as a viable form of alternative religion, and it is this acceptance that leads her to experience sexual gratification. After borrowing and reading from a primer from Marion, the local witch and soothsayer, Joan decides that she will explore this faith in greater depth. While her husband is at work, Jack's wife makes a pilgrimage into the city to buy the paraphernalia that is associated with occult practices.[26] This is the only time within the narrative when she is seen to leave the confines of her suburban universe, for it is only within a modern urban environment that she may be allowed, initially, to explore alternatives to traditionalism in relative anonymity.[27] Returning late in the afternoon, she takes out her small cauldron, candles, incense and other implements, and begins her first ritual.

Once enacted, her empowerment is fully underway. The last step is to embrace this new belief outwardly and to everyone. Witchcraft is alluring and all-encompassing for Joan. Indeed, she is so involved that she forgets the time, and her duties as a mother, as a wife and as a Catholic, roles by which she is defined within her suburban community. As she hears her husband approach, however, she feels the need to hide her foray into this new faith. She just has time to put away her purchases, and to reach into the fireplace to smear ashes on her forehead. This is an outward signifier of Christianity, a tradition whereby on Ash Wednesday one receives the ashes that mark the beginning of Lent, the coming of Good Friday, the death of Christ on the cross and the salvation of the human race. However, while Catholic on the surface, she no longer holds this faith internally. The ashes have not been blessed, and thus she is not internally affected by their sign. Her fatigued and irritable husband enters, and upon seeing her with the mark of the ashes, realizes that he has also forgotten this traditional religious observance. Complaining at having to go to church, he comments, "Well gotta get some ashes. Jesus, I hope that church isn't too crowded."[28]

Indeed, traditional religion appears to have lost its efficacy, being a practice that is not believed, but merely observed outwardly, a trope that was also discussed in relation to Joan's acceptance of her role as a traditional wife and mother. With regard to larger socio-cultural concerns, this scene is an example of two of the debates described above: on the one hand, the need to maintain an outward sign of belonging to the status quo, and on the other, a failure to believe in such social expectations, a rejection that increasingly entered into the public forum during this period.

While Catholicism is thus figured at best as an ineffectual religion and at worst as a stultifying one, Witchcraft is positioned as its opposite, thus establishing another theoretical textual dichotomy. Unlike Catholicism, Witchcraft is articulated as not only being efficacious, but also self-sustaining, and thus worthy of adherence. Indeed, it is female dominated, allowing for a certain freedom of expression that up until this time was disallowed Joan and the other wives of the community. An example of the feminine potential of Witchcraft lies in the genealogical connectivity of this system of belief. While orthodox historical underpinnings for familial and religious connectivity run patrilineally, in the case of Witchcraft, the lines of historical spiritual affiliation are matrilineal in nature, and thus more feminist and female-centric. This is suggested by a quotation voiced by Marion, the film's Wicca practitioner, who suggests:

> It's a religion, really. My mother was a witch and her father belonged. And in today's age where anything goes, people are beginning to take it seriously. Everyone knows there's something out there that we haven't got the power to define.[29]

Equally, the practice yields results. When it is called upon, things happen, even if these results are merely conferring license toward action, another element that is equally denied Joan as a Catholic. In fact, when Joan once again meets with the leader of the coven, this time with the intention of joining, the witch comments, "I thought you were intrigued by it when you were so afraid. Being afraid is necessary for believing."[30] To this Joan replies, "I know that it is real, that it works. I've actually caused things to happen." The Wiccan responds, "It isn't a question of interest. It is a question of knowing, believing."[31]

It is this efficacy, guaranteed by belief, that is also discussed by Joan, her soon-to-be lover, Gregg Williamson, and proved, although unwittingly, by Joan's friend Shirley. In another scene from the film, the group is sitting in the Mitchell living room discussing whether or not occult practice could be used as a means of self-fulfillment. Williamson argues that the only thing really necessary for the practice of any faith is acceptance. Joan questions this, challenging Gregg by suggesting if she were a witch, would her conjuring work simply because she believed it would? Gregg is skeptical, and with this doubt in mind, he conducts an experiment with regard to the power of belief. While Shirley is out of the room, Williamson takes a cigarette, rips off the filter and rolls it up to resemble a marijuana joint. When Shirley returns, Gregg offers her a hit. As she smokes it, Shirley really believes that she is getting high, as is revealed through her speech and actions. Although this experiment is not related directly to spirituality within the universe of *Season of the Witch*, it nonetheless proves the adage that belief is key.

In another scene from the film, the potential of Witchcraft to offer an empowering belief system is made manifest. Joan uses Witchcraft to conjure Gregg for sexual purposes. This is a reversal from an earlier scene, wherein Gregg dominates. Joan first desires information from Williamson about her missing daughter and goes to his classroom to obtain it. Gregg stands at the head of the class behind a lectern, while Joan hovers between the student desks. Although insistent about learning all Gregg knows about her daughter's disappearance, Gregg offers nothing. He, as the teacher, is in control of the dissemination of information—he has the power. However, once she becomes a witch, this dynamic reverses itself. After performing a ritual, whereby she calls upon Williamson to accomplish her will, she prepares herself for the meeting. After waiting for hours, she finally phones him and requests his company for the evening. Because she is convinced that the ritual will yield results, she is equally confident that he will not deny her, and when he does agree, she credits Witchcraft with the result. Even if it is unclear as to whether or not her ritual had any effect within the world of the film, like in *Eye of the Devil, Day of the Arrow, Robin Redbreast*, and *The Wicker Man*, all that is necessary is that the efficacy of the religious practice is believed by the practitioner, unquestionably. Regardless, he now does her bidding—it is she and not he who is in control. In other words, Catholicism is portrayed as having lost the power not only to establish and sustain belief in forces outside the self, but equally to provide an effective moral action with mechanism of identity-building. At the same time, however, there seems to exist a call for these very mechanisms of self-bolstering by the culture that derided traditional religion at this historical moment. It is through these thematic concerns that *Season of the Witch* reveals and disseminates debates that circulated during this era of the late 1960s and early 1970s with regard to a breakdown of traditionalism and the orthodox religion that supported it.

Hungry Wives: Season of the Witch and the Actualization of Sexual Awakening

In addition to an opening up of the power of spiritual connectivity for the establishment of female selfhood, *Season of the Witch* opens up the possibility of a sexual awakening as well. This is especially significant as the main mechanism of what was considered repressive morality by modernity was associated with traditional religion, which holistically denied the possibility of sexual exploration outside of the realm of marriage. Once married, the man and the woman become as one, joined by an edict from God. Not only could they not be separated, but they were also seen as belonging to one another, body and soul. The married couple were thus prohibited from engaging in sexual intercourse with anyone else "as long as they both shall live." In addition to sexual exclusivity, the giving of the self must be complete: to block the sperm is also seen as enacting a separation. The woman in Catholic marriage not only promises to be faithful to her husband, but open to life. This ties her to her husband even more so, as the natural outcome of such a promise is a large family of children that the woman could not support alone, even if divorce were an option. However, in the film, as in the larger culture, religious orthodoxy has come to lose its function as a cultural curb, as discussed earlier in relation to *Rosemary's Baby*. Additionally, as presented in *Rosemary's Baby*, alternatives to religion resulted in alternative lifestyles configured around other mechanisms for self-identification and grounding. These include commodification and political engagement, to name a few. However, as discussed in the previous chapters, to believe in these—or, indeed, to hold no belief at all—was a trait common to modernity, and modernity often resulted in a loss of self-assurance inasmuch as it promised freedom. What has been argued in all the works discussed in this book and has been a common theme in all the Faith Horror films of the late 1960s and 1970s is that it is only through membership in a community of like-minded believers who hold faith in mechanisms outside the self that the self itself can be sustained. This is also a concern of *Season of the Witch*.

This is referenced through the narrative in which the protagonist, Joan, transforms from *Jack's Wife* to an independent and sexually aware witch—a fact that she admits at the end of the narrative. Indeed, during the penultimate scene from the film, Joan is naked and surrounded by a coven of witches. She desires to become a member, and after undergoing a ritual wherein she must ask admittance, allow for each part of her anatomy to be blessed, and then be led into the circle on the end of a symbolic rope, she is granted her wish. In a bookend to the opening scene, a dream that gives voice to her passivity, she is now an active agent, in control of her anatomy, and being led on a leash not to male subjugation, but to female empowerment. She is in control of her body and her destiny as a result of being indoctrinated into a community of believers. She has now taken the final step—she is a witch both outwardly and inwardly, as is revealed by her admitting to this religious affiliation at a social gathering, as described in the opening of this chapter. As a member of a religious community, she is not only effective and powerful, but also unafraid to stand for what she believes in.

However, as has almost always been the case, it is this concern with faith that has been ignored by the contemporaneous reception of these works. This is evident in a review published in the *New York Times*, wherein film critic Vincent Canby suggests of the film:

> *Hungry Wives* has the seedy look of a porn film, but without any of the pornographic action. Everything in it, from the actors to the props, looks borrowed and badly used.... The woman frequently drifts into low budget fantasies that are even more drab than her real-life experiences. These should drive her to the brink of sanity, but they don't.[32]

Thus, the critical reception, while not concerned with the religious depictions of *Season of the Witch*,[33] nonetheless recognizes other elements that make this film a socio-cultural challenge, namely the reference to an opening up of freedom of sexual expression in the cinema. It is significant to note that only one year before *Season of the Witch*, the pornographic film became arguably more socially acceptable following the release of *Deep Throat*.[34] Indeed, this theme regarding depicting a sexual awakening that, up until this point, had been associated with pornography is redoubled in the aesthetics of *Season of the Witch* in likewise being a low budget picture—a fact that Romero himself lamented with regard to production limitations. However, with actors that are at best semi-professional, muted color, and sets and props from real-world locations rather than being made specifically for the film, this work challenges the status quo of Hollywood filmmaking, a media production model not only with its own strict morality, but also its own internal prejudices. Hollywood mainstream film is indeed predominantly a male-centered, morally traditional discourse. This lack of a façade of "legitimacy" could in fact suggest that these mores are restricting, futile and unfulfilling from a creative standpoint as well. However, rather than regarding these divergences as being positive indicators of social subversion on the part of a director known for his sardonic approach to filmmaking, the thematic and aesthetic concerns of *Season of the Witch* are seen at face value and thus discredited as being amateurish and ineffectual.

Extratextual Considerations of *Season of the Witch*

Even though the narrative centers on Joan and her increasing acceptance of this female-empowering faith mechanism, those around her do not equally accept the necessity of faith as a tool for grounding, which may be why they are not awakened in the same way as Joan. Herein a final dichotomy is established between those who believe and those who do not. Clearly, Joan is isolated in a family of unbelievers, as discussed above, but this skepticism infiltrates all those around her as well, with the exception, of course, of those members of the coven to which she will belong. Indeed, her friend Shirley does not seem wholly convinced of the inherent power of Witchcraft, possibly because she herself does not believe in any religion whatsoever. Although she goes to Marion, the witch, for a tarot card reading, she does not accept the faith that allows for this potential for second sight. Shirley, in fact, divorces this practice from the real world by linking it to fictional depictions of Witchcraft. She describes what will become known as a viable "kind of religion" as "the whole *Bell Book and Candle* routine," and equally dismisses the fear experienced by her friend with yet another intertextual reference: "If the mousse tastes chalky don't eat it. You know the *Rosemary's Baby* bit." These references, while on the surface suggesting a lack of belief on the part of Shirley, also on an extratextual level, suggest the centrality of alternative religious practice for this narrative, a fact that Romero himself alludes to when he argues, "You can feel when borrowing is intentional because it's very distinct, very accurate." Indeed, although the two films referenced in *Season of the Witch, Bell Book and Candle* and *Rosemary's Baby*, are essentially diverse in terms of their genre and tone, they nonetheless share a central focus with the occult and its effect upon women, which is equally a concern with this film as well.

During its production distribution span, this film boasted several titles. During production, the film was referred to as *Jack's Wife*, a title that the film's director himself had chosen for this project and which he regarded as being one that suggested the feminist nature of the film. However, disregarding the insistence of the creative mind behind this piece, the distribution company renamed the film at the time of its 1973 release and thus *Jack's Wife* became *Hungry Wives*, a title that production and distribution agents felt would be more marketable as it suggested and foregrounded textual and visual sexual undercurrents. Finally, *Season of the Witch*, by which the film is now referred, was conferred when re-released following the success of *The Crazies*, a film that Romero himself considers as having a more artistic and popular cache. The change in the final title seems to trade less upon the ideas offered up within the film itself and instead connects more firmly to the contemporaneous culture out of which the work was rooted. First, the song that shares a name with the film, *Season of the Witch*, was first released by British pop icon Donovan in 1966, and although never released as a single, achieved a degree of popularity that continues to the present day and might very well be one of his most recognized songs. This same version was also featured in the film, a backdrop to the protagonist's foray into the city to purchase items which she will use in her rituals.

It may also be interesting to note, as was also alluded to earlier in the first chapter's discussion of *Rosemary's Baby*, that at this time, a situation comedy entitled *Bewitched*, which aired from 1964 until 1972 on the American television network ABC, also dealt with similar themes involving a witch who had to assimilate into a suburban lifestyle. However, whereas *Season of the Witch* attempted to address feminist concerns such as an attempt to break free of patriarchal entrapment and the desire to achieve sexual fulfillment, *Bewitched* seemed to conform more readily to existing socio-political norms—more specifically, those surrounding the establishment and maintenance of nuclear families and the reinforcement of traditional gender roles, given the fact that the husband remained the primary breadwinner while the wife, Samantha the Witch, remained a housewife.

As has been argued above, *Season of the Witch* could be considered to engage with textual debates regarding female empowerment as Joan navigates a road from complete subservience to patriarchy to absolute rejection of traditionalism. Further, in enacting this transformation from within culture, this film engages with one method of social reform wherein subjects elicit change while not divorcing themselves completely from the community. This is not, however, the only way in which female empowerment can occur. As will be seen with *The Dark Secret of Harvest Home* and the novel *Harvest Home*, another road toward this result comes not by modifying culture from within but instead by stepping outside of it.

The Dark Secret of Harvest Home: The Role of Traditionalism for Belief

In the final scene of *The Dark Secret of Harvest Home*, the male protagonist, an artist and photographer, becomes completely emasculated, absolutely robbed of discursive agency. Indeed, while the story, up until this point, is told through his eyes, at the end of the film, if not in the novel, he is talked about rather than actively engaged in the storytelling process. Alternatively, his wife, now in a position of apparent control, preparing to leave their house, enters the room where her husband is seated off-camera. She sets down his lunch on a tray near his chair and puts the needle on a phonograph album. Significantly, another narrator begins to speak through the hi-fi system, telling his own tale in a proto-recorded book. As his wife bends to kiss him goodbye, he is revealed for the first time in this scene, shown to be inert, unresponsive and wearing dark glasses. Although not directly stated, connections are drawn between Nick Constantine and others who, throughout the narrative, have in one way or another incurred the wrath of the women of the isolated community in which the film and novel are set. As an artist who relies upon his sight for inspiration and for his profession, he has been castrated. As a man who is not able to actively engage, he is rendered impotent.

The fact that this character's blinding and muting is enacted by a powerful female agency ties into contemporaneous cultural debates with regard to socio-political feminism and feminist film theory forwarded by authors such as Laura Mulvey[35] and Mary Ann Doane,[36] both of whom questioned the efficacy of female agency within a filmmaking process crafted by and inherently positioned for a male subject. Indeed, within feminist film studies patriarchy is regarded as being restrictive and repressive both to the individual and to the culture that (s)he inhabits. In challenging this traditional ethos, this film and its philosophical presuppositions very much fall in line with the countercultural movement, and the contemporaneous feminist debate overall.

It is these concerns regarding inverted gender positioning that will be discussed in a work that had a larger potential audience than any of the works discussed thus far, since it was aired on national American television. Indeed, *The Dark Secret of Harvest Home* may be read as relying upon similar feminist debates involving a strengthening of feminine subjectivity enacted through a rejection of phallocentric traditionalism and an adoption of alternative religious connections such as Witchcraft and Paganism, while at the same time offering up an almost antithetical thematic concern to mainstream traditionalism. All of this is enacted within an essentially mainstream forum.

Once again, like in *Season of the Witch* and *Rosemary's Baby*, certain dichotomies arise, including the old versus the new, the country versus the city, and faith versus a lack of belief. In this case, the former dichotomy is privileged, while the feminine equally comes to dominate over the masculine. This reversal of traditionalism, in turn, opens up connectivity to an archaic universe that excludes itself from its contemporary social and political milieu, enacting a change from without as opposed to from within. Further, in rendering femininity as being efficacious, *The Dark Secret of Harvest Home* and *Harvest Home* alike diverge from the Frazerian Pagan communities seen in *Robin Redbreast, Eye of the Devil, Day of the Arrow* and *The Wicker Man*. Indeed, it could be argued that the titular "dark secret" involves the extent to which this foregrounding of feminine agency exists within this antiquated and isolated community that literally and figuratively castrates men who challenge female dominance.

The Urban, the Rural and the Effect of Modernity

As with the other texts in this section, the opening of *The Dark Secret of Harvest Home* is initially set within an urban landscape,[37] and like in the narratives analyzed herein (with the possible exception of *Eye of the Devil* and *Day of the Arrow*), this modern world is not a happy or fulfilling environment. The teleplay centers on a nuclear family, the Constantines, who, at the beginning of the narrative, reside in New York City. At the opening, Nick, the husband and father, is introduced as having deep regrets regarding an extramarital affair, to which he has recently confessed. The wife and mother, Beth, is sexually frigid as a result of her husband's indiscretion. Finally, the daughter, Kate, lives in fear as a result of a local gang that extorts money in order to grant permission to walk down the very street on which she lives, which induces a panic that results in debilitating asthma. These scenes of physical, moral and spiritual urban blight are intercut with scenes of an agrarian landscape. In what will be revealed to be Cornwall Coombe, the community works together for a common purpose. Husband supports wife, neighbor aids neighbor, and all is encouraged by a nurturing mother figure who bestows praise and guidance. These two worlds meet when, after attending the funeral of Beth's father, a conservative Puritan minister, the Constantine family happens upon a covered bridge that leads them to, essentially, another world. Set up in diametric opposition to the life experienced by the family in New York City, the inhabitants of the village across the "Lost Whistle Bridge" are connected to the land, to their own traditions and to a sense of community that sustains them.

This connectivity extends not only to this isolated community, but also to historical presuppositions regarding the efficacy of familial legacy, ties that bind this community to the past and to each other. While Beth and Nick, initially indicative of an ethos of modernity, stand in antagonism to past generations which dominated their lives to their overall detriment, in Cornwall Coombe, familial history is revered and held close. This is evidenced in a local cemetery, where the headstones tell the story of a collective past centering on generational imperatives. Every grave seems to hold the name of Penrose dating as far back as the foundation of the nation itself. This reverence of the past extends not only to a reverence for family heritage, but also to bygone traditions.

Not unlike the Amish, the locals are antiquated in dress and technology, preferring to use old machinery to till the land, as had their fathers and forefathers. When asked, one member suggests that this shared belief regarding hand tools fosters a sense of the communal and establishes a greater connection to the land. He states that the seeding of the soil is in fact an act of love and must be done by hand for this very reason. These methods are "the ways" to which they all adhere both happily and unquestioningly.

In these ways, Cornwall Coombe lies apart both physically and philosophically, and this apparent separation, at least initially, has a positive effect on the family. Nick, once forced by an antagonistic father-in-law to take a job as an advertising cartoonist to assume financial support of his wife, once in the Coombe begins to adopt his trained role as an artist. He takes photographs of the landscape and its residents, which he uses to sketch scenes of rural life. The family explores the countryside together, laughing and joking around. Their environment is contagious, and if it is unified and unifying, then, for once, so are they. Realizing the change that is taking place, the family inquires as to whether or not the vacant house they discover is for sale. In turn, they are informed that the property is owned by village matriarch Widow Fortune, who is not likely to sell to anyone outside the community. Downhearted, they leave after giving their phone numbers to a local couple who will speak to the Widow on their behalf. Upon returning to New York, the effect of the community of Cornwall Coombe upon this urban family does not altogether dissipate. Beth continues to discuss her infatuation with her therapist. Nick pitches a publication idea to the agency for which he works—a coffee table book composed of drawings of the antiquated country life. In the meantime, the matriarch of Cornwall Coombe, who has been orchestrating everything behind the scenes, grants permission for the Constantines to purchase the house. She suggests to the Coombe residents that the house has chosen them and thus so should they. After receiving a call informing the urbanites that the rural home is theirs should they still want it, it seems as if their fate is sealed and a return to an agrarian lifestyle eminent. Once they arrive, the change is altogether positive. Unlike in *Rosemary's Baby*, wherein Rosemary alone is tasked with the remodel of the family's domestic space, the Constantines continue to function as a team while refurbishing the house, painting the exterior wood of the house white, much like Rosemary oversaw in the earlier film. Once installed, the calm and serene rural life begins to dominate, Beth foregoes any further marriage therapy sessions, and Kate has lost any of the fears she once possessed. Indeed, it seems as if the country air is good for what ails you with regard to modernity.

The Dark Secret of Harvest Home: Cornwall Coombe, Community and the Role of Tradition

However, not everything is as idyllic as it appears on the surface, for, like the contrast between the urban and the rural that opens the teleplay, there is equally conflict within Cornwall Coombe between tradition and modernity. Although the traditions, the "ways" by which the community functions, are irrefutable and ingrained, leading to a definite desire (like in *The Wicker Man*) to live absolutely apart, this separateness is not regarded by everyone in the community as a positive. This is first evidenced by Worthy, the local paper boy, who, in function as well in philosophy represents the new, wants to bring technology to the community. This is a desire that is stopped dead in its tracks by the Widow, who argues, "Why would we want to improve things when everything is just the way we like it?"[38] Indeed, Widow Fortune is regarded not only as a matriarch but also as a spiritual leader, doctor, teacher and counselor. Given her many specialties with both the physical and the psychological, there appears to be no reason to leave the Coombe, and to do so is, in fact, strongly discouraged. In this way, the teleplay is similar to the other Pagan cycle works, but indeed, unlike *Robin Redbreast*, *Eye of the Devil* and *The Wicker Man*, this closed, isolated spiritual community is ruled by a woman, a powerful leader and spiritual figurehead to which everyone is beholden. This role and the duty of women overall becomes clearer as the narrative develops and as the Cornwall Coombe annual cycle of festivals is revealed.

In the home purchased by the Constantines, there is a fireplace with a tiled mantelpiece detailing the various festivals celebrated by the community over the course of the year. The family arrived at the community on planting day, and indeed, this is the first celebration that they witness, one in which the earth is fertilized primarily by the males, who plant their seed in the soil in an act akin to human reproduction, a sexualized act of love. The next observance, Agnes Fair, is one in which the Harvest King is chosen. Although a male is picked for his strength, good looks and community spirit, he is chosen by a female—a young girl named Missy who is possessed with the gift of second sight. This is the first instance wherein it is revealed that while powerful, the Widow Fortune is not wholly dominant. Other festivals include the Day of Seasoning, essentially a church service not unlike Anglican harvest festivals, led first by the local male preacher and then, once the offerings are bestowed, by the Widow, who assumes his place at the altar. Even in this more traditional religious environment, that of the local parish church, it is she who receives the offerings as a spiritual representative.[39] Following these are: Tithing Day, Sheaving Tide, Husking Bee, and finally Corn Play, wherein the fertility of the earth is acted out by the Harvest Lord, the Corn Maiden (his female counterpart) and the children of the community. The ultimate festival, Harvest Home, however, is not only the most important, but the most female-oriented of them all.

As with the Day of Seasoning, this festival begins in the church and once again is led by Widow Fortune, with the community reverend present but not leading the observance. As night falls, the preacher is locked in a room in the church and the Widow passes out farming implements to the female residents. No males are in attendance. Each woman is also given a white robe with a hood to cover her face, thus instilling a sense of equality to all who participate by annihilating difference. The women are undifferentiated as they form a procession to the woods, chanting as they walk. Once they arrive in a remote spot, they form a circle with no one at the head, again alluding to the overall cyclical nature of these rites. The Harvest Lord is brought in blindfolded. His feet are anointed similar to the feet of Christ, the Harvest Lord's Christian counterpart. The Lord is presented to the Corn Maiden, and they engage in sexual intercourse on the earth, in a similar fashion to the community in *The Wicker Man* and for similar purpose: to infect the soil with fertility. At the culmination of the sexual act, the Harvest Lord is separated from the Maiden and beheaded by her using a scythe as a murder weapon. It is thus that he is sacrificed, while his blood, ostensibly like his seed, runs into the earth.

Although practiced with reverence by the female members of the community, Nick, like Worthy, like Constantine's blind male neighbor, have all come to question the ways of the community, and to in fact fight against them.

Nick sneaks into the field and witnesses the Harvest Home rite, seeing what no other man is allowed to witness and live. He not only sees the ritual, but also becomes aware of the fact that the Corn Maiden is in fact his wife, Beth. The screen goes blank as the female members of the community descend upon him. As he loses consciousness, he loses the ability to narrate and we, in turn are left in darkness. Indeed, the fate of Nick is uncertain and remains so until the final scene of the film. With the question as to what has become of Nick left temporarily unanswered, the culmination of the narrative begins with the rest of the family preparing for a picnic. Beth is pregnant, as a result of her coupling with the Harvest Lord and not as a result of sexual intercourse with her husband. Kate has been chosen as the new Corn Maiden and is obviously smitten with the new Lord, Jimmy Minerva. The Widow is there as well, happily interacting with the women in the kitchen of their home. Obviously, the Constantine females have completely adapted to (and in turn been totally adopted by) their community.

In the end, even though the protagonist and narrative storyteller may be regarded as being Nick, as it is through his eyes that the plot develops, at the end of *The Dark Secret of Harvest Home*, he is robbed of this agency. In being blinded and rendered speechless, having had his tongue cut out, he can no longer record or even express what happens around him. His extra-narrative function as storyteller ceases. In the same way, his narrative role as artist and recorder of village ritual is also taken from him. He no longer has agency to affect the world, and instead is isolated from the external world—as apart as Cornwall Coombe is from the modern world which surrounds it. He has been effectively castrated, robbed of his patriarchal agency and rendered complicit at last.

Harvest Home: The Novel and the Role of Religion, History and Feminine Connectivity

In the novel penned by Thomas Tryon, Ned Constantine is more directly revealed to be the central narrator, the point of view told in first person. With the exception of the name (Ned to Nick) and the point of view (first to third person), there are many similarities between the novel and its adaptation. The first of these is the narrative conflict between the modern and the traditional. In both versions of the text, this dichotomy is configured as, on the one hand, an acceptance of the efficacy of spiritual affiliation, and on the other, an inherent skepticism and disbelief that ultimately on both a literal and figurative level result in a loss of agency and a strong sense of self. Likewise, the embodiment of modernity rests with Ned/Nick, while the female characters stand for a tradition rooted in antiquity.

To begin, like in the teleplay, the traditions of Cornwall Coombe are articulated as being ingrained and spiritually motivated. The novel suggests: "There was a sense of veneration for that which had gone before, a rigid disciplined effort to preserve things as they were—even perhaps a reluctance to acknowledge things as they are."[40] Venerated in the community are the land and the "ways" which bestow Cornwall Coombe with fertile crops, a connection to history and a strong sense of community. Whereas this is common to all of the Pagan texts discussed in this section, including *Eye of the Devil, Day of the Arrow, Robin Redbreast* and *The Wicker Man*, unlike these, the village is run by a woman, which is another similarity between the novel and the teleplay. Indeed, although Ned may be regarded as the protagonist, it is the Widow that functions as the central character within the world of the narrative. In the novel, the Widow Fortune is described in the following way: "The Widow Fortune ... was the oldest inhabitant in Cornwall Coombe, a sort of matriarch whom all the villagers respected to the point of reverence."[41] If the land and the ways are revered as suggested above, it is the Widow who sustains them both, making her equally a figure of veneration. In fact, so strong is the role played by the Widow Fortune that upon reading the text, equally venerated Hollywood actress Bette Davis purportedly expressed a desire to portray her should the novel ever be made into a film. However, if the Widow Fortune is discernible as being in a position of power, narratively speaking, equally, the power that she wields (like the reasons behind it) are cloaked, at least until the end of the narrative, when all is made clear.

As in the teleplay, the traditions like the Widow herself are articulated as being ancient and historically entrenched. However, even though there is a separation between this narrative and those British co-productions such as *The Wicker Man, Eye of the Devil*, and *Robin Redbreast* in terms of gender positioning, nonetheless, the shared history between America and its motherland, England, is foregrounded in the novel, unlike in the teleplay, where this connection is alluded to but not clearly addressed. Tryon provides a connectivity between this textual community and their British roots, not only in terms of the name of the community, *Cornwall* Coombe, but also in terms of its shared history, a heritage as well as a shared belief in the supernatural that arose from a common Pagan past: "Most of the villagers ... were descended from farmers who had come from old Cornwall, in England more than three hundred years earlier, and the Cornishmen didn't live who wouldn't trust to charms and omens."[42] And again, later in the novel, with regard to the etymology of the word Coombe and Lost Whistle Bridge, this historical connection is again made manifest:

> It's an English word, Celtic actually.... Means a valley or a sort of hollow. I suppose it implies a certain remoteness, which we are given to hereabouts. There are a number of throwbacks around here, like certain of the names which have an ancient and venerable history. Take the "Lost Whistle Bridge," for instance, which is a corruption of Lostwithiel, one of the towns in old Cornwall.[43]

Thus, in the novel the bridge may be regarded as spanning not only space but equally time, something that is again alluded to but never directly articulated in the teleplay. Indeed, to cross the Lost Whistle Bridge is to cross from a modern world of isolation, discontinuity and loss, as is suggested above, and into a shared and collective British/ American history, an antiquated nature that defines Cornwall Coombe, and equally its pre-modern ethos in which history and tradition are revered. In other words, this nature as coming out of the past also results, as was discussed in the film, as being a rejection of the new, of the modern: "You get plenty of resistance around here to new ways.... Cornwall Coombe has always been a world unto itself."[44]

It is this opposition between the modern and the pre-modern, between historical tradition and a loss of the self-same defining mechanisms that can be located in both the literary and televised texts that make up [*The Dark Secret*] *of Harvest Home*. Although expressed differently, this is a common thread that binds the two texts, thematically speaking. Indeed, if this concern may be located in both works, then arising from this dichotomy is yet another common trope to these Faith Horror narratives, namely an acceptance of the power of spiritual connectivity. As is discussed elsewhere, there is a connection between the Pagan and the Christian, especially with regard to more antiquated beliefs such as those taken from the Old Testament. Indeed, Harvest Home itself quotes from the Bible: "Until I come and take you away to a land like your own land, a land of corn and wine, a land of bread and vineyards, a land of olive oil and of honey, that ye may live and not die."[45]

Another connection that binds faith has to do with ritual, and the meaning and significance behind these observances. This idea ties to *Eye of the Devil,* and thus to the importance of the sacrifice for the sake of the community, a shared belief in *The Wicker Man* and *Robin Redbreast* that is expressed here as well. All of these texts are ultimately concerned with (as Lord Summerisle suggests) the true meaning of sacrifice, and sacrifice forms the basis for not only Paganism, but equally for orthodox Christianity.

Indeed, to be Christian is to revere Christ who died on the cross, a sacrifice to propitiate the sins of humanity. However, whereas in Christianity, the sacrifice described in the New Testament is for the sins of the world, in *Harvest Home,* like in *Eye of the Devil, Robin Redbreast,* and *The Wicker Man,* sacrifice is practiced so as to ensure fertility, thus benefiting the harvest and those who live as a result of that which is sown. Thus, the Pagan and the Christian, like the American and English cultures in which they are practiced, have common roots, and do not necessarily exist in opposition. To return to the novel:

> When they came from Cornwall to the New World, the original settlers were a deeply religious sect.... They were forced to adapt to circumstances, to learn new ways in order to survive. But in learning the new, they refused to give up the old, a faith based on the moon and the stars and the tides, and on

ancient deities they could turn to for succor in time of stress.... They raised themselves up and prayed for help, but not in church, but in the fields, inviting the blessings of the old gods. And the gods answered them. The church and the law have learned that it's a lost cause trying to censure such beliefs. How can you hope to fight them, when it's proved that the old Cornishmen arrived here with the same gods the Indians already had?[46]

However, even while these two faiths may be argued to form an historical continuity wherein, like in *Eye of the Devil*, the Pagan is not forgotten, but instead rests hidden underneath the newer Christian faith, these two spiritual affiliations increasingly become regarded as being dichotomous, especially following the Reformation, wherein the supernatural element that was in many ways foundational to the Catholic Church was rent from practices of worship. It is this more modern form of religious observance, such as that found within Puritan sects, that is then contrasted with more antiquated forms of belief, and which, as is suggested elsewhere in this book, is more efficacious as a faith not only for stabilization of the self, but also for the building of a cohesive community. Ned suggests of his wife and her faith:

She had never been religious; she did not love her father. She had never experienced any warm stream of affection as a child.... In the Puritan ethic ... to be happy was by extension to be sinful, and until we met, I do not think Beth had ever been very happy.[47]

Indeed, like in *Season of the Witch*, these modern faiths are regarded as merely having a restrictive power without any ability to ground or cohere.

Conclusion

If the "ways" presented in *Harvest Home* and *The Dark Secret of Harvest Home* alike can be regarded to represent an alternative belief system that is rooted in spiritual connectivity and historical imperatives, as was argued above, then it may also be suggested that this faith is one that, like in *Season of the Witch* and unlike the rest of the films discussed in this section, is at center female-oriented. This is shown in the film not only through the casting of Bette Davis as the Widow Fortune, a powerful and venerable Hollywood actress assuming an equally reverential role, but also suggested in the narrative itself, as the women assume key positions within the community and the sole positions in the rituals that are shown to sustain the village. Admittedly, there are men allowed to take part in the female-centric rituals, just as they are allowed to take part in similar observances in *Eye of the Devil, Robin Redbreast* and *The Wicker Man*. However, in [*The Dark Secret*] *of Harvest Home*, the only male present is the Harvest Lord, whose sole role is to provide the blood that will nourish the land and restore fertility to the crops. Indeed in [*The Dark Secret*] *of Harvest Home* the male is sacrificed unknowingly if not unwillingly while the men in *Robin Redbreast* and *The Wicker Man* are unwitting sacrifices, and thus assume a less active and more passive role in the Pagan rituals.

Like the Paganism out of which the "ways" were formed, not only is the role of women ancient and connected to the soil, she equally comes to represent the earth in taking the role of the Earth Mother, an essentially feminine position that involves giving birth to the crops, and thus to life itself. The novel argues, "The Earth mother was older than Crete, older than Babylon or Egypt, as old as the dawn of time."[48] Thus, like the religion out of which this role was born, an ancient worship that predates all other faiths, so too can the female in a position of power equally predate the phallocentric culture that is currently in control of the modern universe. Indeed, it is suggested in the text that whereas men are currently in positions of power, this was not always the case, and certainly is not the case currently in the community known as Cornwall Coombe. To return to the novel: "There was something in her, a deeply ingrained sense of something primitive, of the Woman Eternal, who demanded to be served—not just between the legs, but to make man utterly subservient."[49] It is exactly this result that is enacted in the *Season of the Witch, The Dark Secret of Harvest Home,* and *Harvest Home*. As was suggested in the introduction to this chapter, traditional society is turned on its head as the male dominated culture becomes subservient to a female-centered society based on faith, ritual and community and grounded in an agency-building ethos.

Conclusions,
After-Thoughts and Legacies

The Conjuring, The Witch, Midsommar
and the Post-Millennial Faith Horror

> As I grew up, I had access to an 80,000 volume library and I read from that library extensively about religion, all the religions in the world and I was really an atheist at that point when we moved to the farm, but things began to happen in the house....—CAROLINE PERRON

> My Catholic faith is very, very important to me and still is today and that helped me to help others.—LORRAINE WARREN

In a scene from the second film in *The Conjuring* series, psychic investigator Lorraine Warren is comforting a victim of the paranormal whom she and her husband are trying to help. The young girl, Janet Hodgson, is being possessed by a ghost and, as a result, is suffering both emotional and physical distress. These feelings are not only a result of the visitation, however, but also because no one believes that her experiences are genuine. Warren, herself gifted with second sight and thus also prey to similar skepticism, commiserates with Janet. Lorraine recounts a story about visiting a hospital when she was the same age as the young girl. Whilst there, Warren witnessed an angel comforting a sick boy. She confesses that she told doctors, nurses, and even her own family about this encounter; however, no one believed her, either. Like Janet, only she herself was convinced that what she had seen was real. She goes on to relate to young Hodgson that even in the face of such a lack of support, it is important to open up and confide in others. This is demonstrably true, not only because failing to relate warnings from beyond could lead to another being hurt, but equally because the seer might also find someone who empathizes, who understands, who accepts. Lorraine tells Janet that she finally found someone who did come to have faith in her and her gifts. Janet asks what she did once she found this person, to which Warren replies that she married him. In this pivotal scene from *The Conjuring 2*, two things become clear. First, like in all of the films discussed in this book, the key necessity for individual efficacy is belief: to have faith in a higher power, to have the support of family and a community of shared believers, and finally to remain steadfast to both. The second thing that is made manifest is the fact that faith is under constant threat from an outside world of skepticism, which is why belief communities are essential.

Indeed, when focusing on the horror film of the post-millennial age, a shared concern with spiritual affiliation once again comes to light. Many American horror films of this time period, such as *Midsommar*, harken back to British and British-American co-productions of the late 1960s and 1970s as discussed throughout the second section of the book. These more contemporary films, like their antecedents, are set in remote villages wherein the community continues to adhere to ancient Pagan faiths rooted in rituals of propitiation. Also, like the earlier works, a conflict arises when the members of the contemporary world encroach upon these rural landscapes. The skeptical, rational urbanite, upon viewing the rites enacted to appease the gods, might very well regard these rituals as being abhorrent and attempt to arrest their practices, or at least to flee from those who practice them in fear for their lives. Thus, these later films, also like their progenitors, may be said not to be involved with a conflict of beliefs[1] so much as a conflict between faith and a lack thereof. Also, as has equally been suggested throughout *Faith Horror*, the era beginning in the late 1960s and continuing throughout the 1970s was undergoing a vast opening up, not only in terms of more traditional faiths such as Catholicism, but also more alternative faiths, the most radical of which being Satanism. Likewise, following the millennium, works of horror continue to debate the role, method and viability of allegiance to spiritual faith communities, both traditional and alternative. Through a focus on three horror films/film franchises of the present day, *The Conjuring* and *The Conjuring 2*, *The Witch* and *Midsommar*, what will be argued in this final chapter is that in post-millennial horror, there has been a return to a concern with religious debate. However, in the case of these more recent Faith Horrors, this resurgence is not only with regard to a conflict of belief versus skepticism, but also a resurgence of the confrontation of good versus evil, a trope of the classical horror narratives. What will thus be addressed in this concluding chapter is the extent to which these debates might be fostered by, on the one hand, radical changes taking place within the Catholic faith. On the other hand, this reworking of Faith Horror themes might, concomitantly, be due to an increased skepticism of more radical faiths, which may be a result of the increasing threat of terrorism perpetrated by religious extremists and a continued alignment of alternative faith with evil. Further, it will be shown, as was the case with earlier Faith Horrors, it is only with the support of institutions outside the self, whether it be family or spiritual community, that the narrative protagonists within these works become effica-

Impressions of *The Conjuring* and *Midsommar*.

cious. Likewise, when denied this connectivity, these same individuals are rendered impotent within a world that continues to be fraught.

Indeed, with the advent of post-postmodernity, culture saw the beginning of another apocalyptic concern. This time it is not as a result of a fictional overtaking of the world by Satan and his minions, as depicted in *Rosemary's Baby* and *The Omen*, but instead by scientific manmade means. In late June of 1988, climate change became a national issue as the result of testimony given by Dr. James Hansen, then director of NASA's Institute for Space Studies to the U.S. Senate Energy and Natural Resources Committee. According to an article published in the *New York Times*, Hansen stated:

> Global warming has reached a level such that we can ascribe with a high degree of confidence a cause-and-effect relationship between the greenhouse effect and observed warming.... In my opinion, the greenhouse effect has been detected, and it is changing our climate now.[2]

By the mid–1990s, the threat of a natural apocalypse became a well-publicized concern for subjects of post-postmodernity following increased legislation, news coverage and a popular documentary by United States presidential hopeful Al Gore entitled *An Inconvenient Truth*, which was released in 2006. By the 2010s, scientists undisputedly concluded that human contributions of greenhouse gases had a direct influence on the warming of the planet. While there were (and continue to be) groups of people who believe climate change is bogus, experts have nonetheless proven that there has been a growing amount of sea ice loss, accelerated sea level rise, and more intense heat waves in the twenty-first century, threatening a physical end to self and self-interest to add to the angst of a psychological one. Much like during the late 1960s when hippies enacted a return to and a reverence of nature to stave off what they believed to be the detrimental effects of mainstream consumer culture, life-affirming, nature-oriented, contemporary Wiccans typically not associated with apocalyptic visions (as discussed in the second section of this book) have now come to the fore expressing concerns about the lack of concern for Mother Earth that has resulted in this imminent catastrophe. "Wiccan Millenarianism," or "apocalyptic millenarianism," may be defined as a belief in an imminent cataclysmic destruction of society, history, and life. This apocalypse for these Wiccans will be enacted either through a divine supernatural agency, by wholly natural means, or as a result of a combination of the two. This end will be brought about by those who remain skeptical—those who, due to human ignorance, will usher in a total annihilation for all disbelievers. However, much as is the case with the rapture for adherents of the Christian faith, this apocalypse will not bring about an end for all, but will function as the catalyst by which a new, Utopian social order may arise. The emergence of a post-apocalyptic idealized Utopian society, for Wiccan Millennials, will be one wherein those who have spiritually revered and respected nature will be rewarded for such reverence. According to an article on this group written for the peer reviewed academic journal *Nature and Culture*,

> [M]any ecologically conscious Wiccans agreed that "something" was on the verge of changing but were not certain of any details, especially the "whats" and "whens." Typical discourses that I encountered on this topic—in personal conversations, on the Internet, and in Wiccan books—often included an interpretation of environmental degradation, severe weather problems, and the proliferation of natural disasters reported in the news as warning signs that the fragile balance of life on Earth was in imminent danger of destruction. However, the lack of a strong focus on particular events and predictions tended to mitigate Wiccan reactions to their own apocalyptic millenarian ideas.[3]

Indeed, even though spiritually aligned as a community of believers, and thus called into activism by a higher power, this group was equally influenced by their pseudo-modern milieu in their overall lack of common focus. This lack of focus, ironically, might be a result of the self-same technological intervention that they themselves sought to overwhelm.

More generally speaking, the Wicca faith, although becoming more popular, more publicly oriented and increasingly outward facing, still confronts much prejudiced and maligned controversy. One article, published in the *New York Times,* followed a post-millennial May Day celebration held in upstate New York. Even though Wicca and Paganism are two of the fastest growing faiths, according to J. Gordon Melton, Director of the Institute for the Study of American Religion, followers still fear retribution from the general public as a result of their faith. A Wiccan interviewed for the article suggested that the reason behind the festival was one of empowerment: to bring people out of the broom closet. She states:

> So many hide because they feel their children or their jobs will be threatened by the fact that they are witches…. People have strange ideas that witches are bad people and it's absolutely not true. We are a religion like any other. We're earth-based and environmentally conscious. But because of Hollywood and religious propaganda over the centuries, we have a bad rap…. The reasons that people choose Wicca are the same reasons people have always chosen Wicca…. It's a … non-hierarchical religion with a beautiful ritual.[4]

This post-millennial Wiccan faith, much like the hippies that preceded them, desire to commune with nature, connect to the earth, and stave off fears regarding the end of the world as we know it. Likewise, this group has been persecuted by their contemporaneous culture. The pejorative nature of the term "witchcraft" is arguably a result of media representation that links it to Satanism, as was the case with many of the films discussed in the first section of this book. Yet, even given the span of fifty years, questions as to the efficacy and the benefit of this alternative faith is still under debate, both within filmic discourse and contemporaneous culture.

Shutting the Doors and Locking the Windows? Belief in the New Millennium

Simply put, the age of modernity involved a paradigmatic shift from faith in a supernaturally infused religion and culture to the adoption of a rationalist belief in the power of science, arguably as the result of the dual legacies of the Enlightenment and the Reformation. Further, as the descendant of modernity, postmodernity, as has been discussed by authors such as Jean-François Lyotard and Jean Baudrillard, was involved with a further stripping of historical mechanisms of self and social stabilization, what Lyotard referred to as "grand narratives." These included an allegiance to family as well as to faith. In the past, both of these ideally came to provide lessons for how to understand and engage with the surrounding social universe and, in turn, equally provide a basis for how to understand and define the self. However, under the sway of postmodernity, the world became ever increasingly secular, driven even more by radical individualism than by historical or communal engagement. Generational legacy and spiritual alignment gave way to a culture taken up with free market consumerism, wherein these products of consumption became mechanisms of self-identification and reification. In other words, individuals became defined not by those with whom they were associated, but instead by what they owned, thus ultimately becoming products rather than producers of culture, as was the case with Guy in *Rosemary's Baby*. Following this, post-postmodernity, or what Alan Kirby refers to as "pseudo-modernity," occurring at the point of the millennium as a result of emergent information technology, transformed not only the cultural product but also its producer and receiver. If it could be argued, as Kirby does, that the age of modernity and postmodernity equally fetishized the author through their respective glorification and effacement, then pseudo-modernity, according to this theorist,

> re-structured, violently and forever, the nature of the author, the reader and the text, and the relationships between them.... the culture we have now fetishizes the *recipient* of the text to the degree that they become a partial or whole author of it.... *pseudo-modernism* ... makes the individual's action the necessary condition of the cultural product.... By definition, pseudo-modern cultural products cannot and do not exist unless the individual intervenes physically in them.[5]

The age of pseudo-modernity, born of computers wherein control over content is implied if not fully actualized, is thus subsumed within the here and now. Denying the pull of the past and the promise of the future, the subject of pseudo-modernity favors the immediacy of reality TV and a culture equally based on all that is fleeting. Kirby goes on to argue that this world, far from being stable, secure or even satisfying, is instead a place of terror, both literally and figuratively. Kirby argues:

> Pseudo-modernism belongs to a world pervaded by the encounter between a religiously fanatical segment of the United States, a largely secular but definitionally hyper-religious Israel, and a fanatical sub-section of Muslims scattered across the planet: pseudo-modernism was not born on 11

September 2001, but postmodernism was interred in its rubble. In this context pseudo-modernism lashes fantastically sophisticated technology to the pursuit of medieval barbarism—as in the uploading of videos of beheadings onto the internet, or the use of mobile phones to film torture in prisons. Beyond this, the destiny of everyone else is to suffer the anxiety of getting hit in the cross-fire. But this fatalistic anxiety extends far beyond geopolitics, into every aspect of contemporary life; from a general fear of social breakdown and identity loss.[6]

However, while Kirby would assert that it is a specific condition of transitoriness that elicits a trance-like state in the pseudo-modern subject, what this chapter will suggest is that this ever "transitory amnesiac" reacts not to immediacy, but instead to an existential fear and sense of loss brought about by the conditions that the theorist describes above. Indeed, what this irate immediacy lacks, and what the subject of pseudo-modernity has lost but not forgotten, is the momentous import of stable self-identification. According to conservative religious leader, author, and Cambridge-based philosopher Jonathan Sacks in his recent book entitled, *Not in God's Name*, humanity's central role is the search for meaning, and whilst science and technology can provide answers to some questions, it cannot provide answers to every query nor, as Kirby has theorized above, can it provide stability. Sacks, rather than following Kirby's lead, shares the concerns of Gothic writers, as discussed in the introduction to this book, when he argues:

> Science, technology, the free market and the liberal democratic state have enabled us to reach unprecedented achievements in knowledge, freedom, life expectancy, and affluence.... But they do not and cannot answer the three questions every reflective individual will ask at some time in his or her life: Who am I? Why am I here? How shall I live? These are questions which are prescriptive not descriptive, substantive, not procedural. The result is that the twenty-first century has left us with a maximum of choice and a minimum of meaning. Religion has returned because it is hard to live without meaning.[7]

Although, admittedly, spirituality never completely disappears, the role of religion becomes a topic of serious debate during periods of vast paradigmatic shifts. If the printing press assisted in the ushering in of the age of modernity, and broadcasting and consumer culture formed the foundation for postmodernity, then the internet and social media have in many ways come to define the post-millennial, post-postmodern period, as both Kirby and Sacks argue. Information is being circulated faster and in greater quantities than ever before in both the public and the private spheres. Further, the fact that it can be distributed to both realms in anonymity allows for the potential of more radical political, social and religious views to be expressed, regardless of whether the socio-political climate is conservative or liberal. Sacks goes on to assert that if modernity and postmodernity were eras of increasing seculariztion, then the twenty-first century is the age of de-secularization as isolated individuals come to negotiate the information age and its destabilizing effects. Indeed, the term "information society" may be a misnomer. For many, there is not an information "society" at all—only a series of fragmented networks engaged in a global interplay of information. **Broad**casting is also a term that is in need of reclassification, as it has now also been replaced. This "**narrow**casting," rather than speaking to a large mixed public and therefore expressing a range of viewpoints, now targets the specific beliefs of like-minded receivers who are thus further fragmented into delineated special interest groups. This radical change is a force that, for obvious reasons, disorients. Additionally, as was the case at a similar moment at the end of the 1960s when stabilizing "grand narratives" were first being questioned, this current shift has resulted in debates regarding the need for and value of reintegration within communities. In turn, during this time (as was the case one hundred years ago), debates are being circulated as to the potential corrective role of religion in relation to social integration and cultural cohesion, for, as French sociologist Emile Durkheim suggests, to be part of a society is inextricably linked to personhood.

Society, for Durkheim, is "an immense cooperation that extends not only through time, but also through space, combining feelings in a rich and complex set of processes through which we become truly human."[8] One of the main social processes for Durkheim is religion, a system from which all the embodied potentialities of human beings issue forth. In other words, Durkheim's understanding of religion is that it embraces and supports both culture and society, thus offering a corrective to the isolating effects of the information age and the "post-human" technologically infused direction of the world.

Moreover, according to cultural theorist Slavoj Žižek following from Durkheim, Christianity's focus on charity, on love as social solidarity, confronts the processes of dehumanization and social failure present in this era by foregrounding a universal obligation that transcends cultural differences technologically mediated or otherwise. Ultimately, the importance of religion for Durkheim and Žižek is that it not only builds but equally sustains communities, enveloping individuals into a group which is engaged in the pursuit of a shared belief in something larger than the self.

However, even as group identity and social cohesion may be sustained by such beliefs, there is a downside to the benefits of such a social configuration, namely the establishment of theological dualism. When religion becomes the mechanism for unification, those from other alternative beliefs may be perceived as a threat. This attitude becomes dangerous when the cohesion of spiritual societies is endangered by internal forces. When internal conflict jeopardizes a community, an external threat can act to reinforce solidarity, and the greater the threat from outside, the greater the cohesion within. Sacks argues:

> Societies require religion which performs the task of "casting out" the violence of deflecting it away from the group itself by placing it on an external victim, thus turning violence outwards instead of allowing it to turn destructively inwards.[9]

It is this "us versus them" attitude that resulted in the paradigmatic dichotomy of good versus evil, an earlier discussed trope wherein those who consider themselves right-minded view all other religions as being evil. In a more contemporary context, it is this positioning by religious extremists that has come to foster a fear of certain faith communities including Muslims and Evangelical Christians. Indeed, both have been blamed for terrorist activities committed in the service of obtaining a mastery of and dominion over the "other," who is perceived to possess evil attributes.

Aggiornamento, the Church, and the Legacy of the Second Vatican Council

Even as this "us versus them" mentality has increasingly taken hold, especially with regard to religious extremism, there is also, alternatively, an opening up of previously impenetrable barriers within the Catholic Church as a result of the leadership of Pope Francis.

Much like Pope John XXIII, the current leader of the Catholic Church is known for attempts to modernize the faith, its teachings and its practices. According to Georgetown University professor Gerard Manion in *Pope Francis's Agenda for the Future of Catholicism*:

> Many individuals and groups throughout the global church began to voice their perspectives on what the church for today and for the future most needed. This, in itself was not distinctive—for example, one only has to go back to 1958 to see that the Cardinals back then drew up what was, in effect, a job description for the new Pope that the church *of those times* most needed. In many ways, it was, in effect, a description of a Pope who would take the opposite approach to his predecessor on so many important issues. It was certainly, in effect, a description of a Pope who would lead in a very different, more open and engaging style, and who would look out to the

world and encourage dialogue with it rather than preaching down to it and turning the church inward on itself.[10]

Pope John—who called and opened the Second Vatican Council; fought for human rights; sought to establish relationships with the Jewish; and to mend discord within Christianity between Catholics, Protestants and Eastern Orthodoxies—was known for attempting to modernize the Church and to bring people of all faiths together. So too, Pope Francis commits himself to global equality, benefiting the poor and disenfranchised and establishing accord within the Christian faith. Indeed, for the first time since the Reformation, services led by Catholics are taking place in Protestant houses of worship, and vice versa. Francis has thus attempted to make the Church more relevant to post-millennials, including the use of social media, YouTube and live streaming, as well as more traditional means to reach the faithful. His ministry is based on accord and forgiveness for all, regardless of the sins that they might have committed, including forgiveness for women for divorce and abortion. For these reasons, many believe that Francis answered the call issued forth by Pope John XXIII, and indeed, there has been a subsequent rise in those converting to Catholicism and a drop in those who renounce their faith to the Church. Thus, in many ways, the post-millennial culture may be seen to be embroiled in similar debates as those occurring in the late 1960s and 1970s regarding the role of traditional faith and the efficacy of alternatives to this staid religious alignment.

Faith Horror in the Millennium: A Return to Traditionalism

One of the most popular horror franchises to give voice to these aforementioned contemporaneous religious debates, *The Conjuring*, follows the work of Catholic paranormal investigators Ed and Lorraine Warren. The opening shot of the first film identifies these protagonists in the following way:

> Since the 1960s, Ed and Lorraine Warren have been known as the world's most renowned paranormal investigators. Lorraine is a gifted clairvoyant, while Ed is the only non-ordained Demonologist recognized by the Catholic church.[11]

From their introduction at the outset, the prominence of the Warrens within *The Conjuring* universe is clearly articulated, as is the faith that drives, legitimizes and supports their work. Lorraine, for example, credits her religion with giving her psychic powers, and it is with this gift that she helps those in need. It is also her faith that brought her to her husband, the first person to ever believe in these gifts, as described at the opening of this chapter. Once brought together, the two act in tandem, using the powers of righteousness to fight evil under whatever guise it chooses to manifest itself.

This return to traditional religion results in a reduction in sympathetic depictions of alternative belief systems, ostensibly under the guise of a religious dualism, as described above. Thus, any practice that is not Christian is seen as being malevolent, not only in nature but also in intent. This is noted in the reception of the film at the time of its release. According to one review published in the *Religious Studies Review* by critic and film scholar Brian Collins, "The film [*The Conjuring*] operates under the assumption that witches are Satan-worshipping evil doers, not misunderstood outsiders."[12] Further, this alignment is suggestive of the earlier horror works of the classical period, which also regard faithful otherness as evil.

However, even as *The Conjuring* articulates the debates circulating in its contemporaneous culture, it is not commensurate to the culture in which the film is set. Indeed, as discussed previously throughout this book, the films of the mid–1960s and 1970s present a vast range of efficacious alternative beliefs, all of which are literally demonized within this series of texts. Ed Warren, as evidenced in his published case files, seems to acknowledge this conflation. He explains:

> The very word "witchcraft" conjures up many different kinds of impressions to those unfamiliar with its true meanings and with those who practice it. Even today, people found to be practicing witchcraft are persecuted for their beliefs. To the practitioners of this craft, Mother Earth is sacred, and they worship her. [T]hey practice psychic development; long hours of quiet meditation and concentration sharpen their extra senses. Unfortunately, people with this type of knowledge are often considered by others to be strange or even harmful. What we do not understand frightens us.[13]

However, the film does not make this distinction between the practice of Wicca and Satanic worship, much less between good and benevolent white witchcraft and malicious black magic. Also, significantly, Warren notes that the powers of second sight are not evil and should not be aligned with Witchcraft or Satanism unless they are used for this purpose. This is an important consideration for Warren, since it is through these very powers that his wife carries out the Lord's work.

The conflict of good and evil is as clearly defined and delineated as those who will come to represent each side. If Lorraine Warren is regarded as being "good," as is revealed in her accepting of the role as a loyal Christian wife and as nurturing mother, then the antagonist of the film is positioned as Lorraine's other: a wholly malevolent force that renounces her duties as both partner and parent. The antagonist is further discovered to be a witch. However, rather than using her supernatural powers to protect the family, Bathsheba the sorceress uses her gifts to destroy her children as well as the offspring of anyone who comes to occupy her once beloved and now cursed domicile. She does this by possessing mothers' bodies, taking over their souls and then forcing them to kill their children, thus implicating anyone within her reach with her heinous crimes against God and humanity.

Solidifying *The Conjuring* as a case of benevolence versus malevolence fought on a spiritual battleground is its appropriation of scenes and tropes from other famous films of a similar ilk. First, in many ways, the possessing figure of Bathsheba is akin to the demon in the infamous 1970s spiritual horror film *The Exorcist*. In possessing and rendering helpless its victim, the evil spirit destroys both body and soul. It not only weakens its host through a perpetual physical onslaught, but also forces the subject to act in truly heinous ways: the victim curses, self-mutilates, and sexually molests themselves and others, and in the case of *The Conjuring*, forces a mother to commit filicide. Equally, like *The Exorcist*, it is only through the power of Christ channeled by a representative of the Catholic Church that the demon is defeated.

In addition to this manifestation of traditional religious efficacy suggested by an alignment of this film with a seminal 1970s horror text, the first scene of *The Conjuring* is equally reminiscent of the opening of *The Amityville Horror*, another evil possession text from the contemporaneous time in which the later film is set. In both, the introduction to the respective families involves them moving into a house far from urban environs—far beyond their previous experience and far beyond their expense threshold.[14] The families work together as a team, lifting, moving and unpacking boxes so as to make the house into a home. After moving in, both couples make it a point to "christen" their new domicile not with a religious ritual, but by making love. This secular christening is contrasted with a conversation involving the sacred conducted between Ed and Lorraine Warren:

> LORRAINE: Do you remember what you said to me on our wedding night?
> ED: Can we do it again?
> LORRAINE: After that. You said that God brought us together for a reason, right?[15]

Indeed, if Ed and Lorraine are bonded as a family like their textual counterparts, in being married and in having children, they are also bonded through their faith, which gives their lives meaning and purpose, something that the other families do not have. In *The Amityville Horror*, Kathy Lutz is a non-practicing Catholic who marries outside of her faith, while the other "real-life family," the Perrons, upon which the first *Conjuring* film is based, are likewise not religious on or off the screen. In an interview, Caroline Perron states:

> As I grew up, I had access to an 80,000 volume library and I read from that library extensively about religion, all the religions in the world and I was really an atheist at that point when we moved to the farm, but things began to happen in the house.[16]

This is contrasted with Lorraine Warren who, in the same series of interviews relating to the Perron case, asserts, "My Catholic faith is very, very important to me and still is today and that helped me to help others."[17] This connection with faith is of prime importance, as it is only through traditional religious affiliation that evil can be vanquished. This is not a matter for the weak of heart, nor the weak of faith. As is suggested in a conversation between the Warrens and Father Dominic, their liaison with the Church,

> ED: Well....
> FD: Yeah well you weren't kidding. Look, Ed, this is complicated because the kids aren't baptized. And the family are not members of the church. The approval will have to come directly from the Vatican.
> ED: Father, we've never seen nothing like this.
> FD: Yeah.... Well ... neither have I.
> ED: They don't have a lot of time.
> FD: I understand. I'll push it through myself.
> ED: Thank you, Father.[18]

It is in this way that *The Conjuring* harkens back to classic horror films that pre-date the 1960s. In fact, these texts are actually referenced in this work, as the Warrens use the same iconography traditionally used to ward off evil. In a scene from *The Conjuring* wherein the Warrens prepare to battle, Ed begins to decant holy water. He explains that the presence of sacred objects will get a reaction from anything unholy. He states that such items "sort of piss them off." After preparing the holy water, he goes on to place a cross on a shelf in the secular Perron home. A technical assistant hired to document the presence of the supernatural, Drew Thomas, notes that this may be likened to staving off the threat of the vampire, to which Ed replies, "Yeah, exactly. Except I don't believe in vampires."[19] Like in other texts discussed in this book, it is belief that is the key to efficacy, only here there is no room for alternative religion or those that practice such faiths. Good is equated with Christianity and all its trappings, and to be agnostic or atheistic is to be in peril and in need of faith, whilst to practice Paganism or Witchcraft is to be in league with the devil. In one of the final scenes from the film, there is a quote from Ed Warren that makes the threat of these malevolent spirits manifest and further connects them to Satan: "Diabolical forces are formidable. These forces are eternal, and they exist today. The fairy tale is true. The devil exists. God exists. And for us, as people, our very destiny hinges upon which one we follow."[20] In these films, those who are in danger must accept God. Disbelief must be eradicated, for is only through the power of Christianity that evil can be vanquished and order be restored.

This is the same dilemma that surfaces in the Perron eldest daughter's account of her time living on the farm in Rhode Island, a three-volume work entitled *House of Darkness, House of Light: The True Story*. As is suggested in the title of the manuscript, Andrea Perron regards this period in her and her family's lives as involving a battle between the forces of good ("light") versus the forces of evil, or of darkness. Not only is this the central conflict, but as with the classical horrors of which this text is a part, the forces of light are solidly equated with Christianity, even given the fact that the family, at the time of their experiences with the haunting, were admittedly atheists, as is suggested by the quote that opens this chapter. Perron makes use of biblical idioms throughout her series of books that solidify this allegiance, such as in the following: "Carolyn was a beautiful woman, yet, this day her husband gazed at her with a renewed appreciation of grace. She appeared as an ethereal vision, an angel awash in Heavenly Light ... the Lord works in mysterious ways."[21] However, even with this clear delineation, there is still a subtext that suggests that the main battle is not altogether one between good and evil, but instead between belief and disbelief.

A key scene from the film equally establishes this and also concurrently sets up a gendered perceptual divide. Whilst the Warrens, called to investigate the Perron home for supernatural occurrences, set up their equipment, the male chief technological adviser asks the eldest daughter, Andrea, to touch a table and then uses a special light to see the residual handprint. Thus, he manipulates science and technology to look into the past, revealing what the naked eye can't see. It is the same principle that is used by Lorraine, only rather than using technology she relies on clairvoyance or superstition to see. As preparations continue, another device to detect supernatural presences, a bell attached to a door, goes off. The door opens apparently without anyone there, but it is soon revealed that it is the police officer assigned to keep them all safe who is manipulating the entryway. The man looks confused by this unwanted and unwarranted attention, apparently unaware of what is going on around him. He simply states to his audience that he had to "go." Thus, three apparent groups are established and revealed: science, which is usually associated with the technological and is almost always aligned with the male; superstition, which is associated with religion, belief and the irrational (a female attribute); and finally, skepticism, which is usually male and held up in opposition to the previous two.

Andrea Perron seems to echo this in her book as she equally sets up a division between the females in the family, herself, her mother and her sisters on the one side and her father on the other. As part of a conservative nuclear family, the women of the house are the keepers of the home and hearth, with Carolyn, the mother, as the primary carer. The husband, Roger, as the primary breadwinner, is regarded as an outsider, often away for long periods of time on sales trips, leaving his family to fend for themselves at their isolated and purportedly haunted farm. When he does come home, he is tasked with manual labors more suited to male physical strength, such as shoveling the long driveway leading from the farm to the main road. This divide between the tasks of men versus women is redoubled in the film adaptation, *The Conjuring*, wherein the males are in charge of manipulating technology, such as the recording devices used to detect ghosts. Also, it is Ed Warren who helps Roger fix and restore his classic car. On the other side of this divide, it is Lorraine that has the gift of second sight, recording events through personal experience versus technological means. Like Lorraine, Carolyn and her daughters become witness to a myriad of inexplicable phenomena, including the witnessing of shadowy figures, observing objects moving on their own accord, and experiencing feelings of depression and oppression. Roger, due to his absence, does not experience these incidents. Further, and unlike Ed Warren, who equally does not possess the gift of second sight, those signs that he does perceive he denies. It is this skepticism that not only sets him further apart, but in fact drives a wedge between himself and his wife. It is interesting here to note that his coming to an awareness and finally an acceptance of the possibility of the supernatural is referred to as his "coming to the light."

Whilst a division between father and family is exacerbated as a result of a lack of belief, a closeness between mother and daughters is increased as a result of their shared experience. This commonality exists along similar traditional gender distinctions: the male associated with commerce, the public sphere and the rational world, the females with the home, the supernatural and the natural universe. According to Andrea Perron:

> "To everything there is a season and a time for every purpose under heaven." This realization defined a collective, causing the girls to seek time in Nature going forth ... there to behold the wonder, to marvel at the antiquity and

newness of Nature, to worship it as God. Galileo told humanity to look up, his concept of time and space Universal. Whitman told humanity to look down, describing a single blade of grass as the journey work of the stars. Truth be told, everyone must find their own path to travel through life, hopefully one which leads out of the darkness into the light.[22]

This divide along gender lines, between an openness to and a skepticism of the supernatural realm, is one that is common to most of the films of the 1970s, the contemporaneous period in which the film adaptation of the Perron haunting is set. There are indeed many referential moments in *The Conjuring* that tie it to earlier true horror tales, most obviously *The Amityville Horror*. As with the other narratives in this book, it is the differences as well as the similarities that are significant: if *The Conjuring* may be regarded as offering up traditional protagonists, *Amityville* challenges this notion. Although the Lutz family is married, they are a blended family, since the father is not the biological parent. However, aside from this, there are many points of similarity. Like in *Amityville*, the Perron family have purchased a property beyond their means. For the "real-life" Perrons, it was only their ties to the former farm owner that had allowed them the leeway to be able to purchase the property, whereas in the film, the family purchased the property at auction and a far reduced price, ostensibly as a result of the ancient connections between the land and the practice of witchcraft. According to the film, the original farmhouse was built in 1863 by Jedson Sherman, who was married to a woman named Bathsheba, a descendant of one of the women accused of and hung for witchcraft in Salem. In deference to the dark lord, Bathsheba sacrificed her baby when it was seven days old. She not only proclaimed her love to Satan but cursed anyone who tried to take her land. She then hanged herself. Her time of death was 3:07. All the women who live on the land, in turn, seem to sacrifice their offspring and then commit suicide. All the people who took her land seem to be cursed. In the Perron autobiography, the witch makes her presence known by manifesting before Carolyn. The mother perceives this figure as maleficent, desiring to kill, or at the very least to maim, weaken, and drive her victims mad. As she descends upon Carolyn, the living woman mutters a prayer begging God for help, and upon this utterance the evil spirit disappears. She is thus convinced that the spirit of God has intervened on her behalf. The Perron book describes the event as follows:

> Proving to be a powerful prayer, no matter how quiet or brief, Carolyn saved herself with a faithful request of her Savior. Having had the presence of mind to invoke the presence of God in such a moment of crisis, murmuring words possessing potency enough to cause an intervention.... The evil spirit [was vanquished].[23]

As a result of this perceived intervention, the family begins to attend regular Sunday services, rekindling their Catholic faith. It is, moreover, significant that the faith to which they return is Catholicism, because it is the Christian faith that is most associated with the acceptance of the supernatural, as discussed earlier in this book. This is also something that is acknowledged by the eldest sibling of the Perron family when she is confronted with the skepticism that her father adopts in relationship to the haunting of their farmhouse:

> **CAROLYN:** There are many people who do not believe in ghosts.
> **ANDREA:** Why not? The Priest at church talks about God and The Holy Ghost as the greatest spirit of all. At least all Catholics believe in ghosts don't they?[24]

Another connection between *The Conjuring* and a case of purportedly true-life domestic demonic possession involves a scene in the bedroom of the young Perron daughters. One sister believes the other is tricking her by grabbing her foot and farting so as to make the room stink. This is a reference to the Enfield poltergeist, a case from the 1970s that, much like *Amityville*, was investigated by the Warrens and will form the basis for *The Conjuring 2*.

The Conjuring 2, as suggested above, follows another case of demonic possession, first of a place and then of a person. It is also, like *The Amityville Horror* and *The Conjuring*, purportedly based upon the real-life events of a family who were beset by an evil entity. The film begins with the Warrens investigating the Amityville haunting, and as discussed above, the dichotomies between science and superstition and between male and female are clearly established once again.

The scene opens with an unidentified man setting up a camera whilst Lorraine leads a séance. Once again, women are invested with the supernatural, irrational ability to "see," and the men are in charge of science and technology. As this scene of Amityville fades out, an intertitle emerges:

> Ed and Lorraine Warren's investigation into the Amityville haunting sparked a media firestorm and catapulted them into the public eye. Meanwhile, a haunting that many would later compare to Amityville was unfolding thousands of miles away in Enfield, England. It would draw the Warrens into one of their most diabolical cases. Based on a true story.... *The Conjuring 2*.[25]

Just as with *The Conjuring*, the connection between this film and its popular antecedent are made manifest. The case of the Enfield haunting, like Amityville and the Perron farm, involves a family that is trying hard to make financial ends meet. In Enfield, the family is broken—the mother is divorced and attempting to provide for her four children on her own. The environment in the second of *The Conjuring* films is suburban rather than rural or urban, however, which offers the opportunity for community involvement, and thus the family is not quite as isolated in their battle with the supernatural forces that have come to plague them. Although part of a community, the family is a secular one, and thus, like in the other films, they must rely upon Lorraine and Ed to use the forces gifted by God to intervene on their behalf.

The evil manifestation begins when the Hodgson daughters attempt to contact the dead using a spirit board, a device that only the youngest girl, Janet, is successfully able to manipulate. Again, it is the female of the species that is connected to the spiritual realm. The following scene is one in which the Warren family becomes the focus, and it becomes evident that they, like those that they assist, are experiencing attacks by a malevolent spirit. Like with the Hodgsons, the brunt of evil is focused on the youngest female member of the family, the Warren daughter. The film then alternates between following the Warrens and the Hodgson families, and it is thus that the film establishes another clear dichotomy, that between the Hodgsons and the Warrens. While the Hodgsons are a poor, secular, broken family, the Warrens are revealed to be upper-middle class, a traditional nuclear family, and religious, more specifically Catholic in their system of belief, and once again it is this belief that makes their family strong and their work as paranormal investigators efficacious. This is established in a pivotal scene in the film.

In this scene, the Warrens are attempting to prove to the Church that the Enfield case is not a hoax perpetrated by the Hodgsons. With this in mind, they fill Janet's mouth with water and attempt to contact the spirit that has been influencing her. During this interview, the spirit that inhabits Janet, unhindered by the water filling the girl's mouth, identifies himself as Bill. Ed asks Bill why he does not move on and what would be so wrong with going to heaven. Bill replies that he is not a heaven man, to which Ed rejoins that he does not care what the spirit believes in. Ed then proffers his cross and uses this implement to exorcise the spirit. Once again, like the Dracula films of old, and like the more contemporary film *The Exorcist*, it is the power of traditional religious icons wielded by the true believers of the faith that are effective in overcoming evil in all its forms.

Another dichotomy presented in *The Conjuring 2* is that of science versus superstition. Although it could be suggested that science is manipulated in the service of verifying the presence of ghosts, as is the case with the Warren investigations, nonetheless science is usually used as an anathema to superstition and acceptance of the spiritual, whether it be an embodiment or a practice. In the case of *The Conjuring 2*, the figure that represents this side of the division is Anita Gregory, British psychologist and parapsychological debunker who came out publicly accusing the Hodgson family of fraud. In the film, she presents a counterpoint to Lorraine Warren, who, as has been discussed extensively, is aligned with religious and spiritual faith. An exchange from the film conveys this alignment:

> **ANITA (TO LORRAINE):** Honestly, I don't know what was worse, the "demons" or the people who prey on our willingness to believe in them.
> **LORRAINE:** The demons. The demons are worse.[26]

Whereas science is often set up in confrontation against spirituality, the fact of Gregory being a woman and a rationalist is more of a rarity. As suggested above, men are almost always on the side of the skeptics, whilst women are the irrational, supernaturally aligned seers.

Whereas the character of Anita Gregory slightly problematizes the conservative nature of this film in allowing for a female to be an empowered, worldly scientist firmly rooted in the public sphere as an expert and a professional, the final scene of the film assuages this anomaly.

The Conjuring 2, like *The Conjuring*, ends in a similar way as the classical horror films that pre-date it. The protagonists, faithful Christians manipulating their connection to the Church, not only vanquish evil, but also bring the family that has enlisted their aid to the community of believers. In the final scene from the film, Ed and Lorraine are sharing a final conversation with the fraught but now freed Janet Hodgson:

> **ED TO JANET:** You know this has kept me safe since I was a kid. [Gives her his crucifix.] I want you to have it. Then when you grow up, you find someone who needs it, and you give it to them.
> **JANET:** I'm so lucky to find two people who changed everything.[27]

The film concludes with Ed and Lorraine dancing to a ballad recorded by Elvis Presley, "I Can't Help Falling in Love with You." The final shot thus becomes a testament to the power of happy families to overcome everything, and to the power of God that has joined them for this very purpose. The song asks if it would be a sin to stay and allow for love to bloom. As they lyrics state, the answer to this question is that it would not be an act of wrongdoing. It should, however, not be a surprise that this song testifies to the power of love, as manifested through the power of God. Jean-Paul-Égide Martini, the writer of the original song, "The Pleasure of Love (Plaisir d'Amour)," upon which the Elvis ballad was based, was himself trained as a Jesuit. Also, the recording artist himself was a known Pentecostal who averred that it was his love of God that founded his initial inspiration to sing.[28] Once again, it would seem that even in reference to popular culture, this film upholds the power of Christianity.

The Conjuring series, in all its iterations including *Annabelle, Annabelle: Creation, Annabelle Comes Home, The Nun* and *The Curse of La Llorona*, engages in much the same debate, linking this horror universe to conservative classical horror themes. However, this is only one side of an ongoing debate with regard to faith and spiritual affiliation. Unlike *The Conjuring*, which is, as has been argued above, more divisive and conservative in its discourse, other films engage with viable alternative faiths. Some align alternative faiths such as Witchcraft to Satanism, while other post-millennial films present Paganism as efficacious not only for sustaining life, but also for building strong communities.

Another Season for Another Witch

A key example of a post-millennial film that may comfortably be linked with discussions and debates forwarded in the first section of this book would be *The Witch*,[29] the 2015 debut film of director Robert Eggers. In this film, which presents itself as a New England folktale, a Puritan family becomes the victim first of isolation and then of evil corruption. Exiled from their Plymouth colony for mysterious misdeeds, they are forced to strike out into the wilderness of the "New World," finally establishing themselves and their homestead in a field on the border of a large forest. As they pray to God, asking Him to bestow His blessings, eerie music overwhelms their voices as the camera zooms in to the line of trees in the not too distant background. The divide between the world of goodness and light and that of evil and darkness is thus established both aurally and visually. Initially, these realms remain fairly distinct; however, as the narrative progresses, these lines begin to blur as the influence of the coven begins to infiltrate the family. The first indication of the manifestation of evil takes place as the eldest daughter, Thomasin, plays with her baby brother just outside the line of trees. She covers her eyes, engaging him with peekaboo. She repeats this action several times before she uncovers her eyes for the final time to find the baby missing from the blanket on which he was lain. The family searches both the farm and the wood, being drawn in deeper and deeper with the elusive sound of his cooing. As night descends, the perspective shifts and the focus changes to that of a naked woman, completely shaded in darkness as she first rubs her fingers over the naked baby boy and then smooths what appears to be blood into her skin. Although there is no image of the sacrifice, it can only be assumed that the infant has been murdered and then exsanguinated as part of a ritual. The questions that may be asked at this juncture are many, among them being: is this the titular witch, and is she acting alone or as a member of a coven? The scene ends with her silhouette outlined against an impossibly large and full harvest moon. Nothing thus far has been given away.

Even though no questions as to the nature of the witch have been answered, her evil influence is felt. The once obsessively religious family begins to act in ways that are increasingly sinful, and this corruption is revealed not only through their behavior, but in omens that signal demonic intervention. In terms of their sinfulness, they all begin to lie to each other: the father, William, lies to his wife, Catherine, about selling her prized silver cup, letting his daughter instead take the blame for its disappearance. The eldest son, Caleb, lies to the mother about going into the wood in search of food, claiming instead to be in search of apples in the meadow, and the daughter, Thomasin, lies to her younger siblings, twins Mercy and Jonas, about being a witch herself, claiming to be in league with Satan after dancing with him in the forest and signing his book. Mercy and Jonas themselves eschew their responsibilities on the farm, ignore their mother and father, and seem to engage in worshipping "Black Phillip," their ominous male goat. The omens of evil influence include the crops failing to bear fruit, and blood issuing forth from their goats instead of milk. Catherine complains to William that there is something amiss on their farm and that what is occurring is not natural. She goes on to liken their banishment, their isolation and this evil to the trials of Christ, who banished himself into the wilderness for forty days and nights, wherein he faced Satan and the temptation of sin. Evil finally manifests itself physically as a rabbit with strange eyes. William fires upon it, hoping to serve the beast at the dinner table, when his gun misfires, nearly blinding him. The rabbit runs off, only to reappear at the farm where, ostensibly, it influences the livestock, chiefly a black goat, Black Phillip. The goat, to whom the twins and Thomasin talk, is a classic symbol of Satan, and later speaks in his voice, leading the girl to form an alliance with the devil. The family's ultimate demise comes as a direct result of demonic influence. After infant Sam, Caleb is the next to die after disappearing into the wood and coming upon the witch, who seduces him. He returns to the farm naked and unresponsive, finally succumbing after choking up an apple (the symbol of both original sin and his original dishonesty) and claiming to see the face of his savior. The next to go is William. Although he confesses to his sin, he is apparently not forgiven. He dies at the "hand" of Black Phillip, who gores him to death. The next is Catherine. Before she dies, like her husband, she confesses her sin. In her case, it is not dishonesty, but a lack of faith brought on as a result of losing her infant son. Even after admitting her sin, she is visited by evil. This time it is in the form of her dead sons. She believes that Caleb and Sam have returned to her, and in her delusion, she welcomes her children to her and begins to suckle her baby, who is revealed to be not an infant, but a crow who does not suck but tears at her flesh. In the morning, she is shown to be sleeping next to her husband. All the livestock are dead and given the quiet of the farm, it is assumed that the twins have also been killed, although the act was never revealed. The mother accuses Thomasin of destroying the family and attacks her. The two fight and the daughter kills her mother with a scythe. In the final scene of the film, Thomasin removes her bloody clothes and goes into the wood at the bequest of Black Phillip, who has been possessed by the spirit of Satan. In the forest, she meets the coven of witches, who take her in. In the final scene, all of these women ascend into the air. Thomasin laughs as she floats away.

What is particularly significant about this film, unlike *The Conjuring* series, is not so much the alignment of the alternative faith, but instead the outcome of its rituals. In *The Witch*, the symbols combine with the narrative to link Witchcraft to Satanism. However, rather than the forces of righteousness overcoming those of evil, the witches succeed in garnering their final member and destroying all in their path. Much like *Rosemary's Baby*, the coven are successful in their mission of converting Thomasin into *The Witch*. Her name is a key indicator of this transformation; she is a creature born of the sin of questioning faith, like the archetypal doubting Thomas of scripture who forces Jesus to show his stigmata as proof of his identity. Thomasin questions the faith that has led them into an isolated existence, and later renounces it for a belief system that can only exist as part of a closely-knit community—a coven of witches.

Finally, the narrative that most neatly partners with films presented in the last section of this book (i.e., films and media designated as Pagan Horror), would be the 2019 film *Midsommar*, directed by Ari Aster. Indeed, this film has already been identified in the popular press as a work of Folk Horror. However, as has been argued in relation to *The Wicker Man*, *Midsommar* presents themes, narrative forms and visual cues that problematize such a definition. Like *The Witch*, it is a folktale, set in a location that is remote, secluded from mainstream civilization, and like *The Wicker Man* and *Robin Redbreast*, such isolation is necessary for the effective practice of the ancient rites adopted by the village, rituals that include propitiatory human and animal sacrifice. Equally, like all the narratives mentioned above, at the heart of this tale is a strong connectivity to spiritual belief, a faith that is clearly explained and witnessed by select secular urbanite outsiders who, like viewers of this film, are called to share in this centenary nine-day celebration of midsummer.

Midsommar as Pagan Horror

This film opens on a wintery forest landscape. The focus is on the trees, the snow and the stillness. An a cappella chant plays over the images that acts to add a certain sanctity to them. This peaceful reverence of nature is broken by the shrill ring of a telephone, a reminder of the urban modern world which has increasingly come to dominate from the age of modernity until now. Thus, from the start, this film sets up a dichotomy: on one side, the natural world which offers peace and reverent reflection and spiritual connection, and on the other, the technological world that only acts to break contemplative peace. With the ring of the phone, the scene changes to that of a suburban town, also covered in snow. On the surface, these worlds appear similar, but once the surface is scratched away, they could not be more diverse.

The scene continues to close in on one house over all the others—a domicile that stands out above the rest, the only one without lights, and thus lacks warm homeliness. The camera tracks through this home as an answering machine takes a call from the family's worried daughter. Through this message, the family is revealed to be in a state of instability as a result of discord between the parents and one of their two daughters. No one answers the call. The camera zooms in on a computer screen and an email which states, "i cant anymore—everything's black—mom and dad are coming too. Goodbye."[30] Through the use of digital technology, first the telephone answering machine and then the computer, an attempt is being made to establish communication and connectivity. In failing to do so in any meaningful way, the daughter becomes increasingly upset and anxious. She calls her boyfriend and her friend, but she cannot read these conversations because they are once again mediated and not face to face. She is alone and feels this isolation. After speaking to her friend, she becomes even more worried, fearing that both her family and her boyfriend are distancing themselves from her—a fear that is later confirmed in both instances.

First, her family becomes lost to her, as her sister is revealed to have killed herself and her parents, poisoning them with carbon monoxide that has been issued from the family cars in the garage. Snow wafts into the frame as the firefighters and paramedics take care of this murder scene, the emergency lights reflecting onto the white. This image is redoubled in the subsequent shot of the sister, Dani, who is later revealed to be the protagonist of the film. As she moans, screams and cries over her loss, and whilst her boyfriend holds her but fails to share in her grief, the camera zooms into a close-up of the window behind them. The world is dark, and snow is peacefully falling. A final reminder of the peace of the natural versus the technologically mediated world of unconnected grief and loneliness.

Months pass from this crisis. It is no longer the dead of winter, but the advent of summer—the seasons rather than any other indicator signaling this passage of time. During these subsequent scenes, supporting and secondary characters that round out the narrative universe of *Midsommar* are introduced. Dani, as the protagonist, still dominates, but now her boyfriend, Christian, and his friends Josh, Mark and Pelle are revealed. Pelle, a Swedish man who studies in the same university as the others, is planning to take all four of them home with him to attend a nine-day festival held by his community in honor of the summer solstice. He shows the group photos from previous years as he relates to them the theatrical pageantry of this event. Although the rest of the men clearly do not want Dani to join them on their journey, Pelle honestly welcomes her. He admits that he has also lost his parents and empathizes with the grief that she still feels. He also explains that, while he understands the devastation that the loss of one's parents can bring, unlike her, he was embraced by the community to which he belongs. In this way, the division between the world of Pelle, what will come to be known as the ancient agrarian, and the modern urban world of Dani is made manifest. If Pelle is stabilized by his connection to the community, Dani is anything but.

The group then flies to Sweden. As they travel aboard a jumbo jet, the camera once again strays from the main action (as it did in the opening shot of the film), looking out of the window and onto the icy mountains which span endlessly beneath them. Much like the opening scene to the theatrical version of *The Wicker Man*, their journey can only safely be achieved by airplane, so remote and isolated is their destination. Even once they are on the ground, the separation between the urban and the rural increases as the students continue to drive through increasingly isolated landscapes. As they finally reach the border of the town to which they travel, the image inverts itself so that their progress is viewed upside-down. This tracking shot is reminiscent of an earlier film, M. Night Shyamalan's 2010 *Devil*, which also boasts an inverted opening shot, although in the case of the latter, the shot is of an urban as opposed to a natural landscape. As with *Devil*, the normal scenic environment is rendered strange and slightly disturbing as it literally turns the world on its head. These themes of reinvention and renewed perspectives are common threads in both works.[31]

The first stop in what will come to be revealed as a pilgrimage is to a scenic park off the main highway on which they have been traveling. All the younger people from the village commune here, just outside of their village. Pelle is not alone in leaving his birthplace. Many young men and women, all roughly the same age as Pelle, are returning at the same time from their experiences in big cities. Also, like Pelle, each has brought at least one guest. Part of this segment of their pilgrimage involves the ingestion of hallucinogens, which they all must take at the same time so as to share even this internal journey all together. Even in this shared experience, the members of the group react differently—yet another indicator of the divisive themes of the film. Mark, one of their group, worries about being infected by ticks and the pervasive daylight at this longitude, all these elements becoming objects of fear and distress. In direct contrast, Pelle seems completely at ease. This is not hard to fathom; he is home. He asks the group if they can feel the energy coming up from the earth. Dani, still hallucinating, looks down at her hand and perceives grass to be growing from it. Later, Mark, who in the past has also been the most negative about Christian and his relationship with Dani, goes on to say that he truly believes that this circle of friends is his family. This causes Dani to remember her own struggles with her family. She has a bad trip, but rather than turning to her boyfriend, Christian, the most obvious of choices, she instead turns and runs into the forest, where she finds solace and falls into a peaceful sleep. Like Pelle, she is thus connected to the earth. She is on the other side of the divide; unlike Mark, Christian and Josh, she aligned with Pelle and the natural universe—a connection that will be increasingly established as the narrative progresses.

The next day, they continue on their journey to the village. Whereas Dani and Pelle are aligned with the earth, Mark once again stands as their antithesis, as he is increasingly worrying about ticks. If the former group feels embraced by nature, Mark is worried about being infected by it. The group members leave their cars behind and proceed on foot— no technology mediates their procession. The village awaits them. The entrance to the community is marked by a huge sculpture of the sun, an image much like the one from the advertisements for *The Wicker Man*, a structure through which they must pass. All the youth who are returning are embraced. Josh asks Pelle if he knows all of these people, to which Pelle responds, "This is my family."[32] Indeed, whereas Mark seems to have no meaningful relationship to his friends-cum-family, rejecting these ties and sense of obligation that they elicit, Pelle clearly adheres to this connectivity, even though in both cases this family is adoptive and not biological. Dani, on the other hand, is overwhelmed by the link that she feels, possibly as a result of its failure in the past. She is introduced to Pelle's sister and then his stepfather, who welcomes them home and states that they are so happy to have them. Although the statement is accepted by all of Pelle's friends, the message is clearly focused on Dani herself over anyone else. The divisions increase between the friends as it becomes clear who is accepted into the community—who belongs and is embraced, and who will potentially be ostracized.

As the ceremony continues, it becomes increasingly apparent that the celebration is honoring a pantheon of Pagan gods who accept and are appeased through acts of propitiation. In the first ceremony, two elderly members of the community are given flaming torches. The officiant, a middle-aged woman, calls out to the spirits to bring back to the dead as meat and other gifts are sacrificed into the fire, a flame that is tended so that it never dies out. Admittedly, burnt offerings, most commonly of live animals, are common to all ancient pre–Christian religions. Both Pagan and Jewish faiths are based upon making such offerings to the gods that each holds to be sacred; however, it will become evident that these rites are made to the spirits of the earth, as one of the two elderly members of the community who lead this ritual begins to sing, requesting a blessing for the crops. All join in the chant, humming so as to both address and mimic the harmony of nature. This reverence is an integral foundation of this society, taught to children in school: the lessons involving not only caring for the crops and livestock, but also the carving of runes to appeal to the gods for their prosperity. Dani, Christian and their friends are told by Pelle that the children put the images that they have practiced on their pillows to dream of their powers.

Like the ancient tribes that they resemble, this community records their rites and rituals in pictograms—images such as runes and paintings tell the story of their beliefs. In one such text, a series of images links female sexuality and the power of fecundity. The first image is that of the crops, then the sun, then a series involving a pubescent girl who first cuts her pubic hair and then uses the clippings to bake a cake. Then, after menstruating into a cup, the cake and drink are fed to her desired mate. It is a potion that entrances him to fall in love and reproduce. Like the crops that surround and sustain them, potions, ceremonies and spells are likewise used (as will be seen later in the narrative) to propagate the human species as well.

All the indoor spaces are littered with these meaningful drawings that are meant as tools to educate—as lessons to emulate and requests to invigorate. Much like the stained glass of a church that explains the faith to those who are being indoctrinated, the walls of the house in which all the youth of the community reside are decorated with similar symbols. Josh, who is studying the rites practiced by the community, attempts to research the meaning behind the symbols both included in the runes and in the paintings, but cannot connect to the internet to do so. Indeed, this village is radically disconnected from the modern world in which Dani and her friends exist. The people of the village live a communal life enhanced with meaning and purpose that is handed down from generation to generation by word of mouth, by spiritual teaching and visual reinforcement—theirs is a holistic existence. This stands in stark contrast to the world of Dani, which is separate and isolating, and wherein communication and connection are mediated by and broken due to the influence of technology.

Propitiation, ritual and spiritual observance are not the only aspects of this community that honors nature. Life itself is lived like the seasons: spring consists of childhood until the age of eighteen, and it is a time when the young are cared for by the whole community who share the responsibilities of rearing the youth. Then comes summer and a pilgrimage between the ages of eighteen and thirty-six. Following that, from thirty-six to fifty-four is autumn: the working age. Then comes the period of mentorship, a time that begins at fifty-four and ends at seventy-two: the winter years. This is yet another contrast between Pelle's community and Dani's. Whereas each member of this agrarian society knows what is expected of them at every stage of their lives, for the modern youth, this is decidedly not the case. The many examples of this difference include Dani's sister, taking her own life and that of her parents as a result of feelings of confusion, loss and depression; Dani, being too afraid of losing her partner to question his love for her; and Christian's failing to choose a topic for his master's thesis in his final year of the program. All the youths of the modern world are lost, in search of meaning and failing to achieve their quest.

The next morning, the entire community rises together and begins the day with a welcoming of the sun through synchronized movement and song. Then, the whole village shares breakfast at big communal tables. Like the morning ritual, all are in sync as everyone waits to sit until the two elderly members, the couple who led the chants and held the torches the day before, join the meal and sit. All eat once the elders start to eat as an acknowledgment of reverence. After the meal, the couple chant and stand, and when they finish all toast them—yet another sign of the honor reserved for the elderly within this group. After the toast, the couple sit down once again and are carried away in their chairs. All wait and watch. The sun is bright. Horns are blown. The village gathers below a cliff. The couple are brought in on their chairs to the clifftop. The matriarch, who led the celebration the day before, sings from the book of scripture: a combination of runes and paintings. Both elder's hands are then cut, and their blood is spread on the large rune stone. Dani watches as the couple stand at the cliff face. She is hyperventilating just like the old woman, sharing in the anticipation of what will occur next. First the woman and then the man jump off the cliff high above onto a huge rock. The woman dies, smashing her skull, but the man does not. He begins to groan, and all join in mimicking and sharing in his pain. One of the elders uses a huge mallet to hit him, smashing his skull like the woman who lies beside him. As described above, life is a circle, a recycling of the spirit from and back into the earth. Instead of dying in fear and pain, it is explained by the village matriarch, the community give their lives joyfully at the age of seventy-two.

Dani is obviously traumatized by the suicide that she has just witnessed, an event that reminds her of the loss of her own family at the hands of her sister. However, whereas the latter act was one born out of loss of hope and a feeling of meaningless, the former act is seen as being of the greatest significance—not an ending, but ensuring a new beginning for the community, their crops and their life cycle. Pelle pulls Dani aside explaining that he was the most excited for her to come to witness these rites. He comforts her, confiding that he knows what she is going through as he too lost his parents, who burned up in a fire. Like Dani, he is an orphan. However, unlike his friend, Pelle never got the chance to feel lost because he was embraced by all around him, swept up in a community that does not care about what is theirs and what is not theirs. He has always felt held by a family, a real family, which, he stresses to Dani, everyone deserves, including her. He then asks the girl if she feels held by Christian, if he feels like home.

The following day begins like the day that the friends arrived to the village, as the bodies of the elderly are placed in the eternal fire, a burnt offering like the food that was presented early in this ceremony. After this, next rites begin at sundown:

> **MATRIARCH:** In thanks and praise, Great Goddess, we bestow upon you this modest gift. [A ceremonial tree, which is plunged into the river.]
> **MAN OF THE VILLAGE:** Do you hear that rumbling? I think she is still hungry.
> **MATRIARCH:** I hear no rumbling. Do any of you?
> **EVERYONE:** No.
> **MAN:** Ah, well I suppose it could have been my own belly. But I do not wish to risk offending our generous Mother.

MATRIARCH: Nor do I. Yet we have already given our finest jewels and most fruitful tree. What else could we possibly offer?

VILLAGE BOY [BRIOR]: You can use me! [He emerges covered in foliage and trinkets.]

MATRIARCH: You, young Brior wish to offer your life to our beloved Goddess?

BRIOR: If she will have it.

MAN: How brave you are, little Brior.

BRIOR: Brave? What is brave in going home? [They tie weights to his ankles, lift him up, and put a large rock onto his stomach. The two men holding him begin to swing him back and forth at the water's edge.]

ANOTHER WOMAN: No! Leave him be! He has shown his bravery! [They all agree. The men put the child down and Brior runs to the other woman who we now assume is his mother.][33]

Like with the previous propitiatory act that has already taken place, Dani is deeply traumatized. She sees this act like all the rest—devoid of the significance given to sacrifice from ancient times. Rather than an incredibly meaningful, communal, ceremonial act of reverence, she sees it from her own perspective, as meaningless murder, like that perpetrated by her sister against her parents. She goes on to wonder why Pelle has invited them. She believes that her friends have come as an opportunistic act, to better themselves: Josh to complete his thesis, Mark to have sex with as many girls who will let him, Christian to put off ending his relationship with Dani, and finally Dani to escape from her trauma. The community, on the other hand, is obviously Pagan and engaged in human sacrifice. They are both purposeful and spiritually connected, thinking not of themselves but of the community at large and the gods who have made their lives possible. Dani suggests that, as a result of their practices, their very way of life depends upon no one knowing about it. Like the people of Summerisle, intervention from the outside would prove fatal to everything that this group holds sacred. The reason for the friends being welcomed is revealed in the next scene when Christian interviews a member of the community, asking him about their closed system and if inbreeding is ever a concern. He admits that they observe the same taboos regarding incest, and for this reason, they often need to invite outside people to keep the bloodlines pure. Directly following this conversation, Dani is invited to help the other women make food for lunch. It is thus suggested, as it has been intimated throughout, that Dani will be the chosen one.

After this, a series of events ensue that narrow the outsider presence. Josh sneaks out of the communal sleeping quarters to photograph the sacred scriptural text, and he is punished for this transgression, which is regarded as sacrilege. He is hit over the head and killed by a mallet. Mark, who earlier disappeared with a village girl, reappears before Josh is killed. Josh sees him and at first it appears as if Mark is walking around naked, but in close-up it is revealed that the skin of his face has been removed and is being worn as a mask. Finally, Christian, who has been groomed as a stud to procreate with a pubescent girl, as per the pictograms, is first offered a pie with a pubic hair and then a drink that is decidedly redder than anyone else's. The matriarch tells him that he has been approved to mate with the young girl. Not only is he an ideal astrological match, but the girl has fixed her hopes on him even before his arrival, after having seen his photo thanks to Pelle. He is finally drugged and lured away to a hut, wherein twelve female members of the community, all naked, await him. One of the twelve is the girl, who is lying down and also naked. He is disrobed and the girl opens her legs. The women hum as he penetrates her on a bed of flowers. The girl holds out her hand and her mother grabs it. The mother sings to her and the other women join in. As she begins to moan, they all also join in, sharing her ecstasy.

Dani is also led away where she is dressed like all the other women. She is given tea in preparation for a competition to decide the May Queen—a draught that is drugged with hallucinogens. Once again, she looks at her appendages and sees that they are covered in grass, and once again she is revealed to be symbolically connected to the earth.

The May Queen celebration begins with a speech given by the matriarch:

> It was here long ago that the Black One lured the youths of Harga to the grass and seduced them into a dance. Once they began, they could not stop, and they danced themselves to death. Now, in life holding defiance we dance until we fall. And she who survives last will be crowned for her stamina.[34]

While she is dancing, she attempts to talk to the other girls, but she speaks in English, whilst her fellow competitors all only speak Swedish. At first she cannot understand them, for obvious reasons, but then, inexplicably, she begins to speak a common tongue, another of many indications that she has been embraced into the community. All continue to dance until Dani is revealed to be the last woman standing. She has won the contest and will thus be crowned May Queen. She stands on a platform and is carried away by the community. All sing in her honor. She is now fully and irrevocably one of them. She is carried to a table where everyone awaits her. She is placed at the head, in a throne of flowers and foliage—the place of honor. As she sits, so do they. As she eats, so do they. Like with the elderly couple, they all toast to her. A girl sitting next to her tells her that she is now one of the family, that they are all sisters. Following the meal, she is taken away in a carriage with all of her fellow contestants (now her entourage) to bless the crops and livestock.

As Dani returns from bestowing her blessings, she is told to follow one of the women to a place where blessings will now be bestowed upon her. Instead, she hears moaning and chanting and follows the noise. She looks through a keyhole in a hut and sees Christian fornicating with the young village girl. She throws up. Her new sisters carry her away. As she cries inconsolably, all her sisters join in sharing her pain. As she screams, the women hold her and scream, too. She is no longer suffering alone.

Meanwhile, Christian is still having sex. An old woman pushes him in and out until he finishes. The girl exclaims in joy that she can feel the baby growing inside her. Christian runs out of the room naked. He comes upon the community garden, where he sees Josh's foot sticking out from where it has been planted. He enters the henhouse, where Josh, now dead, has been suspended by his own flayed skin, his skin splayed into wings, his eyes replaced by daisies. A man blows a substance into Christian's face that paralyzes him. The man closes his eyes for him, and when he regains consciousness, he is told of his paralysis. The camera pulls back to reveal a figure sitting in a chair covered in flowers. It is Dani.

A speech marks the commencement of the final ceremony:

> On this, the day of our deity of reciprocity we gather together to give special thanks to our treasured sun. As an offering ... we here today surrender nine human lives. For every new blood sacrificed we will dedicate one of our own: four outsiders, four from the village and one to be chosen by our queen. To die and to be reborn in the great cycle. Four new-bloods have already been supplied, two who have already been dedicated and two who have volunteered. [One of them is Pelle's brother.] The queen will choose between a preordained new blood [Christian] and a specially chosen member of the community.[35]

A tombola shoots out a name which will reveal the other potential sacrifice. This person is brought before the queen, along with Christian. Dani looks at Christian. He looks at her.

The final scene takes place in the yellow temple, which is forbidden to outsiders. All the sacrifices are brought in: once human, and now skin shells filled with straw like scarecrows. Where their innards once were, there is now a cornucopia of fruit. They are placed sitting on hay bales. The final victim, Christian, is placed in the skin of the bear, which has been disemboweled.

The speech continues:

> Mighty and awful beast. With you we purge out most unholy affects. We banish you now to the deepest recesses, where you may reflect on your wickedness. They give the living sacrifices bark of the yew tree to feel no fear or pain.[36]

The hay is set alight. Dani sits in her robe of flowers as all around her stand, chant and watch the flames consume all inside the temple. As they scream, so too does everyone, sharing in their pain. The final shot is of Dani smiling.

The narrative offered up in *Midsommar* is thus in many ways the heir apparent to *The Wicker Man*, possibly even more than its rightful sequel, *The Wicker Tree*, a work both written and directed by Robin Hardy. Unlike *The Wicker Tree*, the community in *Midsommar* is isolated, and further it is noted in the text that this separation is indeed a necessity for their practices to thrive and perpetuate. Also, like *The Wicker Man*, the outsiders are brought to the village for the express purpose of being offered as a sacrifice. Even though not willingly offering themselves up like literal lambs to the slaughter, everyone who enters this community nonetheless comes of their own free will, as did Sergeant Howie. Also, much like Howie, Dani is set apart in her natural environment, and she, like the Sergeant, is not able to fully integrate within the modern world. Also, although not sacrificed herself, she is nonetheless enveloped and revered by all around her in this new world. It should also be noted that this world, unlike that of *The Wicker Man*, is not only Pagan, but also matriarchal. The worship of Mother Earth is led by a woman. Like [*The Dark Secret*] *of Harvest Home*, this community has a female leader, although the head of this group shares and makes manifest all the teachings and rites to both male and female followers alike. There may be a dark secret in *Midsommar*, but it is one that is shared by all in the community. Dani's emotions are shared, her burdens lightened, and her losses restored. The ending is rendered even more significant when it is noted that throughout the film, this is one of the first times that she truly smiles.

It has thus been argued throughout this book that works of horror from their ostensible inception with the Gothic up until the present day have actively engaged with contemporaneous debates surrounding religion and spiritual affiliation. Although, as has also been argued, this alignment is not unfraught—not as simple as it at first appears to be. Just like the Gothic literary period, which is commonly agreed to begin with the publication of Horrace Walpole's *The Castle of Otranto* in 1764, following the dual legacies of the Reformation and the Enlightenment, began to question the role of Catholicism and traditional religion, so too did the horrors of the late 1960s and 1970s, following debates within popular culture and the Second Vatican Council, open up a discussion of the possibility of the viability of alternative religions.

These debates, just like the Gothics and the influence of 1970s Faith Horrors, continue to be relevant today, as it appears as if once again debates regarding the role of Christianity and traditional religion come into focus. However, these latest Faith Horrors do not wholly debate the tenets of modernity, as the Gothic were wont to do, nor are they affiliated with debates surrounding postmodernity, and the offering up of a fractured self as a result of the loss of grand narratives nor are they reified as a product of consumer culture, like Guy Woodhouse of *Rosemary's Baby*. Instead, they might be considered, on the one hand, to be products of pseudo-modernity, in the sense of Sacks's definition. On the other hand, these texts offer a return of a concern with traditional spirituality as presented in *The Conjuring Series*. At the same time, in *The Witch*, the battle of good versus evil is fought not in the cities, or even the suburbs, but instead in the countryside. As is the case with classical horror, this film is representative of the cinema of occlusion, a recursive film divorced not only from the here, but also from the now. In being set in colonial America, the link between Witchcraft and Satanism might be connected more to the time of the Salem Witch Trials than to modern representations such as those carefully established as being within their historical and cultural milieu, as was the case with *Rosemary's Baby*. In being set in the distant past, this alignment of faith and the horror that results from it is, on the surface, robbed of cultural connectivity, even though such concerns are just as relevant today as they were during the classical horror era, if not more so. Finally, in setting *Midsommar* in the distant countryside of a distant country, the divide is one of space and not of time; however, as has been argued, this apparent separation does little to challenge its revelation of current debates, conflicts that still circulate in post-millennial pseudo-modern culture as much or even more so than at the apex of modernity fifty years ago. Indeed, questions as to the nature of belief, the value of belief systems in the establishment of self-sustainability, and how these alliances affect perception are ingrained within the human condition, and it is through Faith Horror that these existential queries, both then and now, are given voice.

Chapter Notes

Opening Quotes

1. Robert N. Bellah, Richard Madsen, William M. Sullivan, Ann Swidler, and Steven M. Tipton, *Habits of the Heart: Individualism and Commitment in American Life* (Berkeley: University of California Press, 1985), 142.

2. Victor Sage, *Horror Fiction in the Protestant Tradition* (London: Macmillan Press, 1988), 69.

3. Tony Williams, "An Interview with George and Christine Romero," *Quarterly Review of Film and Video* 18, no. 4 (2001): 52.

Introduction

1. Christopher Lee was an iconic Hammer Horror heavy, first portraying Frankenstein for the studio in the 1957 film *The Curse of Frankenstein*. However, he is more popularly known for his portrayal of *Dracula* starting in the 1958 film *Dracula*. In all, Lee portrayed the Count ten times, seven of which were for Hammer Horror.

2. Anthony Shaffer, *The Wicker Man*. Directed by Robin Hardy (Great Britain and United States: British Lion Productions, 1973).

3. For such works, see David Punter's *The Literature of Terror: A History of Gothic Fiction from 1765 to the Edwardian Age*, and Victor Sage's *Horror Fiction in the Protestant Tradition*, which will be referenced throughout this book.

4. United States Conference of Catholic Bishops, Film Review of *The Omen*.

5. United States Conference of Catholic Bishops, Film Review of *Rosemary's Baby*.

6. The Reformation helped to precipitate a seismic shift in attitudes towards the sacred and supernatural. This evolution of a transcendental and intellectualized religion in which numinous forces were removed from the sphere of everyday life undermined a way of seeing, understanding, and seeking to manipulate the surrounding universe through supernatural means. This process, arguably, culminated in the Age of Enlightenment, whereby all non-scientific means of explaining the world were called into question, even religion itself, leading to a more secular outlook overall.

7. *Paradise Lost* was an undeniable source of inspiration and fascination for the Romantic poets. William Blake's statement that Milton was "of the Devil's party without knowing it" established Satan as the hero as opposed to the villain of *Paradise Lost*. Likewise, in *A Defense of Poetry*, Percy Bysshe Shelley wrote that "nothing can exceed the energy and magnificence of the character of Satan as expressed in *Paradise Lost*." Unsurprisingly the epic poem was also critically influential for Mary Shelley after the poet gave his wife a copy of *Paradise Lost*. As a result, the Shelleys supposedly welcomed Milton to Villa Diodati, where, during the haunted summer, Mary Shelley first conceived the idea for *Frankenstein*.

8. David Punter, *The Literature of Terror: A History of Gothic Fiction from 1765 to the Edwardian Age* (London: Routledge, 1996), 6.

9. *Ibid.*, 8.

10. Garrett Fort, *Dracula*. Directed by Tod Browning (United States: Universal Pictures, 1931).

11. George Baxt, *City of the Dead*.

Directed by John Llewellyn Moxey (United Kingdom and United States: British Lion, 1960).

12. This process of distancing is indeed so strong that the earliest of Gothic authors, Horace Walpole in *The Castle of Otranto*, Anne Radcliffe in *The Italian* and some later novelists (Mary Shelley in *Frankenstein*, for example), frame their narratives around the conceit of a found manuscript that the author merely translates or brings to light. This process of distancing, along with other aesthetic techniques already discussed, allude to the controversial nature of these texts, a nature similar to the reception of the Faith Horror films centuries later.

13. Punter, *The Literature of Terror*, 347.

14. *Ibid.*, 369.

15. Andrew Tudor, *Monsters and Mad Scientists: A Cultural History of the Horror Movie* (Oxford: Basil Blackwell, 1989), 67.

16. *Ibid.*, 95.

17. Stephen Prince, "Introduction to the Horror Film," *The Horror Film*, ed. Stephen Prince (New Jersey: Rutgers University Press, 2004), 4.

18. Robert Bloch, *Psycho* (New York: Tor Books, 1989), 1.

19. Vivian Sobchack, *The Dread of Difference: Gender and the Horror Film* (Texas: University of Texas Press, 1996), 146.

20. Leonard Wolf, "In Horror Movies Some Things Are Sacred," *New York Times*, April 4, 1976, Arts and Leisure Section, Final Edition.

21. Punter, *The Literature of Terror*, 369.

22. Hugh McLeod, *The Religious Crisis of the 1960s* (Oxford: Oxford University Press, 2007), 93.

23. Wolf, "In Horror Movies, Some Things Are Sacred."

24. Vincent Canby, "Hollywood Has an Appealing New Star, Old Gooseberry," *New York Times*, June 25, 1976, Arts and Leisure Section, Final Edition.

25. Roszak, *The Making of a Counter Culture: Reflections on the Technocratic Society and its Youthful Opposition* (New York: Anchor Press, 1969) 124–125.

26. Anton Szandor LaVey, *The Satanic Bible* (New York: Avon Books, 1969).

27. Aleister Crowley, *Magik* (United States: Create Space Independent Publishing Platform, 2014).

28. *Ibid.*, 57.

29. *Ibid.*, 39.

30. *Ibid.*, 33.

31. *Ibid.*, 34.

32. This is not to say that all the sequels were considered, nor were all the novels produced in association reviewed. The time frame and periodization for the book limited those works that were considered. For example, while the first of *The Omen* films in the series is herein analyzed, the final films produced in the 1980s were not. Equally, while *Rosemary's Baby* as an original novel and an adaptive film were studied, the novel produced later in Ira Levin's career, *Son of Rosemary*, was not incorporated herein.

33. Thomas Leitch, "Twelve Fallacies in Contemporary Adaptation Theory," *Criticism* 45, no. 2 (2003): 153.

34. One popular concept has been termed the "Long 1960s," wherein the era is structured around issues related to the civil rights and the counterculture movements. Thus, the 1960s might officially begin, at least within the United States, with the landmark 1954 Supreme Court case *Brown v. Board of Education*, which, arguably, brought issues with regard to equal rights into the public forum in a way not seen since Reconstruction. The end of the "Long 1960s" might then equally have been brought about by the 1972 defeat of the Equal Rights Amendment and the rise of the religious right, two landmarks that signal an end to the "opening up" ethos characteristic of this era. Another conceptualization for this time frame is one that is forwarded within many universities. The span of periodization in this context is even longer still, as the 1960s and 1970s are incorporated into what may be regarded as the Post–War Era. Indeed, many introductory history and film history courses begin, obviously, with the year 1945, and continue into an elusive and ever increasing "present." Still others support a delineation of this time span as beginning in 1960, with the election of John F. Kennedy, a Democratic candidate who, arguably, instilled a sense of hope and new beginnings. Indeed, his presidency is often referred to as Camelot, with

all that this title implies. If 1960 can then be regarded as the beginning of a golden age, for many historians this period of optimism effectively ended in 1968. It was in this year that an increased concern with violent action as opposed to peaceful resistance was signaled by the assassinations of Martin Luther King, Jr., and Robert Kennedy, not to mention the media frenzy that brought the unprecedented violence of the Vietnam War's Tet Offensive and the riots of the Chicago National Convention into American living rooms.

35. Tudor, *Monsters and Mad Scientists*, 56.

36. Philip Loraine, *Day of the Arrow* (Richmond: Valancourt Books, 1964).

37. This sustained growth arguably coalesced around an increasing concern with graphic violence as a chief element of horror following the birth of the slasher film with the release of *Halloween* in 1978. Equally, the horror film seemed less concerned with religion, faith or the occult after the release of *The Amityville Horror* in 1979.

CHAPTER ONE

1. David Thompson, "I Make Films for Adults," *Sight and Sound 5*, no. 4 (1995): 6.

2. Chuck Palahniuk, "Introduction to *Rosemary's Baby*," written by Ira Levin (London: Constable and Robinson, Limited, 2011), vii.

3. *Ibid.*

4. Roman Polanski, *Rosemary's Baby*. Directed by Roman Polanski (Los Angeles: Paramount, 1968).

5. This action is significant and thus worth noting for two reasons. The first is due to the fact that Rosemary and Guy have paid someone to undertake the painting rather than doing it themselves. This unfailing reliance on experts on the part of Rosemary ultimately leads to her downfall, as will be discussed in this chapter. The second reason, which is in many ways allied to the first, is the way in which appearances mask what lays underneath. This is true not only of the decoration of the apartment, but also of those who enter therein.

6. The specific magazine, *House Beautiful*, is only referenced in the novel version of this text. In the film, Rosemary suggests that these ideas were found in "a magazine" without stating which one in particular.

7. *Ibid.*

8. Ira Levin, *Rosemary's Baby* (London: Constable and Robinson, Limited, 2011), 225–227.

9. Renata Adler, "The Screen," *New York Times*, June 13, 1968, Arts and Leisure Section, Final Edition.

10. Mark Jancovich, "Post-Fordism, Postmodernism and Paranoia: The Dominance of the Horror Genre in Contemporary Culture," in *Horror: The Film Reader*, edited by Mark Jancovich (London: Routledge, 2009), 92.

11. Kim Newman, *Nightmare Movies: A Critical History of the Horror Film 1968–1988* (London: Bloomsbury Press, 1990), 39.

12. Sobchack, *Dread of Difference*, 149.

13. Reynold Humphreys, *The American Horror Film: An Introduction* (Edinburgh: Edinburgh University Press, 2002), 87.

14. Ira Levin, "Stuck with Satan: Ira Levin on the Origins of *Rosemary's Baby*," "On Film/ Essays," *Criterion Collection*, 4 November 2012.

15. Punter, *The Literature of Terror*, 4.

16. Levin, *Rosemary's Baby*, 23.

17. *Ibid.*, 13.

18. Both the tour and this scene are left out of the film altogether.

19. Tony Williams, *Hearths of Darkness: The Family in the American Horror Film* (Mississippi: University of Mississippi Press, 2014), 106.

20. *Ibid.*, 99.

21. "The Devil Is Alive and Hiding on Central Park West," *Time*, June 23, 1967, 112.

22. C. S. Lewis, *Mere Christianity* (London: Fount, 1979), 141.

23. Levin, *Rosemary's Baby*, 71.

24. Rosemary is also a housewife, but her relationship with Guy is far less egalitarian, as is evidenced in his decision to sacrifice her body to Satan for fame and material success.

25. Levin, *Rosemary's Baby*, 161.

26. Tony Williams, *Hearths of Darkness*, 102.

27. Beverle Houston and Marsha Kinder, *Close-up, A Critical Perspective on Film* (New York: Harcourt Brace Jovanovich, 1972), 17.

28. Levin, *Rosemary's Baby*, 83.

29. Polanski, *Rosemary's Baby.*

30. *The Holy Bible* (London: Oxford University Press, 1934), 864.

31. Levin, *Rosemary's Baby*, 165.

32. Houston and Kinder, *Critical Perspective*, 19.

33. John F. Kennedy, 1961 Inaugural Address, John F. Kennedy Presidential Library and Museum, http://www.jfk library.org/Asset-Viewer/BqXIEM 9F4024ntFl7SVAjA.aspx (accessed October 19, 2015).

34. Argyron Stavropolous, one of the characters that visits Rosemary's baby, is presented as being decidedly Greek. This character, who appears to woo Rosemary, might stand for Jack Kennedy's "replacement," Aristotle Onassis.

35. Playing the arch–Protestant himself, of which Rosemary seems very proud.

36. Polanski, *Rosemary's Baby.*

37. *Ibid.*

38. Levin, *Rosemary's Baby*, 21.

39. Twiggy, Leslie (Hornby) Lawson, was named the "face of 1966" in the United Kingdom by the tabloid the *Daily Express*, as well as appearing on the cover of popular fashion magazines, including *Vogue* and the *Tatler.* When she first arrived in the United States in March of 1967, the event was regarded as front page news, featured in the headlines of the *New York Times*, *Life* and *Newsweek*, suggesting her appeal to a large swath of the public.

40. Jean Baudrillard, *The System of Objects* (London: Verso Books, 2005).

41. Jean Baudrillard, *For a Critique of the Political Economy of the Sign* (London: Telos Press, 1981).

42. Jean Baudrillard, *The Consumer Society: Myths and Structures* (London: Sage, 2016).

43. Mark Jancovich, *Horror* (London: Batsford, 1992), 89.

44. Bell, *The Cultural Contradictions of Capitalism*, 76.

45. It is later revealed that her doctor, Abraham Sapirstein, is in fact a member of the Satanic coven led by Roman Castevet. This world-renowned obstetrician offered his services to the Woodhouses at a deeply discounted rate so as to ensure the safe birth of what will be the Antichrist. Interestingly, it would appear that while Guy is chiefly concerned with doing all he can to further his career, this doctor is willing to forego the spoils of his notoriety for the sake of his religious belief. This divergence is indeed an important theme of the film and novel alike.

46. Levin, *Rosemary's Baby*, 146.

47. Polanski, *Rosemary's Baby.*

48. Ira Levin, "Stuck with Satan."

49. Emma Lazarus, "The New Colossus," United States National Park Service website, https://www.nps.gov/stli/learn/ historyculture/colossus.htm. Accessed July 2020.

50. Daniel Bell, *The Cultural Contradictions of Capitalism* (New York: Basic Books, 1996), 295.

51. Punter, *The Literature of Terror*, 10.

52. Punter, *The Literature of Terror*, 347.

53. Robert Lima, "The Satanic Rape of Catholicism in *Rosemary's Baby*," *Studies in American Fiction* 2 (1974): 211–22.

54. Levin, *Rosemary's Baby*, 206.

55. Polanski, *Rosemary's Baby* and Levin, *Rosemary's Baby*, 219.

56. *Ibid.*, 228.

57. "*Rosemary's Baby* Given a 'C' Rating by Catholic Office," *New York Times*, June 21, 1968, Arts and Leisure Section, Final Edition.

58. *Ibid.*

59. *Ibid.*

60. Iconic horror producer and director William Castle was the man waiting outside the phone booth that Rosemary uses to call Doctor Hill (Charles Grodin). Castle's gray hair and stature resembling Sidney Blackmer terrifies the protagonist even as those "in the know" chuckle at this reference.

61. It should be noted, although an aside, that in the film and the book, his fame is due largely to his appearance on the national television program *Open End.* This show, hosted by David Susskind, was known for its ideological gamut and widely varying guests. His most famous interviews included the likes of Martin Luther King, Jr., Nikita Khrushchev and seven lesbians in a show entitled "Women Who Love Women."

Chapter Two

1. Christopher Lasch, *The Culture of Narcissism: American Life in an Age of Diminishing Expectations* (New York: WW Norton, 1991), 151.

2. Bellah et al., *Habits of the Heart*, 86.

3. Williams, *Hearths of Darkness*, 13.

4. This is a political incident in two ways: first, being that Thorn is himself a diplomat, this attempted filicide will bring about a scandal. Further, should this news be made public, there will undoubtedly be detrimental ramifications for his office as the ambassador, and the relationship between the United Kingdom and the United States. Secondly, his actions are against the Antichrist, the being who will usher in the end of days and thus socio-political chaos.

5. David Seltzer, *The Omen*. Directed by Richard Donner (United States: 20th Century Fox, 1976).

6. There is, in fact, a strong correlation between the ambassador to the Court of St. James and the United States presidency. Historically, John Adams, James Monroe, John Quincy Adams, Martin Van Buren, James Buchanan, not to mention Joe Kennedy, father to both John and Robert Kennedy, were all once U.S. ambassadors to the United Kingdom.

7. Donner, *The Omen*.

8. Marshall Berman, *All That Is Solid Melts into Air: The Experience of Modernity* (London: Verso, 2010), 13.

9. Tudor, *Monsters and Mad Scientists*, 68.

10. Robin Wood, *Hollywood from Vietnam to Reagan* (New York: Columbia University Press, 1986), 187.

11. *Ibid.*, 186.

12. *Ibid.*, 192.

13. Sobchack, *The Dread of Difference*, 150.

14. It is not only in theoretical and thematic terms that these two texts align. There are indeed many cross referential scenes existing between *The Omen* and *Rosemary's Baby*. These include a scene when Robert and Kathy first move into their stately mansion in England, one that Kathy, like Rosemary, deeply desires for the family. As they look around, the couple waxes amorous, and it is suggested that much like the Woodhouses, they will make love on the bare floorboards of their new home. Also, later in the film, when Thorn discovers that his son has been murdered by Satanists, a fear that drives the actions of Rosemary, he calls out "Murderers.... Murderers!" in much the

same way as Rosemary does when she suspects that her beloved Andy was prey to Satanic sacrifice.

15. Williams, *Hearths of Darkness*, 117.

16. Seltzer, *The Omen* (Film).

17. The sequence of numbers six-hundred and sixty-six (666) is the sign of the Antichrist, and figures prominently not only for Damien, but also all of his followers and acolytes.

18. In this way, Thorn might be shown to be similar to Neil Howie, protagonist of *The Wicker Man*, a work which will be discussed later in this book. Indeed, like Howie, who is specifically recruited by an alternative religious community for his specific allegiances, so too is Thorn.

19. *The Holy Bible*, 301.

20. *Oxford English Dictionary* 3rd Edition (Oxford: Oxford University Press, 2010), 1112.

21. It is interesting that once again, the maternal female is linked with Mary. As discussed in the previous chapter, Roman Polanski, in the film version of *Rosemary's Baby*, makes a point of shooting Rosemary in front of a nativity window display. As she looks through the plate glass, her reflection is seen creating a literal and figurative mirror effect between the mother of the Antichrist and the mother of Jesus.

22. While the other biblical referents in this text appear not to be correlated directly to the Bible, this location, Megiddo, is in fact a real place with a similar significance and history to that which is mentioned in the film.

23. In the first film, the book of the Bible that predicts the end of days is referred to as "The Book of Revelations" rather than "The Book of Revelation"—a point that was discussed by critics and scholars when devaluing the film.

24. It is significant to note that at this birthday party, crammed with family friends, political colleagues, and reporters, the grandparents, aunts, uncles, and cousins of both Robert and Kathy are absent. This is a structuring absence similar to that provided in *Rosemary's Baby*—all the more so, in fact, as so much import has been given to the fact of the Thorn fortune, family and legacy.

25. Seltzer, *The Omen* (Film). This quotation, while purportedly from the Bible, is a fabrication of the screenwriter.

26. *The Holy Bible*, 1041.

27. *Ibid.*, 1050.

28. Richard Eder, "The Screen, Omen Is Nobody's Baby," *New York Times*, June 26, 1976, Arts and Leisure Section, Final Edition.

29. Canby, "Film View; Hollywood Has an Appealing New Star Old Gooseberry," *New York Times*, July 25, 1976, Arts and Leisure Section, Final Edition.

30. United States Conference of Catholic Bishops, Film Review of *The Omen*.

31. Later in life, Heston was known for, among other things, being a member (not to mention the leader) of the National Rifle Association, a hotbed of American conservatism.

32. This may be because the story is a fabrication, but more likely, this omission may be due to the fact of his political reversal later in life, as mentioned earlier.

33. This is an important scene as it not only reveals a necessity to look beyond, but also from a spiritual standpoint. This is one of the two times within the narrative that the family enters into a church, both of which to disastrous results. This scene culminates in Damien panicking at being removed from the car to the church, bruising his mother's face, and his father's reputation as photographers and onlookers make note of the Thorn heir's unacceptable actions. The second time that the Thorns enter a church is when Thorn attempts to kill what he now regards as the Antichrist, again not only bruising the boy, but also his reputation through what is an apparently unspeakable act.

34. It is even more interesting to consider that the disintegration of the family was one of the key ways in which the critics of this work regarded this text as being reactionary. Indeed, if considered as a textual constellation, this might be given more weight analytically.

35. It is Thorn's concern for the feelings of his wife that leads him to adopt the son of Satan in the first place.

36. Seltzer, *The Omen* (London: Futura, McDonald and Company, 1978), 19.

37. *Ibid.*, 9.

38. *Ibid.*, 98–9.

39. *Ibid.*, 167.

40. *Ibid.*, 171.

41. *Ibid.*, 6.

42. *Ibid.*, 11.

43. *Ibid.*, 12.

44. *Ibid.*, 13.

45. *Ibid.*, 13.

46. *Ibid.*, 14.

47. *Ibid.*, 64–5.

48. *Ibid.*, 139.

49. *Ibid.*, 96.

50. *Ibid.*, 137.

51. *Ibid.*, 144.

CHAPTER THREE

1. Bell, *The Cultural Contradictions of Capitalism*, 19.

2. Roszak, *The Making of a Counterculture*, 1.

3. Lasch, *The Culture of Narcissism*, 41.

4. This ethos, as discussed in Chapter One on *Rosemary's Baby*, was aided by an economy based on credit as opposed to cash. Thus, if one desired an item, it could be acquired immediately without having to wait, to work and to save.

5. Marshall Berman, *All That Is Solid Melts into Air*, 67.

6. Cyril Frankel, the director of the film version of *The Witches*, had a particular interest in Africa, and in 1955 released his first feature length film, *Man of Africa*. This docudrama produced by famed documentary director John Grierson was shot on location in Uganda with a crew of just seven. The film became famous not only for its eschewing of stereotypical representations of Africa as a "dark continent," but also for being one of the first films to feature an all-black cast.

7. This representation of the failure of Christianity within a rural British setting is in many ways similar to that presented in *The Wicker Man*. As will be discussed in a subsequent chapter of this book, Summerisle also offers a destroyed church building and a desecrated Christian graveyard wherein the locals practice their pagan rituals. Equally, the heads of these isolated communities are both wealthy members of the landed gentry. Summerisle is a lord, and Bax, although not mentioned as being titled, is nonetheless the village patriarch. Finally, both Lord Summerisle and Bax appear to be the spiritual leaders of these villages. However, while the former is the legitimate head of the island's pagan church, the latter is revealed to be an ersatz clergyman.

8. Nigel Neale, *The Witches*, directed by Cyril Frankel (United Kingdom: British Pathe, 1966).

9. Anton Szandor LaVey, *The Satanic Bible* (New York, Avon Books, 1969), 24.

10. *Ibid.*, 45.

11. *Ibid.*, 47.

12. This scientific study is similar to that enacted by Lord Summerisle's father on the island of Summerisle. Aware of the science of botany and the importance of successful agriculture for the subsistence of the community, the former lord instituted pagan rituals designed to invest the agrarian lifestyle with a spiritual component. In aligning the monetary and the spiritual, the success of the crops became all-important to the villagers. While the former lord did not believe in the rites, however, his son not only adopted and adhered to these rituals, but came to have faith in them. This is similar to Stephanie, who at first approached the rites out of scientific curiosity, but then came to have faith in their efficacy.

13. Nigel Neale, *The Witches*.

14. *Ibid.*

15. Howard Thompson, "The Devil's Own in Neighborhood Houses," *New York Times*, March 16, 1967, Arts and Leisure Section, Final Edition.

16. Adam Scovell, *Folk Horror* (London: Auteur Publishing, 2017), 132.

17. Michael Wood, "Witches and Demons: The Occult in Two Hammer Films from the 1960s," *Monstrum* 1, no. 1 (April 1, 2018): 135.

18. Peter Shelley, *Grande Dame Guignol Cinema: A History of Hag Horror from Baby Jane to Mother* (Jefferson, NC: McFarland, 2009).

19. Michael Wood, "Witches and Demons," 145.

20. Norah Lofts, *The Devil's Own* (New York: Arrow Books, iBook Edition, 2011), 480.

21. *Ibid.*, 109.

22. *Ibid.*, 285.

23. *Ibid.*, 201.

24. *Ibid.*, 336.

25. *Ibid.*, 491.

26. *Ibid.*, 925.

27. This characterization is completely different from her depiction in the film, wherein she is indeed the most powerful antagonist.

28. Nora Lofts, *The Devil's Own*, 143.

29. *Ibid.*, 1007.

30. *Ibid.*, 310.

31. *Ibid.*, 370.

32. *Ibid.*, 555.

33. *Ibid.*, 681.

34. It is interesting to note that while falling in line with a Folk Horror tradition in this regard, the idea of the safety of the urban and the danger inherent in the rural presents an antithesis to what occurs in *Rosemary's Baby* and *The Omen*. Indeed, in both texts, it is the big urban metropolis, New York in the former and Rome in the latter, that deters the detection of the satanist and his coven.

35. Norah Lofts, *The Devil's Own*, 1109.

36. Joseph McBride, "Race with the Devil," *Variety*, December 31, 1974. Final Edition.

37. Beth Bailey, *Sex in the Heartland* (Cambridge: Harvard University Press, 2002), 141.

38. Interestingly, not only does Oates characterize the members of the satanist coven as being hippies, he also suggests as he battles these antagonists that he is too old for this.

39. Oates suggests of his wife, "She is the woman I know I'll love forever."

40. Peter Fonda, Dennis Hopper and Terry Southern, *Easy Rider*, directed by Dennis Hopper (United States: Columbia Pictures, 1969).

41. It is interesting that the sheriff badge, a five or in some cases a six-pointed star, is similar to the icon used to symbolize the satanist movement or indeed the occult in general: the pentacle also being a five-pointed star.

42. Film theorists like Linda Williams note that it was not until the release of *Deep Throat* in 1972 that representations of sexuality became more culturally acceptable outside of a strictly pornographic definition.

43. Bailey, *Sex in the Heartland*, 155.

44. *Ibid.*, 157.

45. Wes Bishop, *Race with the Devil*, directed by Jack Starett (United States: 20th Century Fox, 1975).

46. Vincent Canby, "The Screen: In Race with the Devil, Witches Are Hunters," *New York Times*, July 10, 1975, Arts and Leisure Section, Final Edition.

47. Robbyn Grant and Barry K. Grant, "Race with the Devil: A Brief Vacation on the Open Road," *Jump Cut: A Review of Contemporary Media* 10–11 (June 1976): 20.

48. This inclusion of a tank, although odd narratively, could be understood as a cultural referent to the Vietnam War. Indeed, scenes of violence involving tanks were common fare in the news and newsreels of the period.

49. William Welch, *The Brotherhood of Satan*, directed by Bernard McEveety (United States: Columbia Pictures Corporation, 1971).

50. This separation, instituted by the "nepotists" in *The Brotherhood of Satan*, completely isolates this village in a way similar to *Robin Redbreast*, *The Wicker Man* and *The Dark Secret of Harvest Home* so as to safeguard the perpetuation of an alternative lifestyle against outside persecution. Likewise, the isolation also closes off departure for those living within these societies so that word of their practices cannot spread to a secular world that almost certainly would condemn such propitiatory practices as human sacrifice.

51. Roger Greenspun, "Horror film," review of *The Brotherhood of Satan*, *New York Times*, August 7, 1971, Arts and Leisure Section, Final Edition.

Chapter Four

1. David Thompson, "Cult TV Pick: Robin Redbreast," *Film Comment* 49, no. 6 (2013): 76.

2. Bellah et al., *Habits of the Heart*, 154.

3. Ironically, the teleplay was originally produced in color. During its telecast, however, an electrician's work to rule prevented transmission to all regions, and so the following February, the teleplay was re-aired, making this the first *Play for Today* to be repeated. As was BBC practice, there was no concern with archiving materials, however, so when rebroadcast, only the black and white version was available to air. Thus, whereas the characters are revealed in their true colors, the teleplay was not.

4. Adam Scovell, *Folk Horror*, 10.

5. Born Robin Philip Loraine Estridge, Philip Loraine was one of the pen names of this author, the other being Robin Estridge. The former was used for the novel *Day of the Arrow*, and the latter used for the screenwriting credit on the adaptive film *Eye of the Devil*. In the film credits, there is an acknowledgment of the fact that the screenplay is based on the Loraine novel, but there is no indication that Robin Estridge and Philip Loraine are indeed the same person.

6. "Criminals at Large," *New York Times*, March 1, 1964, Arts and Leisure Section, Final Edition.

7. Bill Ellis, *Raising the Devil: Satanism, New Religions and the Media* (Lexington: University of Kentucky Press, 2000), 157.

8. Jonathan Rigby, "Robin Redbreast," *Sight and Sound* (January 2014), 94.

9. Sam Binkley, *Getting Loose: Lifestyle Consumption in the 1970s* (Durham: Duke University Press, 2007), xiii.

10. It is important to note that this was not only a time of getting loose, a time of an acceptance of a panoply of faiths by the counterculture, but also a time that saw the rise of the religious right—for example, the incredibly popular and pervasive ministry of Billy Graham and his Evangelical movement.

11. Scovell, *Folk Horror*, 134.

12. Ramsay MacMullen, *Christianity and Paganism in the Fourth to Eighth Centuries* (New Haven: Yale University Press, 1997).

13. Scovell, *Folk Horror*, 64.

14. "The Hippies" *Time*, July 7, 1967, 2–3.

15. Scovell, *Folk Horror*, 10.

16. According to *Time*, Morning Star represents a major new development in the hippie world. This rural commune became a prototype for some thirty such communities which now exist from Canada through the U.S. to Mexico.

17. Binkley, *Getting Loose*, 133.

18. Berman, *All That Is Solid Melts into Air*, 41.

19. Indeed, the urban is inexorably linked with the rise of modernity, for according to Max Weber, the foundation of Western rationalism was laid with "urban revolution" (Weber, *The Protestant Ethic and the Spirit of Capitalism*, 321).

20. It is interesting that while the loca-

tion symbolizes modernity, the inclusion of the harp adds a contradictory element. The harp is one of the symbols of Diana, as is the bow and arrow, the latter of which will figure prominently in this film.

21. Robin Estridge, *Eye of the Devil*, directed by J. Lee Thompson (United Kingdom: Metro Goldwyn Mayer, 1966).

22. The links between this image and Christianity can be located in the Old Testament of the Bible, wherein offerings were often made to God as restitution for sin in the form of fatted calves, lambs, or even doves and pigeons. Not only this, but in the Psalms, another reference is made that not only equates the spirit of God to a bird, but also suggests that his love will protect against the sting of an arrow: "He will cover you with His pinions, And under His wings you may seek refuge; His faithfulness is a shield and bulwark. You will not be afraid of the terror by night, Or of the arrow that flies by day; Of the pestilence that stalks in darkness, Or of the destruction that lays waste at noon" (Psalm 91). Equally, the use of candles and the donning of robes suggest a debt to traditional Christian practices of worship.

23. Estridge, *Eye of the Devil.*

24. *Ibid.*

25. Ramsay MacMullen, *Christianity and Paganism in the Fourth to Eighth Centuries* (New Haven: Yale University Press, 1997).

26. The *Apocrypha* is an ancient collection of writings included in early versions of the Bible until the Puritan revolution of the 1600s excised it.

27. Sydney Carter, "Lord of the Dance," *Hymnary.org*, http://www.hymnary.org/text/i_danced_in_the_morning_when_the, accessed March 16, 2016.

28. Interestingly, Carter's legacy rests not only in the creation of this potentially controversial hymn, but also in his contributions to television, and more specifically a satire series for the American ABC television network entitled *Hallelujah!* and *Don't Just Sit There*, for which he wrote a song, "The Devil Wore a Crucifix." While "Lord of the Dance" won him praise, apparently, according to the *Telegraph* obituary, this collaboration did not win such universal approval.

29. "Sydney Carter Obituary'" *Telegraph*, March 16, 2004, Obituaries Section, Final Edition.

30. Estridge, *Eye of the Devil.*

31. *Ibid.* This quotation is also used in the original literary text, *Day of the Arrow.*

32. Bosley Crowther, "Screen: 'Eye of the Devil' Begins Run: Deborah Kerr Appears with David Niven 5 Other Films Arrive in Local Theaters East-West Twin Bill Local Double Bill," *New York Times*, December 7, 1967, Arts and Leisure Section, Final Edition.

33. It is interesting that the true nature of the screenplay writer, like the practices that he describes, are equally obscured as to their true identity.

34. An addition to the filmic work is a literary protagonist, James Lindsay, who, like Françoise (Catherine in the film), equally represents tendencies toward modernity.

35. It is interesting that in the novel version of this extended text there is not only the addition of a protagonist, but in fact a Scottish protagonist. As will be discussed later, this country has a unique and specific history of religious belief that ties it to not only the foundations of Catholicism, but also the roots of Paganism.

36. This age is also significant for the contemporaneous "Yippie" movement, whose leader Abbie Hoffman, as suggested in an earlier chapter, warned not to trust anyone over thirty, as this was the time when adulthood and a concomitant acceptance of traditionalism took hold.

37. Loraine, *Day of the Arrow*, 14.

38. *Ibid.*

39. *Ibid.*, 41.

40. *Ibid.*, 43.

41. *Ibid.*, 7.

42. *Ibid.*, 60.

43. *Ibid.*, 35.

44. This connection is not surprising, as one of the many inspirations for the novel was Frazer's *The Golden Bough*, a commonality between this work and the subsequent texts discussed in this section. As with *The Wicker Man*, there was also a desire on the part of the filmmakers to portray the religious devotions depicted consistently and correctly, which is why an expert in Paganism, Alex Sanders, "King of the Witches," was called in as a consultant. Were such concerns equally

a part of *The Omen*, potentially the film might not have been panned by critics.

45. Loraine, *Day of the Arrow*, 59.

46. *Ibid.*, 106.

47. *Ibid.*, 118.

48. *Ibid.*, 119.

49. *Ibid.*, 98.

50. This idea of the rural retreat is one which is common to many horror narratives. As discussed elsewhere in this book, Rosemary, in the literary version of the text *Rosemary's Baby*, leaves for the country after a fight with her husband. Interestingly, however, while in this earlier work, the country is regarded as a safe haven (the city being inhabited by the coven), in this and other works of horror, the country is regarded as being the location of the frightening pre–modern world of insanity, Witchcraft, Satanism and Paganism, as evidenced in such works as *Psycho*, *The Witches*, *Eye of the Devil/ Day of the Arrow* and *The Wicker Man*, to name only a few.

51. John Griffith Bowen, *Robin Redbreast* (United Kingdom: British Broadcasting Corporation, BBC 1, 1970).

52. For a horror aficionado, this request resonates with more classical horror texts, namely the vampire narrative in which, according to superstition, the Evil One must ask permission before being allowed entrance to any location.

53. Vic Pratt, *Hunting for Sherds* (London: British Film Institute, n.d.), 1.

54. Indeed, not only does she assume his family name and title, she is also dependent upon her husband financially.

55. According to many financial publications, 1960s English women could expect to make 61 pence for every £1 a man made. The wage gap hovered at around sixty percent until 1970, when it surpassed seventy percent, arguably making England slightly less occupationally segregated than other first world countries such as the United States, however, significantly segregated, nonetheless.

56. Daniel Bell, *The Cultural Contradictions of Capitalism*.

57. Sir James George Frazer, *The Illustrated Golden Bough* (London: Macmillan, 1978), 28.

58. The first time that Norah and Rob are introduced it is for the express purpose of his killing the field mice that have invaded the cottage attic. Again, like in all the other cases, this meeting, and indeed even the infestation, was prearranged with a specific goal in mind.

59. Frazer, *The Golden Bough*, 27.

60. Pratt, *Hunting for Sherds*, 1.

61. Bowen, *Robin Redbreast*.

62. *Ibid.*

63. Pratt, *Hunting for Sherds*, 1.

64. A craft name is a secondary religious name often adopted by Wiccan practitioners. Much like those of the Catholic faith who adopt a saint's name upon confirmation and upon being named Pope, Wiccans adopt a magical name as an expression of religious devotion. Such a name also protects the privacy of the practitioner from those who would persecute them (hiding Wiccan allegiance is known ironically as being in the broom closet), or from those who might curse them.

65. Linda and Rod Dubrow-Marshall, "How Cult Leader Charles Manson Was Able to Convince His Family to Commit Murder," *Journal of the International Cult Studies Association*, November 20, 2017.

66. Oliver Wake, "James MacTaggart, 1928–1974: Producer, Director, Writer," BFI Screen On-line, Retrieved 09/21/2019. (http://www.screenonline.org.uk/people/ id/1343392/index.html)

Chapter Five

1. Andrew Abbott and Russell Leven, *Burnt Offering: The Cult of the Wicker Man* (United Kingdom: Nobels Gate, 2001).

2. *Ibid.*

3. Allan Brown, *Inside the Wicker Man* (Edinburg: Polygon, 2017).

4. Shaffer, *The Wicker Man*.

5. *Ibid.*

6. *Ibid.*

7. *Ibid.*

8. *The Holy Bible*, 829.

9. Adam Scovell, *Folk Horror: Hours Dreadful and Things Strange* (London: Auteur Press, 2017).

10. *Ibid.*, 81.

11. Several times throughout this film, Howie identifies himself as being a member of the West Highlands Constabulary. Although not named, the city in which Howie makes his home is most likely Fort William, the second largest city in the

highland region, and the largest city in the West Highlands. Determining the exact city is, however, less important than the fact of it being in the Highlands of Scotland. The Highlands are distinct in being more associated with antiquity than the Scotch Lowlands. The highlands were the domains of the last of the clans, and the last location to speak Scotch Gaelic. Although not as geographically separated, the Highlands are thus associated with the Hebrides, where the last vestiges of ancient Scottish culture remained long after the rest of the country assimilated into the United Kingdom. This is significant as it might close the gap a bit between the conflict offered up between Howie and Summerisle. Although at odds, they are more alike vis-à-vis the rest of their contemporaneous culture than they are different, as will be seen in the analysis that follows.

12. Shaffer, *The Wicker Man*.

13. Robin Hardy and Anthony Shaffer, *The Wicker Man* (London: Pan Books, 2000), 37.

14. *Ibid.*

15. *Ibid.*

16. *Ibid.*, 202.

17. *Ibid.*, 207.

18. Lucius Shepard, "Something Wicker This Way Comes," *The Magazine of Fantasy and Science Fiction* 112, no. 1 (January 1, 2007): 128.

19. McLeod, *The Religious Crisis of the 1960s*, 244.

20. *Ibid.*, 1.

21. Andrew Abbott and Russell Leven, *Burnt Offering: The Cult of the Wicker Man* (United Kingdom: British Film Institute, 2001).

22. *Ibid.*

23. Alan Brown, "Introduction to *The Wicker Man*," in *The Wicker Man*, written by Robin Hardy and Anthony Shaffer (Glasgow: Pan Books, 2000), xi. This does not take into account other horror films from the period that deal with spirituality such as *Rosemary's Baby* and *Eye of the Devil*, both of which preceded *The Wicker Man* by more than five years, not to mention the myriad other films that are discussed within this book.

24. Andy Boot, *Fragments of Fear: An Illustrated History of British Horror Films* (London: Creation Books, 1999), 236.

25. Hardy and Shaffer, *The Wicker Man*, 5.

26. Janet Maslin, "Screen: 'The Wicker Man,' About a Fertility Cult: Strange Happenings," *New York Times*, March 26, 1980, Arts and Leisure Section, Final Edition.

27. Hardy and Shaffer, *The Wicker Man*, 64–65.

28. Hardy and Shaffer, *The Wicker Man*, 62.

29. David Pinner's novel *Ritual* was one basis for the film, although obliquely. While the rights to the text were acquired, *The Wicker Man* cannot be said to be an adaptation of *Ritual*, for director Robin Hardy never even read the book, and Anthony Shaffer states the novel "could not be made into a movie." This is only one of the two elements that found its way into the final version of the film, the other being the idea of transmutation. As Rowan Martin ostensibly becomes a March hare in the film, in the opening of Pinner's work, a young girl who is also potentially murdered comes back to life as a butterfly.

30. Pinner, *Ritual*, 116–118.

31. Interestingly, in the film, the scene is framed so that the actress, as she sings, directly addresses the camera, thus, arguably, attempting to seduce the spectator as much as the character within the narrative. This begs the question as to whether or not we as the audience would resist her wiles as Howie, through prayer, has managed to do, especially given an apparent lack of belief in anything beyond self-interest, a condition intrinsic to the modern world and its inhabitants, as discussed by Hardy and Shaffer above.

32. Hardy and Shaffer, *The Wicker Man*, 197.

33. *Ibid.*, 182.

34. *Ibid.*, 265.

35. Shaffer, *The Wicker Man*.

36. Abbott and Levin, *Burnt Offerings*.

37. Hardy and Shaffer, *The Wicker Man*, 202.

38. Frazer, *The Golden Bough*, 135.

39. *Ibid.*, 196.

40. *Ibid.*, 74.

41. Hardy and Shaffer, *The Wicker Man*, 118–119.

42. Frazer, *The Golden Bough*, 58.

43. Hardy and Shaffer, *The Wicker Man*, 135.

44. Frazer, *The Golden Bough*, 248.

45. Hardy and Shaffer, *The Wicker Man*, 136.

46. *Ibid.*, 147.

47. *Ibid.*, 13.

48. *Ibid.*, 32.

49. *Ibid.*, 132.

50. Brown, *Inside the Wicker Man*, 61.

51. Interview with Dennis Wheatley (British Broadcasting Corporation, 1970). Accessed 27 August 2016. https://dangerousminds.net/comments/satanism_was_basically_anything_horror_writer_dennis_wheatley_didnt_agree.

52. Roger Ebert, *Death Wish* film review, RogerEbert.com. Accessed 28 September 2019. https://www.rogerebert.com/reviews/death-wish-1974.

53. Christopher Lee, *Tall, Dark and Gruesome* (London: W&N, 1997), 97.

54. Brown, *Inside the Wicker Man*, 46.

55. This use of instruments was foregrounded in the original director's cut of the film, wherein, in a cutaway shot during the song "The Landlord's Daughter," the musicians are shown playing these traditional instruments. This foregrounding is redoubled during the fertility rite and the song "Gently Johnny" in the final scene as the same musicians appear again.

56. *Ibid.*, pp. 30–31.

57. *Ibid.*, xiv.

Chapter Six

1. Thomas Tryon, *Harvest Home* (London: Coronet Books, 1980), 167.

2. *Ibid.*, 351.

3. Whereas this is not directly stated in the film, it is suggested in a voice over. Responding to the call of a domestic disturbance, the police detective suggests, "Whether she's lying or not, she'll get away with it. We'll run a check on insurance. Goddamn women, they get it all in the end. They wind up with everything."

4. "Jack's Wife" was one name for the film bandied about by producers.

5. George A Romero, *Season of the Witch*, directed by George A. Romero (United States: Jack A. Harris Enterprises, 1973).

6. This supposedly conferred an element of legitimacy and professionalism not experienced since the making of his first feature length film, *Night of the Living Dead.*

7. While produced in the United Kingdom and starring primarily British actors, these films were largely funded by American dollars, making their national origin divided. This is not the case, however, with *Robin Redbreast*, a BBC teleplay produced in the UK with British financing, cast and writers.

8. Catholicism has often been derided as privileging men over women, as only men can assume positions of power within the Church. Whereas male clergy can become Priests, Bishops, or even Pope, women can only achieve the status of nun, a wife of God rather than an active agent with regard to the dissemination, articulation and enaction of His word. This is because the faith is in many ways represented in gender-based terms. God is the Father, Christ, his Son, the Priest, God's representative on earth, and therefore also male, and finally the Church as the female bride, wed to Jesus and to the Priest as his stand-in.

9. Significantly, if not unproblematically, following the publication of Betty Friedan's *The Feminine Mystique* in 1963, the mid–1960s were popularly discerned to be the beginning of the second wave of the feminist movement. This periodization, admittedly, is not without flaw for a number of reasons, one of them being the fact that Friedan herself not only garnered many of her ideas and primary research from female-oriented popular magazines, but also published in the same before coalescing these articles into a single monograph. Equally as is suggested by June Meyerowitz in her book, *Not June Cleaver*, second-wave feminism could be considered not to be a secondary movement subsequent to the first wave, but instead a socio-political struggle that never ceased, a fact that can be noted when considering the working and lower-middle classes.

10. John Skow, "Sweet Corn," *Time* 101, no. 26 (June 25, 1973): 92.

11. Owen Davies, *Paganism: A Very Short Introduction* (New York: Oxford University Press, 2011).

12. Owen Davies, *America Bewitched: The Story of Witchcraft after Salem* (Oxford: Oxford University Press, 2013), 5.

13. "Visited" in this context, of course, means to be impregnated.

14. Although, admittedly, many Christian faiths have accepted women into the clergy, the liturgy is still highly stratified along gendered lines. God is figured as being male, as is His Son, Jesus. The Priest or pastor, in being God's human representative, is thus equally aligned with the masculine, even if the actual gender of the reverend is female. Finally, the church takes on a feminine characteristic. This allows for God's/Jesus's love of the church to mirror human love in marriage: God, the groom, and the church His bride, for which He sacrificed His life, as we are meant to do.

15. Bailey, *Sex in the Heartland*, 14.

16. Such a call was by no means novel, beginning in the middle 1800s, as a platform for the American Civil War and the first-wave American feminist movement's Seneca Falls Convention.

17. Thomas A. Harris, *I'm Okay—You're Okay* (London: Arrow, 2012).

18. The website for the Women's Liberation Front. https://womens liberationfront.org. Accessed 16 September 2020.

19. It could be suggested that by killing her husband, Michell was indeed literally "bringing down the man." However, the film itself makes it unclear as to whether this act was intentional or accidental. Also, while being a witch, Joan still attends parties and still lives in her suburban home.

20. Tryon, *Harvest Home*.

21. Sigmund Freud, *The Interpretation of Dreams* (Hertfordshire: Wordsworth Editions, 1997).

22. *Hungry Wives* film trailer, DVD, directed by George A. Romero (United States: Jack H. Harris Enterprises, 1973).

23. Williams, "An Interview with George and Christine Romero," 403.

24. *Ibid.*

25. Romero, *Season of the Witch*.

26. This appears to be one answer to the question posed in the trailer for *Hungry Wives*: what does a wife do while her husband is at work? Apparently, she buys implements of the occult and begins to practice witchcraft.

27. This articulation of the city as a modern environment with a positive affect is unique to these texts discussed throughout this book. Indeed, the other narratives present the urban as being a groundless world that robs the individual of essential subjectivity.

28. Romero, *Season of the Witch*.

29. *Ibid.*

30. *Ibid.*

31. *Ibid.*

32. Vincent Canby, "Thalia Twin Bill," *New York Times*, December 12, 1980, Arts and Leisure Section, Final Edition.

33. This is not uncommon with the secular reception of these works, wherein either the religious is downplayed as being an incorrect depiction, or simply framed as indecipherable and confusing.

34. Jerry Gerard, *Deep Throat*, DVD, directed by Jerry Gerard (United States: Bryanston Pictures, 1972).

35. Laura Mulvey, "Visual Pleasure and the Narrative Cinema," *Screen* 16, no. 3 (1975).

36. Mary Ann Doane, "Film and the Masquerade: Theorizing the Female Spectator," *Screen* 3, no. 4 (1982).

37. Although one might argue that this is not the case with *The Wicker Man*, as the theatrical version opens with the protagonist flying to the island, in the director's cut, Howie is shown in an urban environment on the beat in the big city.

38. Tryon, *The Dark Secret of Harvest Home* (film).

39. In much the same way as in *Eye of the Devil* and *Day of the Arrow*, the church is figured more as a mask than as an independent religious entity.

40. Tryon, *Harvest Home* (novel), 31.

41. *Ibid.*, 35.

42. *Ibid.*, 61.

43. *Ibid.*, 183–4.

44. *Ibid.*, 88.

45. *Ibid.*, 105.

46. *Ibid.*, 184–5.

47. *Ibid.*, 139.

48. *Ibid.*, 179.

49. *Ibid.*, 252.

Conclusions

1. This is the case for all of the films discussed in this book, with the exception of *The Wicker Man*. However, even though the main conflict is undoubtedly between the pagan residents of

Summerisle and Howie, their Christian sacrificial victim, both of whom share strong beliefs, these two are held in opposition not only to each other, but also to the wider world, which seems to have no place for either.

2. Phillip Shabecoff, "Global Warming Has Begun, Expert Tells Senate," *New York Times*, June 24, 1988.

3. Shawn Arthur, "Wicca, the Apocalypse, and the Future of the Natural World," *Journal for the Study of Religion, Nature & Culture* 2, no. 2 (June 2008): 199–217.

4. Mary Reinholz, "An Alternative Rite of Spring," *New York Times* (1923–Current File), May 09, 2004.

5. Alan Kirby, "The Death of Postmodernism," *Philosophy Now* 58 (September 2020): 2.

6. Kirby, "The Death of Postmodernism," 4–5.

7. Jonathan Sacks, *Not In God's Name: Confronting Religious Violence* (London: Hodder and Stoughton, 2015), 19.

8. Emile Durkheim, *Sociology and Philosophy* (New York: New York Free Press, 1974), 12.

9. Sacks, *Not In God's Name*, 75.

10. Gerard Manion, *Pope Francis's Agenda for the Future of Catholicism* (Cambridge: Cambridge University Press, 2017).

11. Chad Hayes and Carey W. Hayes, *The Conjuring*, DVD, directed by James Wan (United States: New Line Cinema, 2013).

12. Brian Collins, *The Conjuring* film review, *Religious Studies Review* 39, no. 4 (December 2013): 254.

13. J.F. Sawyer, *Deliver Us from Evil: True Cases of Haunted Houses and Demon Attacks* (Spain: Canary Islands Publishing, 2009), 21.

14. Made during the onset of postmodernity, to falsely associate oneself with objects beyond one's means might be linked with the adoption of a false identity. For, as Baudrillard would argue, it is through objects acquired that subjects are defined, judged and indeed reified, turned themselves into objects of conspicuous consumption.

15. Hayes, *The Conjuring*.

16. *The Conjuring: Face to Face with Terror* (added feature included as part of *The Conjuring* Blu-ray edition).

17. *Ibid.*

18. Hayes, *The Conjuring*.

19. *Ibid.*

20. *Ibid.*

21. Andrea Perron, *House of Darkness, House of Light: The True Story*, Volume One (Indiana: Author House, 2011).

22. *Ibid.*, 69.

23. *Ibid.*, 187.

24. *Ibid.*, 393.

25. Chad Hayes, Carey W. Hayes, James Wan and David Leslie Johnson, *The Conjuring 2*, directed by James Wan (United States: New Line Cinema, 2016).

26. Hayes, *The Conjuring 2*.

27. *Ibid.*

28. It is, of course, duly noted that Elvis died as the result of a drug overdose after divorcing his wife. However, the drugs that he was taking, according to his biography, were prescribed by his doctor and not obtained by elicit means.

29. Robert Eggers, *The Witch*, directed by Robert Eggers (United States: A24, 2015).

30. Ari Aster, *Midsommar*, directed by Ari Aster (United States, Sweden and Hungary: A24 and Nordisk Films, 2019).

31. In *The Devil*, five individuals become trapped in an elevator, one being Satan. Members of the group are systematically murdered as they await rescue, a situation that causes each to turn against the other as suspicions as to the identity of the killer mount. Their perceptions of one another and indeed themselves are altered as they are forced to face their deepest fears and their most grievous sins. The last to survive is the only one to make it out alive after he confesses to his crimes and begs redemption. It is this idea of obtaining grace and unity with a higher power, leaving the past behind and assuming a new life, that is common to both works.

32. Aster, *Midsommar*.

33. *Ibid.*

34. *Ibid.*

35. *Ibid.*

36. *Ibid.*

Bibliography

Works Cited

Adler, Renata. "The Screen: 'Rosemary's Baby,' a Story of Fantasy and Horror: John Cassavetes Stars with Mia Farrow 2 Other Movies Open at Local Theaters." *New York Times*, June 13, 1968. Arts and Leisure Section, Final Edition.

Arthur, Shawn. "Wicca, the Apocalypse, and the Future of the Natural World." *Journal for the Study of Religion, Nature & Culture* 2, no. 2 (June 2008): 199–217.

Bailey, Beth. *Sex in the Heartland*. Cambridge: Harvard University Press, 1999.

Baudrillard, Jean. *For a Critique of the Political Economy of the Sign*. London: Telos Press, 1981.

_____. *The Consumer Society: Myths and Structures*. London: Sage, 2016.

_____. *The System of Objects*. London: Verso Books, 2005.

Bell, Daniel. *The Cultural Contradictions of Capitalism*. New York: Basic Books, 1996.

Bellah, Robert N., Richard Madsen, William M. Sullivan, Ann Swindler, and Steven Tipton. *Habits of the Heart: Individualism and Commitment in American Life*. Berkeley: University of California Press, 1996.

Berman, Marshall. *All That Is Solid Melts into Air: The Experience of Modernity*. London: Verso, 2010.

Binkley, Sam. *Getting Loose: Lifestyle Consumption in the 1970s*. Durham: Duke University Press, 2007.

Bloch, Robert. *Psycho*. London: Hale, 1960.

Boot, Andy. *Fragments of Fear: An Illustrated History of British Horror Films*. London: Creation Books, 1999.

Botting, Fred. The *Gothic (Essays and Studies)*. New York: Boydell & Brewer Ltd., 2001.

Box Office Mojo. https://www.boxoffice mojo.com/movies/?id=omen.htm. Accessed August 9, 2019.

Brown, Alan. *Inside the Wicker Man*. Edinburgh: Polygon, 2017.

_____. "Introduction to The Wicker Man." in *The Wicker Man*, written by Robin Hardy and Anthony Shaffer, ix–xiii. Glasgow: Pan Books, 2000.

Calhoun-Brown, Allison. "Upon this Rock," *PS: Political Science and Politics* 33, no. 2 (2000): 169–174.

Canby, Vincent. "Film View: Hollywood Has an Appealing New Star Old Gooseberry." *New York Times*, July 25, 1976. Arts and Leisure Section, Final Edition.

_____. "Screen: Damien Back in 'Omen II': 'Born Unto a Jackal.'" *New York Times*, June 9, 1978. Arts and Leisure Section, Final Edition.

_____. "The Screen: In Race with the Devil, Witches Are Hunters." *New York Times*, July 10, 1975. Arts and Leisure Section, Final Edition.

_____. "Thalia Twin Bill." *New York Times*, December 12, 1980. Arts and Leisure Section, Final Edition.

Carroll, Noel. *The Philosophy of Horror or Paradoxes of the Heart*. New York: Routledge, 1990.

Carter, Sydney. "Lord of the Dance." Hymnary.org. http://www.hymnary.org/text/idancedinthemorningwhenthe.

Clover, Carol. *Men, Women and Chainsaws: Gender in the Modern Horror Film*. Princeton: Princeton University Press, 1992.

Collins, Brian. *The Conjuring* film review.

Religious Studies Review 39, no 4 (December 2013).

Creed, Barbara. *The Monstrous Feminine: Film, Feminism and Psychoanalysis.* London: Routledge, 1993.

Crowley, Aleister. *Magik.* United States: Create Space Independent Publishing Platform, 2014.

Crowther, Bosley. "Screen: 'Eye of the Devil' Begins Run: Deborah Kerr Appears with David Niven 5 Other Films Arrive in Local Theaters East-West Twin Bill Local Double Bill." *New York Times*, December 7, 1967. Arts and Leisure Section, Final Edition.

Davies, Owen. *America Bewitched: The Story of Witchcraft After Salem.* Oxford: Oxford University Press, 2013.

_____. *Paganism: A Very Short Introduction.* New York: Oxford University Press, 2011.

"The Devil Is Alive and Hiding on Central Park West." *Time*, June 23, 1967.

Doane, Mary Ann. "Film and the Masquerade: Theorising the Female Spectator." *Screen* 3, no. 4 (1982): 74–87.

Driscoll, Paul F. "Going to the Opera." *Opera News*, October 1997.

Dubrow-Marshall, Linda, and Rod Dubrow-Marshall. "How Cult Leader Charles Manson Was Able to Convince His Family to Commit Murder." *Journal of the International Cult Studies Association* (November 2017).

Durkheim, Emile. *Sociology and Philosophy.* New York: New York Free Press, 1974.

Ebert, Roger. *Death Wish* film review. RogerEbert.com. Accessed September 28, 2019. https://www.rogerebert.com/reviews/death-wish-1974.

Eder, Richard. "The Screen, Omen Is Nobody's Baby." *New York Times*, June 26, 1976. Arts and Leisure Section, Final Edition.

Ellis, Bill. *Raising the Devil: Satanism, New Religions and the Media.* Lexington: University of Kentucky Press, 2000.

Elsaesser, Thomas. *The Last Great American Picture Show: New Hollywood Cinema in the 1970s.* Amsterdam: Amsterdam University Press, 2004.

Fisher, Lucy. "Birth Traumas: Parturition and Horror in *Rosemary's Baby.*" *Cinema Journal* 31, no. 3 (1992): 3–18.

Frazer, Sir James George. *The Illustrated Golden Bough.* London: MacMillan, 1978.

Freud, Sigmund. *The Interpretation of Dreams.* Hertfordshire: Wordsworth Editions, 1997.

Grant, Robbyn, and Barry K. Grant. "Race with the Devil: A Brief Vacation on the Open Road." *Jump Cut: A Review of Contemporary Media* 10–11 (June 1976): 20.

Green, Leroy, and Ron Kersey. "Disco Inferno." In *Disco Inferno*, recorded by The Tramps. Philadelphia: Atlantic Records, 1976.

Greenspun, Roger. "Horror Film." *New York Times*, August 7, 1971. Arts Section, Final Edition.

Hardy, Robin, and Anthony Shaffer. *The Wicker Man.* London: Pan Books, 2000.

Harris, Thomas A. *I'm Okay, You're Okay.* London: Arrow, 2012.

"The Hippies." *Time*, July 7, 1967, 2–12.

The Holy Bible. London: Oxford University Press, 1934.

Houston, Beverle, and Marsha Kinder. *Close-up: A Critical Perspective on Film.* New York: Harcourt Brace Jovanovich, 1972.

Interview with Dennis Wheatley. British Broadcasting Corporation, 1970. Accessed August 27, 2016. https://dangerousminds.net/comments/satanism_was_basically_anything_horror_writer_dennis_wheatley_didnt_agree.

Jagger, Mick. "Sympathy for the Devil." In *Beggar's Banquet.* London: Decca, 1968.

Jancovich, Mark. *Horror.* London: Batsford, 1992.

_____. "Post-Fordism, Postmodernism and Paranoia: The Dominance of the Horror Genre in Contemporary Culture." In *Horror: The Film Reader.* Edited by Mark Jancovich. 83–126. London: Routledge, 1992.

Kennedy, John F. "Inaugural Address." January 20, 1961. John F. Kennedy Presidential Library and Museum, http://www.jfklibrary.org/AssetViewer/BqXIEM9F4024ntFl7SV AjA.as`px.

King, Martin Luther, Jr. "Speech from the March on Washington." In *A Testament of Hope: The Essential Writings and Speeches of Martin Luther King, Jr.*

Edited by James Melvin Washington. 217–221. San Francisco: Harper, 1991.

Kirby, Alan. "The Death of Postmodernism." *Philosophy Now* 58 (September 2020): 2–23.

Kristeva, Julia. *Powers of Horror: An Essay on Abjection.* Translated by Leon S. Roudiez. New York: Columbia University Press, 1982.

Lasch, Christopher. *The Culture of Narcissism: American Life in an Age of Diminishing Expectations.* New York: W.W. Norton, 1991.

LaVey, Anton Szandor. *The Satanic Bible.* New York: Avon Books, 1969.

Lazarus, Emma. "The New Colossus." United States National Park Service website. Accessed July 2020. https://www.nps.gov/stli/learn/history culture/colossus.htm.

Lee, Christopher. *Tall, Dark and Gruesome.* London: W&N, 1997.

Leitch, Thomas. "Twelve Fallacies in Contemporary Adaptation Theory." *Criticism* 45, no. 2 (2003): 149–171.

Levin, Ira. *Rosemary's Baby.* London: Constable and Robinson, Limited, 2011.

_____. "'Stuck with Satan': Ira Levin on the Origins of *Rosemary's Baby*." *Criterion Collection.* November 4, 2012.

Lewis, C. S. *Mere Christianity.* London: Fount, 1979.

Lima, Robert. "The Satanic Rape of Catholicism in *Rosemary's Baby*." *Studies in American Fiction* 2 (1974): 211–22.

Lofts, Norah. *The Witches.* New York: Arrow Books, Ibook Edition, 2011.

Loraine, Philip. *Day of the Arrow.* Richmond: Valancourt Books, 2015.

Lyotard, Jean-François. *The Postmodern Condition: A Report on Knowledge.* Translated by Geoff Bennington and Brian Massumi. Manchester: Manchester University Press, 1984.

MacMullen, Ramsay. *Christianity and Paganism in the Fourth to Eighth Centuries.* New Haven: Yale University Press, 1997.

Mannion, Gerard. *Pope Francis and the Future of Catholicism.* Cambridge: Cambridge University Press, 2017.

Maslin, Janet. "Screen: 'The Wicker Man,' About a Fertility Cult: Strange Happenings." *New York Times,* March 26, 1980. Arts and Leisure Section, Final Edition.

McLeod, Hugh. *The Religious Crisis of the 1960s.* Oxford: Oxford University Press, 2013.

Monaco, Paul. *History of the American Cinema: The Sixties.* New York: Charles Scribner's, 2001.

Morris, Aldon D. *The Origins of the Civil Rights Movement.* New York: Simon & Schuster, 1986.

Mulvey, Laura. "Visual Pleasure and the Narrative Cinema." *Screen* 16 no. 3 (1975): 6–18.

Murray, Patrick. *The Deer's Cry: A Treasury of Irish Religious Verse.* Dublin: Estate of Patrick J. Murray Press, 1986.

Newman, Kim. *Nightmare Movies: A Critical History of the Horror Film, 1968–1988.* London: Bloomsbury, 1988.

Oxford English Dictionary. 3rd ed. Oxford: Oxford University Press, 2010.

Palahniuk, Chuck. "Introduction to *Rosemary's Baby*." In *Rosemary's Baby,* written by Ira Levin. vii–x. London: Constable and Robinson Limited, 2011.

Perron, Andrea. *House of Darkness, House of Light: The True Story.* Vol. 1. Indiana: Author House, 2011.

Pinner, David. *Ritual.* Bath: AudioGO Ltd, 2012.

Pratt, Vic. *Hunting for Sherds: Robin Redbreast.* London: British Film Institute, nd.

Prince, Stephen. "Dread, Taboo, and the Thing." In *The Horror Film.* Edited by Stephen Prince. 118–131. New Jersey: Rutgers University Press, 2004.

_____. "Introduction to *The Horror Film*." In *The Horror Film.* Edited by Stephen Prince. 115. New Jersey: Rutgers University Press, 2004.

Punter, David. *The Literature of Terror: A History of Gothic Fictions from 1765 to the Present Day.* New York: Longman, 1980.

Reigler, Thomas. "We're All Dirty Harry Now: Violent Movies for Violent Times." *At the Interface/Probing the Boundaries* 70 (November 2010): 18–41.

Reinholtz, Mary. "An Alternative Rite of Spring." *New York Times* (1923–Current File), May 09, 2004.

Rigby, Jonathan. "Robin Redbreast," *Sight and Sound* (January 2014), 94.

"'Rosemary's Baby' Given a 'C' Rating by Catholic Office." *New York Times,* June

21, 1968. Arts and Leisure Section, Final Edition.

Roszak, Theodore. *The Making of a Counter Culture: Reflections on the Technocratic Society and Youthful Opposition*. London: Faber & Faber, 1969.

Sacks, Jonathan. *Not in God's Name: Confronting Religious Violence*. London: Hodder and Stoughton, 2015.

Sage, Victor. *Horror Fiction in the Protestant Tradition*. London: Macmillan Press, 1988.

Sawyer, J.F. *Deliver Us from Evil: True Cases of Haunted Houses and Demon Attacks*. Spain: Canary Islands Publishing, 2009.

Scoville, Adam. *Folk Horror: Hours Dreadful and Things Strange*. London: Auteur Press, 2017.

Shabecoff, Phillip. "Global Warming Has Begun, Expert Tells Senate." *New York Times*, June 24, 1988. Final Edition.

Shelley, Peter. *Grande Dame Guignol Cinema: A History of Hag Horror from Baby Jane to Mother*. Jefferson, NC: McFarland, 2009.

Shepard, Lucius. "Something Wicker This Way Comes." *Magazine of Fantasy and Science Fiction* 112, no. 1 (2007): 124–130.

Skow, John. "Sweet Corn." *Time* 101, no. 26 (June 25, 1973): 92.

Sobchack, Vivian. "Bringing It All Back Home: Family Economy and Generic Exchange." In *Dread of Difference: Gender and the Horror Film*. Edited by Barry Keith Grant. 143–163. Austin: University of Texas Press, 2015.

Sontag, Susan. "On Culture and the New Sensibility." In *Against Interpretation*. Edited by Susan Sontag. 293–304. London, England: Penguin Classics, 1964.

"Sydney Carter Obituary." *Telegraph*, March 16, 2004. Obituary Section, Final Edition.

Thompson, David. "Cult TV Pick: *Robin Redbreast*." *Film Comment* 49, no. 6 (2013): 76.

_____. "I Make Films for Adults." *Sight and Sound* 5, no. 4 (1995): 11–19.

Thompson, Howard. "The Devil's Own in Neighborhood Houses." *New York Times*, March 16, 1967. Arts Section, Final Edition.

"Toward a Hidden God." *Time*, April 8, 1966.

Tudor, Andrew. *Monsters and Mad Scientists: A Cultural History of the Horror Movie*. Oxford: Basil Blackwell, 1989.

Twichell, James B. *Dreadful Pleasures: An Anatomy of Modern Horror*. Oxford: Oxford University Press, 1995.

United States Conference of Catholic Bishops. "Film Review of *Rosemary's Baby*." United States Conference of Catholic Bishops Archive. Accessed June 5, 2016. http://archive.usccb.org/movies/r/rosemarysbaby1968.shtml.

_____. "Film Review of *The Omen*." United States Conference of Catholic Bishops Archive. Accessed June 5, 2016. http://archive.usccb.org/movies/o/omenthe1976.shtml.

Wake, Oliver. "James MacTaggart, 1928–1974: Producer, Director, Writer." BFI Screen On line. Accessed September 21, 2019. http://www.screenonline.org.uk/people/id/1343392/index.html.

Weber, Max. *The Protestant Ethic and the Spirit of Capitalism: With Other Writings on the Rise of the West*. Translated by Stephen Kalberg. New York: Oxford Press, 2009.

Website for the Women's Liberation Front. https://womensliberationfront.org. Accessed September 16, 2020.

Williams, Tony. *Hearths of Darkness: The Family in the American Horror Film*. New Jersey: Fairleigh Dickinson University Press, 1996.

_____. "An Interview with George and Christine Romero." *Quarterly Review of Film and Video* 18 no. 4 (2001): 397–411.

Wolf, Leonard. "In Horror Movies Some Things Are Sacred." *New York Times*, April 4, 1976. Arts and Leisure Section, Final Edition.

Wood, Michael. "Witches and Demons: The Occult in Two Hammer Films from the 1960s." *Monstrum* 1, no. 1 (April 1, 2018): 135–62.

Wood, Robin. *Hollywood from Vietnam to Reagan*. New York: Columbia University Press, 1986.

Works Consulted

Anson, Jay. *The Amityville Horror*. New York: Pocket Star, 2005.

"Any God Will Do." *Time*, March 19, 1965.

"The Atheist Rabbi." *Time*, January 29, 1965.

Bassett, Ronald. *Witchfinder General*. New York: Macmillan, 1968.

Bede. *A History of the English Church and People*. Translated by Leo Sherley-Price. Baltimore: Penguin Books, 1961.

Benjamin, Phillip. "At the Fair: Goodbye, Goodbye." *New York Times*, November 5, 1965. Section A, Final Edition.

Berenstein, Rhona. "Mommie Dearest: *Aliens, Rosemary's Baby* and Mothering." *Journal of Popular Culture* 24 no. 2 (1990): 55–74.

"Beyond Transubstantiation: New Theory of Real Presence." *Time*, June 2, 1965.

"The Bible as Living Technicolor." *Time*, January 15, 1965.

"The Bishop's Agenda." *Time*, September 24, 1965.

Blatty, William Peter. *The Exorcist*. New York: Harper, 2013.

Boorstin, Daniel J. *Democracy and its Discontents: Reflections on Everyday America*. New York, Random House, 1974.

Bork, Robert H. *Slouching Toward Gomorrah: Modern Liberalism and American Decline*. New York: Reagan Books: 2003.

Butler, Ivan. *The Cinema of Roman Polanski*. London: Zwemmer, 1970.

_____. *Horror in the Cinema*. London: Zwemmer, 1970.

"Changing Guard at Justice." *Time*, January 1, 1965.

"Changing the Confession." *Time*, February 26, 1965.

"Christ's Sexuality." *Time*, April 9, 1965.

"Church and Birth Control: from Genesis to Genetics." *Time*, July 16, 1965.

Clarens, Carlos. *An Illustrated History of the Horror Film*. New York: Capricorn Books, 1968.

Cook, David A. *Lost Illusions: American Cinema in the Shadow of Watergate and Vietnam 1970–1979*. Berkeley: University of California Press, 2000.

Coubro, Gerry. *Hammer and Horror: Bad Taste and Popular British Cinema*. Sheffield: Sheffield Hallam University Press, 1995.

"Death and Transfiguration." *Time*, March 5, 1965.

"A Deity De-personified." *Time*, September 17, 1965.

Delitta, Frank. *Audrey Rose*. London: Pan Books, 1982.

DeQuincey, Thomas. *Suspiria de Profundus and Other Writings*. United States: Digireads Classics, 2011.

Derry, Charles. *Dark Dreams: A Psychological History of the Modern Horror Film*. South Brunswick: A.S. Barnes, 1977.

"Division on Birth Control." *Time*, April 2, 1965.

"Ecumenism: Those Who Don't Want It." *Time*, August 27, 1965.

"Faith: Healthy versus Neurotic." *Time*, April 2, 1965.

Foster, Hal. *The Anti-aesthetic: Essays on Postmodern Culture*. New York: W.W. Norton, 1988.

Frank, Allan G. *The Movie Treasury: Horror Movies*. New York: Octopus, 1974.

Fuentes, Carlos, *Aura*. Translated by Barbara van Becht. London: Deutsch, 1990.

Gent, George. "Papal Pilgrimage; 100 Million Viewers Get a Front Seat at a Historic Moment in Fatima." *New York Times*, May 14, 1967. Section A, Final Edition.

"God and Man at 800 Campuses." *Time*, January 15, 1965.

"God Is Changing." *Time*, May 7, 1965.

Halliwell, Leslie. *The Dead that Walk*. London: Grafton Books, 1986.

"Hooray for the Lord." *Time*, January 1, 1965.

"How to Succeed though Married." *Time*, April 9, 1965.

Humphreys, Reynold. *The American Horror Film: An Introduction*. Edinburgh: Edinburgh University Press, 2002.

Hutchings, Peter. *Hammer and Beyond: The British Horror Film*. Manchester: Manchester University Press, 1993.

Huxley, Aldous. *The Devils of Loudun*. London: Vintage Classics, 2005.

Jackson, Shirley. *The Haunting of Hill House*. New York: Penguin, 1984.

Jong, Erica. *How to Save Your Own Life: A Novel*. London: Secker and Warberg, 1977.

King, Geoff. *New Hollywood Cinema: An Introduction*. London: I.B. Tauris Publishers, 2007.

Konvitz, Jeffrey. *The Sentinel*. London: Star, 1982.

Koontz, Dean. *Demon Seed*. London: Headline, 1998.

Larrington, Carolyne. *The Land of the Green Man: A Journey Through the*

Supernatural Landscapes of the British Isles. London: I. B. Tauris, 2015.

"The Lasting Vision of Pope John Paul." *Time*, February 26, 1965.

Leiber, Fritz. *Conjure Wife.* New York: Orb Books, 2009.

"Less Ecumenism, Please." *Time*, March 12, 1965.

"Life in a De-fatalized World." *Time*, April 2, 1965.

Lindsay, Hal. *Satan Is Alive and Well on Planet Earth.* New York: Harper Books, 1992.

"Little Sex Without Love." *Time*, April 9, 1965.

"Love in the Place of Law?" *Time*, March 5, 1965.

Marasco, Robert. *Burnt Offerings.* New York: Dell Publishing, 1988.

Maxford, Howard. *Hammer House of Horror: Behind the Screams.* London: Batsford, 1996.

Mills, C. Wright. *White Collar: The American Middle Classes.* Oxford: Oxford University Press, 1967.

"Parables for Cool Squares." *Time,* March 5, 1965.

Pirie, David. *A Heritage of Horror: The English Gothic Cinema 1946–1972.* London: Gordon Frasier, 1973.

"Pope Will Say Mass at Yankee Stadium." *New York Times*, October 2, 1965. Section A, Final Edition.

"A Priest's Protest." *Time*, January 8, 1965.

"The Promised Land." *Time*, January 15, 1965.

"A Quick Lent?" *Time*, March 12, 1965.

Reich, Charles A. *The Greening of America.* London: Allen Lane, 1971.

Riesman, David. *The Lonely Crowd: A Study of the Changing American Culture.* New Haven: Yale University Press, 2001.

Rose, James. *Beyond Hammer: British Horror Cinema Since 1970.* Leighton Buzzard: Auteur Publishing, 2009.

Rubin, Jerry. *Growing Up at Thirty-Seven.* New York: M. Evans, 1976.

Stuart, Ramona. *The Possession of Joel Delaney.* London: Macmillan, 1972.

"Surf, Snow, Sex and Protest." *Time*, April 2, 1965.

Tryon, Thomas. *The Other.* New York: NYRB Classics, 2012.

"Values in Oklahoma." *Time*, May 14, 1965.

"The Vietnam Debate." *Time*, January 15, 1965.

Waller, Gregory A. *American Horrors: Essays on the American Horror Film.* Urbana: University of Chicago Press, 1987.

"The Womb Clingers." *Time*, June 25, 1965.

"Worship Where Life Is." *Time*, August 27, 1965.

Films Cited

Anger, Kenneth. *Lucifer Rising.* Directed by Kenneth Anger. United Kingdom and United States: Kenneth Anger Productions, 1972.

Aster, Ari. *Midsommar.* Directed by Ari Aster. United States, Sweden and Hungary: A24 and Nordisk Films, 2019.

Baxt, George. *City of the Dead.* Directed by John Llewellyn Moxey. United Kingdom and United States: British Lion, 1960.

Bernhard, Harvey. *Damien: The Omen II.* Directed by Don Taylor. United States: Twentieth Century Fox, 1978.

Bishop, Wes, and Lee Frost. *Race with the Devil.* Directed by Jack Starrett. United States: Twentieth Century Fox, 1975.

Blatty, William Peter. *The Exorcist.* Directed by William Friedkin. United States: Warner Brothers, 1973.

Bowen, John Griffith. *Robin Redbreast.* Directed by James MacTaggart. United Kingdom: British Broadcasting Corporation, 1970.

Christensen, Benjamin. *Haxan.* Directed by Benjamin Christensen. Sweden: Svensk Filmindustri, 1922.

Cohen, Lawrence D. *Carrie.* Directed by Brian De Palma. United States: United Artists, 1976.

The Conjuring: Face to Face with Terror. DVD Bonus Feature from *The Conjuring* DVD. Directed by James Wan. United States: Warner Bros. Entertainment.

Craven, Wes. *The Hills Have Eyes.* Directed by Wes Craven. United States: Vanguard Monarch Releasing Company, 1977.

Crawford Kinkle, Chad. *Jug Face.* Directed by Chad Crawford Kinkle. United States: Moderncine, 2013.

Curtis, Peter. *The Witches.* Directed by

Cyril Frankel. London, England and United States: Hammer Film Productions and Twentieth Century Fox, 1966.

De Felita, Frank. *Audrey Rose.* Directed by Robert Wise. United States: United Artists, 1977.

Deutsch, Helen, Dorothy Kingsley, and Harlan Ellison. *The Valley of the Dolls,* Directed by Mark Robson. United States: Twentieth Century Fox, 1967.

Eggers, Robert. *The Witch.* Directed by Robert Eggers. United States: A24, 2015.

Estridge, Robin, and Dennis Murphy. *Eye of the Devil.* Directed by J. Lee Thompson. United Kingdom and United States: Filmways Pictures and Metro Goldwyn Mayer, 1966.

Fonda, Peter, Dennis Hopper, and Terry Southern. *Easy Rider.* Directed by Dennis Hopper. United States: Columbia Pictures, 1969.

Foote, Horton. *To Kill a Mockingbird.* Directed by Robert Mulligan. United States: Universal Pictures, 1962.

Fort, Garrett. *Dracula.* Directed by Tod Browning. United States: Universal Pictures, 1931.

Gates, Tudor. *Lust for a Vampire.* Directed by Jimmy Sangster. United Kingdom and United States: Hammer Films and American International Pictures, 1971.

_____. *Twins of Evil.* Directed by John Hough. United Kingdom and United States: Hammer Films and Rank Productions: 1971.

Gerard, Jerry. *Deep Throat.* Directed by Jerry Gerard. United States: Bryanston Pictures, 1972.

Goldman, William. *The Stepford Wives.* Directed by Bryan Forbes. United States: Columbia Pictures, 1975.

Hardy, Robin. *The Wicker Tree.* Directed by Robin Hardy. United Kingdom: British Lion, 2011.

Hayes, Chad, and Carey W. Hayes. *The Conjuring.* Directed by James Wan. United States: New Line Cinema, 2013.

Hayes, Chad, Carey W. Hayes, James Wan, and David Leslie Johnson. *The Conjuring 2.* Directed by James Wan. United States: New Line Cinema, 2016.

Jones, L.Q., and Sean MacGregor. *The Brotherhood of Satan.* Directed by Bernard McEveety. United States: Columbia Pictures Corporation, 1971.

Kermode, Mark. *Burnt Offering: The Cult of the Wicker Man.* Directed by Andrew Abbott and Russell Leven. United Kingdom: Nobel's Gate, 2001.

Miller, Victor. *Friday the 13th.* Directed by Sean S. Cunningham. United States: Paramount Pictures, 1980.

Newman, David, and Robert Benton. *Bonnie and Clyde.* Directed by Arthur Penn. United States: Warner Brothers, 1967.

Paul, Jeremy. *Countess Dracula.* Directed by Peter Sasdy. United Kingdom and United States: Pinewood Studios and Twentieth Century Fox, 1971.

Polanski, Roman. *Rosemary's Baby.* Directed by Roman Polanski. Los Angeles: Paramount Pictures,1968.

Romero, George A. *Dawn of the Dead.* Directed by George A. Romero. United States: United Film Distribution Company, 1978.

_____. *Night of the Living Dead.* Directed by George A. Romero. United States: Continental Distributing, 1968.

_____. *Season of the Witch.* Directed by George A. Romero. United States: Jack H. Harris Enterprises, 1973.

Russell, Ken. *The Devils.* Directed by Ken Russell. United Kingdom and United States: Warner Brothers, 1971.

Sacks, Sid. *Bewitched.* Directed by William Asher. United States: American Broadcasting Channel, 1964–1972.

Seltzer, David. *The Omen.* Directed by Richard Donner. United Kingdom and United States: Twentieth Century Fox, 1976.

Shaffer, Anthony. *The Wicker Man.* Directed by Robin Hardy. United Kingdom and United States: British Lion Pictures, 1973.

Stefano, Joseph. *Psycho.* Directed by Alfred Hitchcock. United States: Paramount Pictures, 1960.

Tryon, Thomas. *The Dark Secret of Harvest Home.* Directed by Leo Penn. United States: Universal Television, 1978.

Wallant, Edward Lewis. *The Pawnbroker.* Directed by Sidney Lumet. United States: Allied Artists, 1965.

Yordan, Phillip. *El Cid.* Directed by Anthony Mann. United States: Allied Artists, 1961.

Films Consulted

Argento, Dario, and Daria Nicolodi. *Suspiria*. Directed by Dario Argento. Italy and United States: Seda Spettacoli, 1977.

Beaumont, Charles. *The Haunted Palace*. Directed by Roger Corman. United States: American International Pictures, 1963.

Bloch, Robert. *The House that Dripped Blood*. Directed by Peter Duffell. United Kingdom and United States: Cinerama Releasing, 1971.

_____. *Torture Garden*. Directed by Freddie Francis. United States: Columbia Pictures, 1967.

Bockman, Michael. *Nurse Sherri*. Directed by Al Admanson. United States: Independent International Pictures, 1978.

Brown, William O. *The Witchmaker*. Directed by William O. Brown. United States: Excelsior Company, 1969.

Cammell, Donald. *Performance*. Directed by Nicholas Roeg. United States: Warner Brothers, 1970.

Clark, Greydon. *Satan's Cheerleaders*. Directed by Greydon Clark. United States: World Amusements, 1977.

Clemens, Brian. *Dr Jekyll and Sister Hyde*. Directed by Roy Ward Baker. United Kingdom and United States: Hammer Films, 1972.

Cohen, Larry. *God Told Me To*. Directed by Larry Cohen. United States: New World Pictures, 1976.

Comport, Brian. *The Fiend*. Directed by Robert Hartford-Davis. United States: World Arts Media, 1972.

Coppola, Francis Ford. *Dementia 13*. Directed by Francis Ford Coppola. United States: American International Pictures, 1963.

Cronenberg, David. *They Came from Within*. Directed by David Cronenberg. Canada and United States: Cinepix, 1975.

Curtis, Dan. *Burnt Offerings*. Directed by Dan Curtis. United States: United Artists, 1976.

Damiano, Gerard. *Legacy of Satan*. Directed by Gerard Damiano. United States: Beaumont Film, 1974.

Davis, Walt. *Evil Come Evil Go*. Directed by Walt Davis. United States: Conde Films, 1972.

De Concini, Ennio. *Black Sunday*. Directed by Mario Bava. Spain and United States: American International Pictures: 1960.

Dillon, Robert. *The Old Dark House*. Directed by William Castle. United States: Columbia Pictures, 1963.

Durston, David E. *I Drink Your Blood*. Directed by David E. Durston. United States: Cinemation, 1971.

Essoe, Gabe. *Devil's Rain*. Directed by Robert Fuest. United States: Bryanstan Films, 1975.

Fine, Harry. *Vampire Lovers*. Directed by Roy Ward Baker. United Kingdom and United States: Hammer Films, 1970.

Forbes, Bryan. *Séance on a Wet Afternoon*. Directed by Bryan Forbes. United States: Rank Films, 1964.

George, Barry. *Death Bed: The Bed that Eats*. Directed by Barry George. United States: CAV Films, 1977.

Gidding, Nelson. *The Haunting*. Directed by Robert Wise. United Kingdom and United States, Argyle Entertainment, 1963.

Girard, Bernard. *A Name for Evil*. Directed by Bernard Gerard. United States: Penthouse Productions, 1973.

Girdier, William, and Patrick J. Kelly. *Asylum of Satan*. Directed by William Girdler. United States: Studio One Productions, 1972.

Goldman, William. *Magic*. Directed by Richard Attenborough. United States: Twentieth Century Fox, 1978.

Goodheart, William. *The Exorcist II: The Heretic*. Directed by John Boorman. United States: Warner Brothers, 1977.

Gordon, Bert I., and Gail March. *Necromancy*. Directed by Bert I. Gordon. United States: Zenith International, 1972.

Gordon, Leo. *The Terror*. Directed by Roger Corman. United States: American International Pictures, 1963.

Higgins, John C. *Daughters of Satan*. Directed by Hollingsworth Morse. United States: United Artists, 1972.

Houghton, Don. *The Satanic Rites of Dracula*. Directed by Alan Gibson. United Kingdom and United States: Hammer Films, 1973.

Humphreys, Dave. *The Haunting of Julia*. Directed by Richard Loncraine. Canada and United States: Discovery Films, 1977.

Huyck, Willard, and Gloria Katz. *Messiah of Evil*. Directed by Willard Huyck. United States: International Cine Film Corporation, 1973.

Jackson, Donald G., and Jerry Youkins. *Demon Lover*. Directed by Donald G. Jackson and Jerry Youkins. United States: Wolf Lore Cinema, 1977.

Jaffee, Robert. *The Demon Seed*. Directed by Donald Cammell. United States: Metro Goldwyn Mayer, 1977.

Karpf, Stephen, and Elinor Karph. *Devil Dog: The Hound of Hell*. Directed by Curtis Harrington. United States: Columbia Broadcasting System, 1978.

Kelly, Tim, and Christopher Wicking. *Cry of the Banshee*. Directed by Gordon Hessler. United States: American International Pictures, 1970.

Maddow, Ben. *Mephisto Waltz*. Directed by Paul Wendkos. United States: Twentieth Century Fox, 1971.

Matheson, Richard. *The Strange Possession of Mrs Oliver*. Directed by Gordon Hessler. United States: National Broadcasting Company, 1977.

McGillivray, David. *Satan's Slave*. Directed by Norman J. Warren. Canada, United Kingdom and United States Monumental Pictures, 1976.

Mikels, Ted V. *Blood Orgy of the She Devils*. Directed by Ted V. Mikels. United States: Occult Films, 1973.

Moncada, Santiago. *Hatchet for the Honeymoon*. Directed by Mario Bava. Spain and United States: American International Pictures, 1974.

Nolan, William F. *Trilogy of Terror*. Directed by Dan Curtis. United States: American Broadcasting Company, 1975.

Ovidio, Assonitis. *Beyond the Door*. Directed by Robert Barret. United States: Film Ventures International, 1974.

Rivto, Rosemary, and Alfred Sole. *Alice Sweet Alice*. Directed by Alfred Sole. United States: Allied Artists Pictures, 1976.

Robinson, Matt, and Irene Kamp. *The Possession of Joel Delaney*. Directed by Waris Hussein. United States: Paramount Pictures, 1972.

Ross, Arthur A. *Satan's School for Girls*. Directed by David Lowell Rich. United States: American Broadcasting Company, 1973.

Rudkin, David. *Penda's Fen*. Directed by Alan Clarke. United Kingdom: British Broadcasting Company, 1974.

Sandor, Stern. *Amityville Horror*. Directed by Stuart Rosenberg. United States: American International Pictures, 1979.

Sangster, Jimmy. *Maniac*. Directed by Michael Carreras. United Kingdom and United States: Columbia Pictures, 1963.

_____, Patrick Tilley, and Paul Wheeler. *The Legacy*. Directed by Richard Marquand. United States: Universal Pictures, 1979.

Vernick, William. *The Redeemer: Son of Satan*. Directed by Constantine S. Gochis. United States: Dimension Pictures, 1978.

Wanzer, Orville. *The Devil's Mistress*. Directed by Orville Wanzer. United States: Holiday Pictures, 1966.

Wicking, Christopher. *Demons of the Mind*. Directed by Peter Sykes. United Kingdom and United States: Hammer Films, 1972.

_____. *To the Devil a Daughter*. Directed by Peter Sykes. United Kingdom and United States: Hammer Films, 1976.

Winner, Michael. *The Sentinel*. Directed by Michael Winner. United States: Universal Pictures, 1977.

Woods, Jack. *Equinox*. Directed by Jack Woods. United States: Tonylyn Productions, 1970.

Wynne-Simmons, Robert, and Piers Haggard. *The Blood on Satan's Claw*. Directed by Piers Haggard. United Kingdom and United States: Tigon Pictures, 1971.

Index

Abiquito, New Mexico 168
abortion 63, 96, 132, 204
Abraham 55, 70
Academy Awards 52, 72
acquisitive impulse *see* consumerism
action movies 159
activism 16, 72, 170–171, 199
The Actor's Studio 53, 72
adaptation 6, 10, 18–19, 32, 44–45, 47, 59, 73–74, 76, 80, 85, 114, 124, 128, 166, 171, 189, 209–210
Adler, Renata 32
Adonis 154
adultery 175, 185
Africa 82
African Americans 170, 171
The Age of Reason 157
Aggiornamento 14, 85, 203
agnosticism 16, 76, 207
alcoholism 174
Aldrich, Robert 87
Alice, Sweet Alice 8
Allen, Woody 53
altruism 10, 87, 88
America Bewitched: The Story of Witchcraft after Salem 168; *see also* Davies, Owen
American Academy of Dramatic Arts 53
American Broadcasting Company (ABC) 183
American dream 47
The American Horror Film: An Introduction 33; *see also* Humphreys, Reynold
American Independent Pictures 53
Amish 186
The Amityville Horror 206–207, 210–211
amnesia 92, 201
Anacin 44
Anger, Kenneth 16, 95, 106
The Anglican Church 56, 112, 137, 139, 187
Anglo-American 22, 111, 166, 170, 196
Annabelle 214
Annabelle Comes Home 214

Annabelle Creation 214
Antichrist 7, 34, 39, 41–42, 50, 57, 58, 60, 62–70, 74, 75, 80, 87, 96, 106; desegregation protests 72
anxiety 174, 201,
apocalypse 21, 57, 58, 61, 66, 67, 68, 70, 75, 87, 127, 142, 172, 197–198
apocalyptic millennialism *see* Wiccan Millennialism
The Apocrypha 121
Apollo 135
The Apostles 87, 121–122
archetypes 41, 81, 85, 94, 216
Armageddon *see* apocalypse
Armstrong, R.G. 100
art-house cinema 52
Ash Wednesday 177
Aster, Ari 216
astrology 224
atheism 14, 16, 195, 207, 208
Augustine 121
authority 8, 33, 36, 61, 64, 65, 73, 117, 153
avarice 48
The Awful Truth 52

The "B" Film 21, 52, 53, 114
Baby Boomers 148
Babylon 193
Bacchae 135
Bailey, Beth 94, 96–97, 170; see also *Sex in the Heartland*
Banishment 215
Bankhead, Tallulah 54
Baptism 84, 85, 154
Barnard College 72
Batman (TV series) 52
Baudrillard, Jean 44–45, 200
The Beatles 16
Beckett, Samuel 73
Bell, Book and Candle 182
Bell, Daniel 45, 48, 78, 132, 175; see also *The Cultural Contradictions of Capitalism*

Bellah, Robert 36, 56, 111; see also *Habits of the Heart*
Bellamy, Ralph 52
Beltane 161
Ben Hur 72
Berman, Marshall 60, 81, 118
Bethlehem 154
Bewitched 52, 183
The Bible 40, 41, 57, 65, 66, 68, 69, 70, 75, 84, 142, 153, 154, 191
The Big Sleep (film) 52
Binkley, Sam 115, 117, 118; see also *Getting Loose*
bird watching 155
Black Magic 205
The Black Mass 114
The Black Panthers 171
black shuck 140
Blackmer, Sidney 52
blended families 210
The Blood on Satan's Claw 8, 143, 144
The Book of Lies 97; see also Crowley, Aleister
Boot, Andy 149
bourgeoisie 61
Bowen, John 111, 139
The Bowery 146
Brechtian theatre 73
British Broadcasting Company 19, 22, 111, 129, 139, 140, 159
The British Empire 88, 139, 157, 196
British Lion Films 162
broadcasting 201, 202
Broadway 52
The Brotherhood of Satan 22, 78, 80, 102–106, 107, 113
Brown, Allan 141, 149, 158; see also *Inside the Wicker Man*
Brown v Board of Education 72
Buddhism 16, 148
Burns, Robert 161
Burnt Offerings 154, 220, 222

Cagney, James 52
Callan 160
Canada 135, 146
Canby, Vincent 15, 71, 181
Candlemas 161
capitalism 48, 61, 73
Carrie (film) 7, 107
Carrie (novel) 107
Carter, Sydney 121; see also *The Lord of the Dance*
Cassavetes, John 29, 52
Castle, William 27, 53
Castle of Otranto 225; see also Walpole, Horace

castration 171, 183–184, 185, 189
Catholicism 21, 30, 33, 36–42, 46, 47, 53, 54, 59, 60, 62, 63, 64, 76, 77, 84, 85, 102, 104, 112, 116, 120–123, 127, 128, 129, 137, 150, 154, 158, 168, 169, 175–180, 195, 196, 203–204, 207, 211, 212, 226
celibacy 145
Celts 97, 136, 148, 155, 158, 190
chaos 159
Christ see Jesus Christ
Christian Feast Days 161
The Chrysler Building 49
Cilento, Diane 160
Citizen Kane 73
City of the Dead 10–11
The Civil Rights Act of 1964 72
The Civil Rights Movement 72, 170, 172
Cixous, Helene 169
Classical Horror 61, 86, 91, 104, 144, 147, 149, 158, 196, 207, 208, 212, 213, 227
climate change 197
Collins, Brian
Come Back Little Sheba 52
commodification see consumerism
The Conjuring 23, 195, 196, 204–211, 213, 215, 227
The Conjuring II 195–196, 211–214, 215, 227
Connery, Sean 161
conspiracy theory 21, 33, 56, 75
consumerism 18, 21, 27, 29, 30–32, 33, 34, 43, 44, 45, 46–48, 49, 52, 59, 80, 100, 173, 180, 198, 200, 201, 209, 227
contraception 180; see also oral contraceptives
Cook, Elisha 52
Corman, Roger 163
"Corn Rigs Are Bonnie" 161
Cornwall 190, 191
The Counterculture Movement 18, 22, 29, 61, 79, 94, 95, 96, 97, 98, 99, 101, 103, 114, 115, 118, 125, 148, 184
Countess Dracula 151
Cox, Wilma 54
Crawford, Joan 87, 89
The Crazies 182
Creed, Barbara 34; see also *The Monstrous Feminine*
Crete 193
the crone 132, 169, 173
Crowley, Aleister 16–17, 97, 138
Crowther, Bosley 123, 124, 126
cult of youth 21, 61, 78, 80, 81, 94, 101
The Cultural Contradictions of Capitalism 48, 78, 132; see also Bell, Daniel
The Culture of Narcissism 56, 65; see also Lasch, Christopher
The Curse of La Llorona 214

The Dark Secret of Harvest Home 20, 22, 147, 166, 169, 171, 172, 183–189, 191, 192, 193
Dark Shadows 100
Datsun Motor Company 99
David, King of Israel, and Judea 65
Davies, Owen 168; see also *America Bewitched: The Story of Witchcraft After Salem*
Davis, Bette 87, 89, 190, 192
Dawn of the Dead 7
Day of the Arrow 20, 22, 113, 114–115, 116, 117, 122, 124–129, 131, 132, 137, 138–140, 142, 142, 144, 146, 160, 163, 166, 179, 184, 185, 189, 190
the death of God 104
Death Wish 159
Deeley, Michael 162
Deep Throat 181
De Havilland, Olivia 87
demonology 204, 208
denial 69
desecration 93, 94
determinism 18, 68
The Devil 218
The Devils 7
The Devil's Own 81; see also *The Witches*
digital technology 217
Dionysian 134, 135
Disney 52
Doane, Mary Ann 184
dogma 93
Donner, Richard 7
Donovan 182
Don't Look Now 162
Dorian, Angela 55; *see also* Vetri, Victoria
Doubting Thomas 216
Dracula 6, 10
Dreadful Pleasures 32; *see also* Twitchell, James B.
drug culture 61, 159
The Druids 136, 140, 155
Dubrovnik 50
Durkheim, Emile 202

Eastertide 135, 137, 154
Easy Rider 95, 98, 99, 100
Ebert, Roger 159
eco-naturalism 148
Eder, Richard 71
Eggers, Robert 214
Egypt 193
Ekland, Britt 152, 160
El Cid 72
Ellis, Bill 114; see also *Raising the Devil*
Ellis Island 47
emasculation *see* castration

Emergo 53
EMI 162
empathy 98
Empire State Building 49
Enfield poltergeist 211
England 126, 153, 158, 190, 191
The Enlightenment 9, 114, 156, 200, 226
Episcopalianism 137
the establishment 61
Estridge, Robin 124, 138; *see also* Loraine, Philip
Etruria 77
Eucharist *see* Holy Communion
European Economic Community 58
Evangelicalism 203
Evans, Maurice 52
Evil Children Narratives 8, 61–62
evil eye 140
evolution 156, 156
existential crisis 201
The Exorcist (film) 7, 8, 206, 212
exploitation 151
extratextuality 60, 98, 100, 181
Eye of the Devil 20, 22, 112, 113, 114, 115, 116, 117–124, 127, 129, 131, 132, 136, 137, 138–140, 142, 143, 146, 147, 163, 166, 179, 184, 185, 187, 189, 190, 191, 193

A Face in the Crowd 72
Faithfull, Marianne 16
familial breakdown 60, 67, 74, 101
familial legacy 59, 62, 64, 65, 66, 71, 74, 80, 81, 103, 122, 124, 126, 133, 176, 178, 185, 200
Farrow, Mia 27, 29, 53
fascism 159
Faust 81
The Feminine Mystique 20; *see also* Friedan, Betty
feminism 18, 20, 22–23, 50, 166, 168, 172, 175, 177, 182, 183, 184
feminist theory 88, 166, 167, 168, 174, 184
femme fatale 88
filicide 206
Firestone, Shulamith 171
first person point of view 50
Folk Horror 8, 88, 89, 93, 111, 114, 116, 143, 144, 145, 216
Folk Horror: Hours Dreadful, Things Strange 88; *see also* Scovell, Adam
folkloric traditions 131, 139, 140, 214, 216
Fonda, Peter 95, 98, 99, 100
Fontaine, Joan 87, 89
The Food and Drug Administration 96
the fool 153
Fortune Magazine 46
France 128

Frankenstein 6

Frazier, Sir James 22, 116, 134, 135, 137, 139, 153, 155, 156, 166, 167, 169, 184; see also *The Golden Bough*

free will 62, 67, 80, 120, 153

Freud, Sigmund 172

Friday, Nancy 170

Friday the 13th 7

Friedan, Betty 20, 170, 171; see also *The Feminine Mystique*

Friedkin, William 7

fundamentalism 67

Gable, Clark 52

Galileo 210

The Garden of Eden 155

Gatiss, Mark 143

gender positioning 80, 167, 173, 183, 184, 209, 210, 211

"Gently Johnny" 151

Georgetown 203

Germanic faiths 97

Germany 77

Getting Loose: Lifestyle and Consumption in the 1970s 118; see also Binkley, Sam

The Ghost of Frankenstein 52

A Ghost Story for Christmas 129, 139

Giovanni, Paul 161

global warming 197

The Goddess 165

Goethe 81

The Golden Bough 22, 113, 116, 134, 137, 139, 153, 154, 155, 156, 157, 167–168; see also Frazier, Sir James

Good Friday 177

Gordon, Ruth 29

Gore, Al 198

Gothic 6, 9–14, 48, 49, 50, 51, 55, 77, 89, 144, 155, 201, 226, 227

Graham, Billy 15, 107

grand narratives 200, 202, 227

Grande Dame Guignol 89; see also Hags-ploitation

Grant, Cary 52

great auks 156

Great Britain 129

greenhouse effect 197, 198

Greenspun, Roger 105

Gregory, Anita 213

Gun Control Act 72

Habits of the Heart 36, 56, 111; see also Bellah, Robert

Haggard, Piers 143

Hagsploitation 87–88, 89

Halloween 8

hallucinogenic drugs 219

Hammer House of Horror 88, 149, 151, 159, 160

Hansen, Dr. James 197

Hardy, Robin 139, 141, 148, 149, 150, 159, 160, 161, 162, 169

Harley Davidson Motorcycle Company 99

Harlow, Jean 52

Harvest Festival 137, 139, 161, 187

Harvest Home 166, 167, 169, 171, 172, 183, 184, 189–193, 226; see also Tryon, Thomas

Harvest King 135, 187, 193

The Hayes Code 96

Hearths of Darkness 33, 36, 56; see also Williams, Tony

Hebrides (Scottish) 141, 145, 146, 148, 163

hedonism 48, 83, 87, 91, 97, 104, 105, 106, 159

Hemmings, David 113, 160

Hermetic Qabalah 138

Herne the Hunter 111

Herod (King) 77

Heston, Charlton 72

heteronormativity 96

hierarchy 169

Hinduism 16, 148

The Hippie Movement 114, 115, 117, 118, 147, 198, 199

Hitchcock, Alfred 7, 13

Hodgson, Janet 195–196

Hoffman, Abbie 94

HOG (Harley Davidson Owners Group) 99

Hollywood (cinema) 11, 52, 71, 88, 149, 181, 192, 199

Hollywood (location) 53, 54

Holy Communion 85, 93, 127, 154, 162

Holy Roman Empire 57, 58

The Holy Spirit 169

Honda Motor Company 99

Hopper, Dennis 16, 99

House Beautiful Magazine 28, 44

House of Darkness, House of Light: The True Story 208

The House on Haunted Hill 53

Houston, Beverle 39, 41; see also Kinder, Marsha

Humphreys, Reynold 33, 34; see also *The American Horror Film*

Hungry Wives 174, 181, 182; see also *Season of the Witch*

"I can't help falling in love with you" 213

I'm Okay, You're Okay 170

Imbolc 161

imperialism 88

incest 223

An Inconvenient Truth 198

individualism 48, 62, 80, 85, 87, 88, 91, 98, 99, 120, 126, 129, 149, 200
indulgences 47
industrialism 59
information age 202
information technology 200, 202
inner-city 159, 162
The Inquisition 168
insanity 49, 82
Inside the Wicker Man 158; *see also* Brown, Allan
The Institute for the Study of American Religion 199
The Interpretation of Dreams 172
invasion 98
Iona, Scotland 148, 158
Islam 55, 70, 148
isolation 98, 103, 106, 111, 129, 130, 141, 143, 144–158, 166, 174, 176, 184, 185, 187, 189, 190, 202, 209, 214–216, 221
Israel 58, 200
Italy 58, 62, 77

Jack's Wife 165, 172, 180, 182; see also *Season of the Witch*
Jagger, Mick 16, 95, 106
James Bond (films) 160
Jancovich, Mark 8, 33, 45
Jesuit 213
Jesus Christ 65, 66, 67, 68, 69, 75, 93, 121, 127, 128, 134, 142, 145, 149, 150, 151, 153, 154, 158, 177, 191, 205, 215, 216
Joseph of Nazareth 65
Judaism 55, 57, 58, 70, 204, 220
Judeo-Christianity 128
Jump Cut Magazine 101

Kawasaki Motor Company 98
Kelly, Patsy 54
Kennedy, John F. 33, 36, 41–42
The Killing 52
Kinder, Marsha 39, 41; *see also* Houston, Beverle
King, Martin Luther, Jr. 20, 170
King for a Day 153
Kirby, Alan 200
Kubrick, Stanley 52

Lammas Night 161
Lancaster, Burt 43
"The Landlord's Daughter" 161
Lasch, Christopher 56, 65, 81, 82; see also the *Culture of Narcissism*
Latin (language) 85, 106, 122, 155, 168
LaVey, Anton 16–17, 84, 85, 97; *see also* The Satanic Bible
Lee, Christopher 5, 141, 149, 159, 162–163

Leggett, Paul 11
lesbianism 54
Letich, Thomas 18
Levin, Ira 27, 33, 35, 37, 38, 42, 43, 46, 47, 49, 51
Lewis, C.S. 37–38; see also *Mere Christianity*
liberal humanism 72
Life Magazine 45–46
liminality 144
Lincoln, Abraham 55
Lisbon, Portugal 125
The Literature of Terror 48; *see also* Punter, David
Lofts, Nora 87
London 90, 93, 125, 129, 131, 132
Loraine, Philip 113, 124; *see also* Estridge, Robin
The Lord of the Dance 121, 122; *see also* Carter, Sydney
Luce, Henry 45
Lucifer Rising 16; *see also* Anger, Kenneth
Lughnasadh 161
Lust for a Vampire 151
Luther, Martin 47
Lutheranism 137
Lutz, Kathy 207
the Lutz family 210
Lyotard, Jean-François 200

Macabre 53
machismo 99
MacTaggart, James 140
madness *see* insanity
the maiden 169, 188
mainstream 184
Malcolm X 171
male domination 173
the male gaze 171
Manhattan 49
Manion, Gerard 203
Mansfield, Jayne 106
The Manson family 138
marginalization 170
marijuana 178
Martin, Troy Kennedy 140
Martini, Jean-Paul-Egide 213
Martinmas 161
martyrdom 141, 142
Mary, mother of Jesus 66
M.A.S.H. 100
Maslin, Janet 150
matriarchy 167, 186, 221–225
May Day 153, 154, 199
May Queen 224
McCullen, Ramsay 121
McLeod, Hugh 14–15, 148, 175

"Me" Generation 17
mediated communication 217–218, 221
Melton, J. Gordon 199
Meon Hill 140
Mere Christianity 37–38; see also Lewis, C.S.
Messiah 66, 138
method acting 53, 72
Methodism 90, 137
the middle class 46, 52, 61, 95, 99, 100, 101, 166, 172, 212
Midsommar 23, 195, 196, 216
Midsummer celebrations 90, 217
Milton 9
Mithra 128
monasticism 148, 158
Monotheism 138, 169
The Monstrous Feminine 34; see also Creed, Barbara
Monstrum horror journal 88
The Morningstar Commune 118
Mother Earth 113, 114, 165, 168, 169, 193, 198, 205, 222, 226
Mulvey, Laura 184
Muslims 200, 203
mysticism 157, 158, 175

narcissism 104
narrative closure 98
narrowcasting 202
National Aeronautics and Space Administration 198
National Association for the Advancement of Colored People (NAACP) 170
National Catholic Office of Motion Pictures 51; see also National Legion of Decency
National Legion of Decency 7; see also National Catholic Office of Motion Pictures
The National Organization for Women (NOW) 170, 171
Native American peoples 168
naturalism 18
Nature and Culture 198
nemus 155
nepotism 103, 104
New England 214
New Hollywood Cinema 100, 101
The New Left 96
New York 13, 31, 32, 36, 38, 42, 43, 46, 47, 53, 72, 125, 146, 185, 199
The New York City Blackout 34
The New York Times 14, 15, 32, 51, 71, 87, 100, 105, 113, 122, 150, 181, 197, 199
The New Yorker Magazine 44
Newman, Kim 33; see also Nightmare Movies

Nightmare Movies 33; see also Newman, Kim
Niven, David 124
Nixon, Richard 60
non-conformism 73
nostalgia 144
Not in God's Name 201; see also Sacks, Jonathan
nuclear family 59, 80, 95, 103, 119, 183, 209, 212
nudity 150, 151, 160, 180, 214, 224, 225
The Nun 214

oak tree (in Paganism) 155
Oates, Warren 95, 98, 100
occlusion 227
the occult 101, 135, 137, 138, 139, 144, 159, 175, 177, 178, 182
Odeon Theatres 160
Oklahoma 72
Omaha, Nebraska 36
The Omen (film) 7, 8, 21, 33, 51, 55, 56–77, 79, 80, 87, 88, 91, 103, 105, 112, 114, 127, 142, 172, 197
The Omen (novelization) 73, 74–77, 159
omens 215
open endings see narrative closure
oral contraceptives 96
orgy 86, 87, 93, 96
original sin 155
Orientalism 88, 89; see also Said, Edward
orthodoxy 62, 64, 65, 68, 76, 77, 80, 82, 92, 93, 98, 148, 169, 179, 191, 204
Osborne, John 73
The Oscars see Academy Awards
O'Sullivan, Maureen 53
Oxford English Dictionary 66

paganus 168
Page, Jimmy 16
Palahniuk, Chuck 27
pantheism 157, 169, 220
Paradise Lost 9
Paramount Pictures 52
Paranoia 88
the paranormal 204
Paris, France 118, 119, 124, 125, 131
Parker, Lara 100
patriarchy 61, 62, 89, 166–167, 170, 171, 172, 174, 175, 176, 183, 184
Peck, Gregory 7, 57, 71
Peckinpah, Sam 100
Pentecost 122, 161
Pentecostal 213
The Perils of Pauline 52
Perron, Andrea 208, 209–210
Perron, Caroline 195, 207, 210
Perron, Roger 209

the Perron family 210–211
Persia 128
phallocentrism 166, 169, 181, 184, 193
pictograms 220
the pill *see* oral contraceptives
Pinches, George 160
Pinner, David 151, 152, 158, 159, 162; see also *Ritual*
Pitt, Ingrid 159, 160
Pittsburgh, Pennsylvania 175
Planet of the Apes 72
Play for Today 111, 129, 139, 140
Playboy Magazine 54
Plymouth 214
Polanski, Roman 7, 12, 15, 27, 40, 49, 52, 56, 138
polytheism 168, 169
Pope Francis 203, 204
Pope Francis's Agenda for the Future of Catholicism 203
Pope John XXIII 19, 203–204
Pope Paul IV 19–20, 38, 42, 46
pornography 96, 151, 160, 181
possession 61, 87, 94, 195, 205, 211
post-millennial horror 196
post-millennialism 201, 204, 227
postmodernity 12, 17, 29, 200–202, 227
postpartum syndrome 50
post-postmodernity 197, 198, 201
potsherds 130
Pratt, Vic 131, 137
predestination 21, 56, 59, 60, 62, 63, 65–69, 71, 76
Presbyterianism 175
Presley, Elvis 213
Prince, Stephen 7, 13, 135
private sphere 61, 166, 167, 170, 173, 174
profanity 93
promiscuity 175
prophecy 56, 58, 60, 63, 66, 68, 69, 70, 75, 76
propitiation *see* sacrifice
Protestantism 21, 22, 35, 48, 84, 116, 137, 149, 156, 204
prurient interest 150
pseudo-modernity 200–201, 227
Psycho 7, 8, 13
psychoanalysis 173
psychoanalytic theory 34, 172–174; *see also* Freud, Sigmund; *The Interpretation of Dreams*
Psychobiddy 89; *see also* Hagsploitation
public service announcements 146
public sphere 59, 167, 170, 174, 209, 213
Punch 153
Punter, David 10, 12–13, 35, 48, 49; see also *The Literature of Terror*
Puritanism 48, 90, 185, 214

Quinton 139

Race with the Devil 22, 79, 80, 94–102, 103, 112
radicalism 171, 172
radio broadcast 146
Raising the Devil 114; *see also* Ellis, Bill
Rank Organisation 160
the rapture 198
rationalism 51, 86, 89, 111, 123, 135, 156, 196, 199, 209, 213
reactionaryism 67
Reagan, Ronald 20
reality television 200
rebellion 82, 97
The Reformation 9, 84, 114, 156 , 200, 204, 226
regression 157
religious extremism 197, 203
The Religious Studies Review 205
Remick, Lee 72
repression 172–174, 179, 184
Rigby, Jonathan 115, 116
Rio de Jannero 125
rites of passage 151
Ritual 151–152, 153, 155, 158, 159; *see also* Pinner, David
Robin Redbreast 19, 22, 111, 112, 113, 114–115, 116, 117, 118, 120, 129–140, 142, 143, 144, 162, 166, 179, 184, 187, 189, 191, 193, 216
Roe vs Wade 96
The Rolling Stones 16, 95
The Romans 128, 168
Rome, Italy 77, 125, 158
Romero, George 166, 168, 174–175, 181, 182
Rosemary's Baby (film) 7, 8, 12–13, 15, 21, 27–55, 56, 58, 60, 61, 64, 66, 67, 71, 73, 77, 79, 80, 87, 88, 91, 96, 100, 103, 104, 105, 111, 112, 114, 115, 127, 128, 135, 138, 142, 169, 172, 180, 182, 183 184, 186, 197, 200, 216, 227
Rosemary's Baby (novel) 27–55, 60, 61
Roszak, Theodore 16, 78
Royal Academy of Dramatic Art 160
Rubin, Jerry 97; *see also* Yippie Movement
the rule of thumb 173
runic symbols 97, 220, 221

Sacks, Jonathan 201, 202, 203, 227; see also *Not in God's Name*
sacrifice 70, 78, 89, 93, 94, 96, 97 101, 104, 112, 115, 116, 120, 122, 123, 126, 127, 134, 135, 136, 140, 141–158, 163, 188, 191, 193, 210, 214, 216, 220–223, 225
sacrilege 223
Said, Edward 88; *see also* Orientalism

Salem witch trials 168, 210
Samhain 161
Sanders, Alex 138; *see also* Verbius
Santa Fe, New Mexico 168
Sassoon, Vidal 27, 44
Satan 68, 69, 75, 78, 84, 87, 100, 103, 104
The Satanic Bible 16–17, 83, 97; *see also*
    LaVey, Anton
Scandinavian 157
scientific method 157
Scorsese, Martin 53
Scotland 141, 145, 148, 149, 158, 161, 162
The Scottish Highlands 145
Scottish Term (Quarter) Days 161
Scovell, Adam 8, 88, 111, 115, 116, 139, 143,
    144, 145; see also *Folk Horror: Hours
    Dreadful*; *Things Strange*
Seagram's Gin 45
Season of the Witch (film) 22, 165–166, 168,
    169, 171, 172–183, 184, 192, 193; see also
    Jack's Wife
Season of the Witch (song) 182–183
The Second Vatican Council 14, 15, 20, 22,
    85, 122, 204, 226
second wave feminism 169; *see also* femi-
    nism; feminist theory
secularism 21, 59, 61, 64, 67, 69, 75, 78, 83,
    103, 120, 156, 164, 168, 200, 202, 206, 212
Seltzer, David 74, 75, 76
separatism 171, 172
September 11, 2001 201
Sex in the Heartland 94, 170; *see also* Bai-
    ley, Beth
sex magik 97; *see also* Crowley, Aleister
sexual promiscuity 174
Shadows 53
Shaffer, Anthony 139, 141, 148, 149, 150,
    153, 158, 159, 160, 161, 162
The Shakers 121
Shelley, Peter 89
Shepard, Lucius 147
shopping cart faith 98, 148
Shyamalan, M. Night 218
Sinatra, Frank 53, 54
Sistine Chapel 42
skepticism 82, 86, 103, 111, 115, 116, 126,
    129, 136, 164, 178, 182, 189, 195, 196, 197,
    198, 209, 210, 213
Skow, John 167
slasher films 8
Sleuth 159
Sobchack, Vivian 13, 33, 61, 67
social media 201, 204
Songs of Praise 132
Southern Christian Leadership Confer-
    ence 171
Soylent Green 72

Spikings, Barry 162
spinsters 88
Sports Illustrated Magazine 46
Spring Maiden 153
Star of Bethlehem 66, 75
The Statue of Liberty 47
Steinem, Gloria 170
Stephens, Harvey 57
Stewart, Rod 160
Stratford-on-Avon 139
subjugation 174
suburbia 165, 166, 177, 183, 212, 217, 227
suicide 222
summer solstice 218
the supernatural 127, 129, 133, 135, 139,
    156, 157, 198, 199, 205, 207, 208, 209,
    210, 211, 212
superstition 126, 137, 144, 158
Sweden 218
switching 173
Switt, Loretta 100
symbolism 83, 85, 136, 154, 155, 173, 180,
    215, 216, 221

taboos 223
tarot cards 182
Tate, Sharon 138
The Telegraph 121
television 132, 139, 144, 146, 160, 175, 183,
    184
The Ten Commandments 72, 175
Tennant, Ann 139
terrorism 197
The Texas Chainsaw Massacre 8
Thelema 16, 97, 138; *see also* Crowley,
    Aleister
Thirteen 114
Thompson, David 111
Thompson, Howard 87, 88
Time Magazine 13, 37, 45–46, 117, 118,
    167
The Tingler 53
To Kill a Mockingbird (film) 72
Tom Jones (film) 160
Tom Jones (play) 73
The Tony Awards 52, 159
transitory amnesia 201
transubstantiation 85, 154
Treaty of Rome 58
the triune Goddess 169, 173
Troughton, Patrick 57
Tryon, Thomas 165, 166, 167, 189, 190; see
    also *Harvest Home*
Tudor, Andrew 12–13, 19, 20, 60
Twiggy 44
Twins of Evil 151
Twitchell, James B. 11, 32

the unconscious 174
The United Kingdom 58, 147
The United States Conference of Catholic Bishops 7, 51, 71, 150
United States Senate Energy and Natural Resources Committee 197

vampires 207
The Vatican 47, 62, 207
Verbius 138; *see also* Sanders, Alex
Vetri, Victoria 54, 55; *see also* Dorian, Angela
The Victorian Era 49, 157
vigilantism 159
the Vikings 157
virginity 151, 153
Vodun 82
von Sydow, Max 7
Voodoo 82, 89

Walton, Charles 139–140
Walpole, Horace 226; see also *The Castle of Otranto*
Warner, David 67, 73, 159
Warren, Ed 204
Warren, Lorraine 195–196, 204
The Warren Commission 33, 60
Warwickshire 139
Welles, Orson 73
West Side Story (film) 54
What Ever Happened to Baby Jane 87
Wheatley, Dennis 114, 158–159
Whitelaw, Billie 57, 73
Whitman, Walt 210
Whitsun 161
Wicca 89, 97, 138, 139, 165, 169, 173, 174, 175, 177, 198–199, 205
Wiccan Millenarism 198
The Wicker Man (film) 5, 7, 8, 22, 97, 103, 111, 115, 116, 139, 140, 141–164, 172, 184,

187, 188, 190, 191, 193, 216, 218, 219, 223, 226
The Wicker Man (novelization) 146–14
The Wicker Tree 226
Williams, Tony 7, 56, 33, 34, 36, 39, 56, 61–62, 67, 175; *see also Hearths of Darkness*
Winner, Michael 159
Winnie the Pooh (tv series) 52
wish fulfillments 172–173
The Witch 23, 195, 196, 214–217, 227
the witchdoctor 82
The Witches (film) 22, 79, 80, 81–89, 97, 100, 101, 103, 104, 106, 127, 128, 133
The Witches (novel) 89–94
Witchfinder General 8, 144
witch's coven 159, 166, 169, 178, 180, 182, 215, 216
witch's familiars 85, 140
Wolf, Leonard 13–15
The Wolfman 52
The Women's Liberation Front 171
Wood, Michael 88
Wood, Natalie 54
Wood, Robin 8, 61, 67
Woodward, Edward 5, 149, 160, 162
working class 98
working through 174
World War II 77
wyrd 144

Yale University 121
Yamaha Motorcycle Company 28, 44, 100
Yankee Stadium 20, 42
The Yellow Wallpaper 50
The Yippie Movement 97; *see also* Rubin, Jerry
Youtube 204

Žižek, Slavloj 202
Zion 57, 58